A WORLD BANK COUNTRY STUDY

Kyrgyzstan

The Transition to a Market Economy

The World Bank
Washington, D.C.

World Bank Country Studies are among the many reports originally prepared for internal use as part of the continuing analysis by the Bank of the economic and related conditions of its developing member countries and of its dialogues with the governments. Some of the reports are published in this series with the least possible delay for the use of governments and the academic, business and financial, and development communities. The typescript of this paper therefore has not been prepared in accordance with the procedures appropriate to formal printed texts, and the World Bank accepts no responsibility for errors.

The World Bank does not guarantee the accuracy of the data included in this publication and accepts no responsibility whatsoever for any consequence of their use. Any maps that accompany the text have been prepared solely for the convenience of readers; the designations and presentation of material in them do not imply the expression of any opinion whatsoever on the part of the World Bank, its affiliates, or its Board or member countries concerning the legal status of any country, territory, city, or area or of the authorities thereof or concerning the delimitation of its boundaries or its national affiliation.

The material in this publication is copyrighted. Requests for permission to reproduce portions of it should be sent to the Office of the Publisher at the address shown in the copyright notice above. The World Bank encourages dissemination of its work and will normally give permission promptly and, when the reproduction is for noncommercial purposes, without asking a fee. Permission to copy portions for classroom use is granted through the Copyright Clearance Center, 27 Congress Street, Salem, Massachusetts 01970, U.S.A.

The complete backlist of publications from the World Bank is shown in the annual *Index of Publications*, which contains an alphabetical title list (with full ordering information) and indexes of subjects, authors, and countries and regions. The latest edition is available free of charge from the Distribution Unit, Office of the Publisher, The World Bank, 1818 H Street, N.W., Washington, D.C. 20433, U.S.A., or from Publications, The World Bank, 66, avenue d'Iéna, 75116 Paris, France.

ISSN: 0253-2123

Library of Congress Cataloging-in-Publication Data

Kyrgyzstan : the transition to a market economy.
       p.   cm. — (A World Bank country study, ISSN 0253-2123)
    "This report is based on the work of an economic mission that
visited Kyrgyzstan in April 1992"—Pref.
    ISBN 0-8213-2525-6
    1. Kyrgyzstan—Economic conditions. 2. Kyrgyzstan—Economic
policy. 3. Post-communism—Kyrgyzstan.   I. International Bank for
Reconstruction and Development.   II. Series.
HC420.7.K98   1993
338.958'43—dc20
                                                      93-27903
                                                        CIP

PREFACE

Kyrgyzstan became a member of the World Bank on September 18, 1992. This report is based on the work of an economic mission that visited Kyrgyzstan in April 1992 and subsequent visits by World Bank sectoral staff. The report was discussed with the authorities in October 1992 and distributed to the first Consultative Group (CG) meeting for Kyrgyzstan, which took place on December 15, 1992. The mission wishes to thank the authorities in Kyrgyzstan for their excellent support and cooperation.

The report was prepared by a team led by Sanjay Dhar and comprised Craig Andrews, Howard Barnum, Brian O'Connor, Jean-Charles Crochet, John Edelman, Ann Ishee, Donald Keesing, Henk Koppen, Dhananjaya Kumar, Guy Le Moigne, Dan Mozes, Barbara Ossowicka, Herve Plusquellec, Joseph Saba, Marcel Scoffier, Kutlu Somel, Michael Stevens, Stephen Taylor, Milan Vodopivec, Jeurgen Voegele and Peter Whitford. Thomas Daves, Klaus Lorch, Michael Mills, Michael Rathnam and Salvatore Schiavo-Campo also contributed to the report. The work was carried out under the general supervision of Kadir Tanju Yurukoglu.

Since the report was distributed to the CG, many reform measures, addressing key areas discussed in this report, have been undertaken by the Government. This preface provides a brief update on key developments in recent months, while the rest of the report remains as it was presented to the CG meeting at the end of last year.

Important structural reforms that have been approved since this report was distributed to the CG include: (i) the adoption by Parliament of a Concept Note for privatization of small and medium scale enterprises in December 1992. By January 1993, about 2300 enterprises, accounting for about 12 percent of total fixed assets, had been privatized. The majority of these, around 2000, were small-scale enterprises in the trade and services sectors; (ii) the elimination of most legal and institutional barriers to private sector participation in trade and distribution, including state orders; (iii) the elimination of most previously granted tax privileges and exemptions by December 1992 (further fiscal measures were approved by Parliament and are included in the IMF standby program); (iv) the adoption of new central bank and commercial banking laws, establishing a two-tier banking system and empowering the National Bank of Kyrgyzstan with increased supervisory authority; and, (v) the approval of a new constitution in May 1993.

In May 1993, Kyrgyzstan left the ruble zone in order to pursue an independent monetary policy and macroeconomic stabilization. The introduction of the national currency, the Som, was approved by Parliament on May 3, 1993, and actual conversion took place on May 10, 1993.

An IMF stand-by arrangement for Kyrgyzstan was approved on May 12, 1993, covering an eleven month period starting in June 1993. Kyrgyzstan was the first recipient of the IMF's new Systemic Transformation Facility, which was also approved on May 12, 1993. The stabilization program targets sharp reductions in the budget deficit (from 15 percent of GDP in 1992 to 7 percent in 1993) and the growth of broad money and domestic credit. The program envisages no central bank financing of the fiscal deficit after the introduction of the new currency. With no domestic borrowing capacity, the fiscal deficit is to be entirely funded by external financing inflows.

The World Bank approved an Import Rehabilitation Credit for Kyrgyzstan on May 13, 1993 for an amount of US$60 million.

For 1993, the expected financing requirement of about US$400 million is evenly split between FSU and non-FSU areas. Following the CG meeting in late 1992, a pledging session was held in April 1993. US$200 million of grant and concessional financing for balance of payments support and US$114 million of export credits from non-FSU sources were pledged, together with US$44 million from the IMF and a Rub131 billion credit tranche from the Russian Federation. Kazakhstan, Azerbaijan and Uzbekistan have also agreed to provide Kyrgyzstan with Rub73 billion of trade credits.

GLOSSARY OF ABBREVIATIONS

ACU	-	Aid Coordination Unit
AMC	-	Antimonopoly Committee
BAC	-	Bank Advisory Committee
CBR	-	Central Bank of Russia
CEE	-	Central and Eastern Europe
CG	-	Consultative Group
CIS	-	Commonwealth of Independent States
CMEA	-	Council for Mutual Economic Assistance
CPI	-	Consumer Price Index
DSR	-	Debt Service Ratio
FDI	-	Foreign Direct Investment
FIB	-	Foreign Investment Bureau
FSU	-	Former Soviet Union
G-7	-	Group of Seven Industrial Nations
GDP	-	Gross Domestic Product
GNP	-	Gross National Product
Goskominvest	-	State Committee on Foreign Investments and External Assistance
Goskompriroda	-	State Committee for Environmental Protection
Goskomstat	-	State Committee on Statistics
ILO	-	International Labor Organization
IMF	-	International Monetary Fund
MEF	-	Ministry of Economy and Finance
MLT	-	Medium and Long Term
MOC	-	Ministry of Communications
MOH	-	Ministry of Health
MOU	-	Memorandum of Understanding
NBK	-	National Bank of Kyrgyzstan
NMP	-	Net Material Product
OECD	-	Organization for Economic Cooperation and Development
PAS	-	Procurement and Audit Service
PDA	-	Privatization and Denationalization Act
PIP	-	Public Investment Program
SB	-	Savings Bank
SOE	-	State Owned Enterprise
SPF	-	State Property Fund
TACIS	-	Technical Agreement for CIS
UNICEF	-	United Nations Children's Fund
VAT	-	Value-Added Tax
WHO	-	World Health Organization
WPI	-	Wholesale Price Index

CURRENCY EQUIVALENTS

RUBLES PER $

Period		Official Exchange Rate Rate (Average)	Auction/ MIFCE Rate (Average)
1987		0.6328	n.a.
1988		0.6080	n.a.
1989		0.6274	8.9
1990		0.5856	18.8
1991		0.5819	59.0

		(end of period)	(end of period)
December	1991	0.5571	169.2
January	1992	n.a.	230.0
February	1992	n.a.	139.0
March	1992	n.a.	160.3
April	1992	n.a.	143.5
May	1992	n.a.	113.0
June	1992	n.a.	144.0
July	1992	n.a.	161.2
August	1992	n.a.	205.0
September	1992	n.a.	254.0
October	1992	n.a.	398.0
19 November	1992	n.a.	448.0

COUNTRY DATA - KYRGYZSTAN

GNP per Capita in $US in 1991	1,550

General
Area (square km)	198,500.0
Population, 1991 (thousands)	4,422.2
Growth Rate, 1979-1991 (percent)	2.3
Density, 1991 (per square km)	22.3

Social Indicators

Population Characteristics
Crude Birth Rate, 1991 (per 1,000)	29.1
Crude Death Rate, 1991 (per 1,000)	6.9

Health
Infant Mortality Rate 1991 (per 1,000)	29.6

Life Expectancy at Birth, 1990
Male	64.2
Female	72.6

Gross Domestic Product

	Current Prices (million rubles)		Real Growth Rate[a] (annual % change)	
	1990	1991	1990	1991
GDP at Market Prices	7,325.0	16,900.0	3.2	-3.9
Total Consumption	5,947.0	12,000.0	-2.2	-13.0
Gross Domestic Investment	2,785.0	5,200.0	-21.4	-6.4
Net Export	-1,407.0	-300.0		

a/ Based on data in 1983 prices.

Output, Employment and Productivity

	GDP in 1991		Employment in 1991[a]		GDP per Worker	
	mln Rub	% of total	thousands	% of total	rubles	% of avg
Agriculture	4,800.0	28.4	384.9	22.0	12,470.8	128.9
Industry	6,400.0	37.9	332.8	19.0	19,230.8	198.8
Construction	1,200.0	7.1	151.7	8.7	7,910.3	81.8
Transport	700.0	4.1	56.4	3.2	12,411.3	128.3
Services[b]	3,800.0	22.5	821.3	47.0	4,626.8	47.8
Total/Average	16,900.0	100.0	1,747.1	100.0	9,673.2	100.0

a/ Excluding working on private plots and at home.
b/ Including services in material and nonmaterial sphere.

Government Finance

	Consolidated General Government, 1991	
	bln Rub	% of GDP
Total Revenues	5.4	32.1
Total Expenditures	4.7	28.0
Overall Balance	0.7	4.1

Money, Credit and Prices

	1991	June 1992
	(billion rubles)	
Net Foreign Assets		
Foreign Exchange	0.0	-0.7
Net Domestic Assets	10.0	16.5
Credit to Government	-0.5	-1.2
Credit to the Economy	8.3	19.7
Other Items, Net	2.2	-2.0
Money Stock	10.0	15.8
Currency Outside Banks	2.8	5.6
Deposits	7.2	10.2

Balance of Trade in Domestic Prices

	1990	1991
	(million rubles)	
Non-FSU Trade		
Exports	53	41
Imports	1,043	1,374
Balance	-990	-1,333
FSU Trade		
Exports	2,446	6,505
Imports	2,863	5,409
Balance	-417	1,096

Composition of Exports and Imports in World Prices in 1990 (million rubles)

	Interrepublic		Extrarepublic		Total Trade	
	Exports	Imports	Exports	Imports	Exports	Imports
Electric Energy	101	51	0	0	101	51
Oil and Gas	34	605	0	0	34	605
Coal	21	36	0	0	21	36
Ferrous and Nonferrous Metals	244	345	32	5	276	350
Chemical and Petrochemical	19	269	1	37	20	306
Machine Building	1,099	906	13	79	1,112	985
Lumber and Paper	2	80	0	9	2	89
Industrial Construction Materials	13	64	0	3	13	67
Light Industry	174	200	2	90	176	290
Food Industry	182	103	3	477	185	580
Other industries	16	43	0	5	16	48
Agriculture	31	93	1	53	32	146
Others	20	114	0	1	20	115
TOTAL	1,956	2,910	52	759	2,006	3,669

CONTENTS

Text Boxes

Text Figures

EXECUTIVE SUMMARY

Background

1.   Kyrgyzstan is confronted by highly adverse circumstances in which to initiate the transition to a market economy. Historically, it was among the poorest of the republics of the former Soviet Union (FSU). Its economy was characterized by heavy dependence and excessive specialization through trade with the FSU. Official transfers from the Union averaged 10 percent of GDP during 1989-91, and additional direct financing for enterprises was available from their parent organizations elsewhere in the FSU. The trade deficit averaged about 14 percent of GDP during this period, and trade was predominantly conducted within the FSU. Exports to the rest of the world amounted to less than two percent of total exports over the past three years, and convertible currency imports exceeded such exports by a factor of over 20. Foreign exchange reserves are negligible as is the institutional capacity for importing directly from outside the ruble area. While there is adequate domestic production of most food items including meat, fruits and vegetables, Kyrgyzstan has been a substantial net importer of grains, including wheat, and does not produce any modern pharmaceuticals. It is also almost entirely dependent on imported oil and gas, though it exports hydroelectric power to neighboring states.

2.   This level of dependence renders Kyrgyzstan highly vulnerable to macroeconomic and trade developments in the FSU, over which it has little or no control. Of particular concern in the first half of 1992 was the shortage of cash supply from the Central Bank of Russia (CBR) in the face of the massive and largely externally determined shifts in the structure and level of prices. The cash shortage has eased in recent months. However, the breakdown of payments arrangements for interrepublican trade and the resulting contraction of trade and build-up of arrears among trading enterprises is of continuing concern. In addition, the recent and prospective increases in the relative prices of imported oil and gas will adversely impact the productive sectors of the economy for several years.

3.   In common with most republics of the FSU, the ability of Kyrgyzstan to respond to these shocks is constrained by the inexperience of the recently created institutions needed for the governance of an independent nation. Also, given its geographical location, the country has been relatively isolated from exposure to practices common in market based economies. Hence, the task of building the skills and institutions for the efficient functioning of a market economy will perhaps require even greater effort than elsewhere in the FSU.

4.   Several attributes however favor the country's long-term development potential. Literacy levels and the skills base appear high relative to the level of development. Agriculture is relatively well diversified, and, with an improved incentive framework, could yield higher output and productivity. There are reported to be substantial deposits of natural gas and a wide range of unexploited mineral resources. The potential for increased hydroelectric production and tourism is also significant.

Developments in 1992

5.   Being a small country in the ruble area, macroeconomic developments have been dominated by developments in Russia and elsewhere in the Commonwealth of Independent States (CIS). Following a contraction of output by about 4 percent in 1991, the decline accelerated considerably in 1992 as supply disruptions became pervasive and trade contracted. Industrial enterprises were particularly

susceptible given their heavy dependence on trade and the higher relative prices for imported energy. Real GDP for the year is estimated to decline by 24 percent. This output decline has been associated with a larger decline in real disposable income -- estimated at 36 percent -- in light of the terms of trade deterioration and loss of Union transfers. However, a large swing from surplus to deficit is estimated for the current account balance, moderating somewhat the decline in domestic absorption.

6.   Following the liberalization of most prices on January 4, 1992, consumer prices rose 3.8 times in the first quarter, while wholesale prices were up by a factor of nine, driven by a much larger (twenty fold) increase in fuel prices. Price increases between May and August moderated considerably, with the monthly rise in the CPI averaging under 6 percent. However, in September both consumer and wholesale prices rose substantially, by 27 percent and 48 percent, respectively. Fuel prices in September were 60 times their level of a year earlier, yet remained far below international levels if converted at the market exchange rate. A fourteen fold increase in the GDP deflator is estimated for 1992.

7.   Fiscal resources were drastically reduced in the first half of 1992 with the cessation of official transfers from Moscow and the adverse impact on revenue of the price and output trends. Constrained by inadequate financing, public expenditures were forced to contract in a parallel and damaging manner producing an approximate balance on a cash basis at the end of the first half. Delayed payments of wages and pensions are indicative of the severity of the Government's financial predicament. The budget deficit rose rapidly in the second half of the year, reflecting a partial recovery of wages, a transfer of liability for defense expenditures from Russia, relief outlays for natural disasters, a repayment of government arrears, and the cost of settling inter-enterprise arrears. Financing of the deficit in the second half of 1992 was facilitated by increased availability of cash from the CBR. Government revenues in 1992 are expected to fall to 12 percent of GDP, from a level of 32 percent in 1991. Even with a cut in real expenditures of about 35 percent, a 1992 budget deficit of about 12.5 percent of GDP is estimated to emerge.

8.   Kyrgyzstan's participation in the ruble zone effectively removes actions on the exchange rate and money supply from national control. A key determinant of the supply of money and credit is the issue of currency by the CBR to Kyrgyzstan. During the first half of 1992, the stock of rubles issued to Kyrgyzstan doubled, whereas nominal GDP rose about six fold. Moreover, deposit liabilities of banks rose by only 42 percent. This massive contraction in real terms in part was a consequence of the inability of banks to convert deposits into cash. As a result, there was a severe liquidity squeeze, with velocity rising by four times, the real stock of bank credit shrinking by two thirds, and a rapid build-up of inter-enterprise debt. The liquidity situation improved in the third quarter, however, with an increased supply of cash from the CBR.

9.   Kyrgyzstan was one of the first of the former Soviet republics to initiate a program of structural reform to facilitate the development of a market economy. A plethora of laws and decrees have been enacted, new institutions created, and an ambitious set of privatization targets developed by the reform-minded leadership. With the serious deterioration in economic conditions -- double digit rates of decline in consumption are estimated in both 1991 and 1992 -- the opposition to market oriented reforms has strengthened, resulting in some slippage in the pace of reform. Limited technical and institutional capacity and the unfamiliarity and resistance within government and among the workers and managers of enterprises and farms may also constrain the pace at which reform can be implemented. Notwithstanding these limitations, in July 1992, Kyrgyzstan's Parliament approved a comprehensive program of economic adjustment and reform, designed to accelerate the transition to a market economy.

Policy Priorities during the Transition

Macroeconomic Policy

10.   If Kyrgyzstan elects to remain in the ruble zone, there will be a need for closer coordination of monetary, fiscal and trade policies with Russia and the other countries using the ruble. Such coordination will, however, be difficult unless joint efforts to reduce fiscal deficits and inflation meet with greater success than in 1992. If a new currency is introduced, Kyrgyzstan's fiscal and monetary policies will become the primary determinant of domestic inflation. In either case, a tightening of financial policies relative to the second half of 1992 will be required. Without a substantial reduction in inflation, progress on structural reform is likely to be slowed, delaying the economic recovery.

11.   To reduce the budget deficit to a level compatible with moderate inflation, the tax base will need to be widened, tax administration strengthened and non-essential government expenditures further reduced. Since tax revenues from the enterprise sector may be slow to recover in the short term, several additional revenue enhancing measures should be considered. Reinstating the excise tax on gasoline, extending it to other fuels, and raising rates on tobacco and alcohol should be considered. A reduction of the VAT rate should be resisted and most existing exemptions to the VAT eliminated. Exemptions from the personal income and profit tax should also be minimized, and contributions to the Employment Fund adjusted to allow the Fund to remain self-financing. User fees for services such as transportation, telecommunications and irrigation should be raised to cover the economic cost of providing the public service (including capital costs), and environmental costs should increasingly be incorporated. Electricity pricing should eventually be based on long-run marginal cost. Until an appropriate structure is devised, electricity prices should be adjusted on a cost-plus basis to at least maintain the profitability of the relevant providing enterprises. Finally, rents should be increased to at least cover operations and maintenance costs.

12.   Expenditure cuts should focus on phasing out transfers to nonviable enterprises in a manner compatible with social constraints. Wage increases in public enterprises should be limited initially by decree and subsequently through tax incentives and penalties, while real wages in government may also have to be reduced from their level of November 1992. Consumer subsidies on items still subject to price controls will have to be reduced in real terms, in conjunction with a schedule for the elimination of most such controls. Increases in imported energy prices should be passed on fully to both industry and consumers, and subsidies on coal should be eliminated. However, expenditures on critical social services (such as primary health care and basic education) and the social safety net should be protected.

13.   The need for reduction in existing expenditures is underscored by the fact that new requirements will emerge during the transition. Expenditure on unemployment benefits can be expected to rise while the current level of government investment, at one percent of GDP, will not suffice if adequate resources are to be channeled to build the infrastructure for a market economy. The priorities for such investment include constructing a telecommunications network that permits the expansion of trade and communications outside the CIS and training in areas such as banking, management and marketing.

14.   To promote hard currency export growth from its currently very low base, the after tax profitability of such exports should be at least as great as for ruble exports. Ideally a rational incentive framework for hard currency exports should be coordinated across the ruble zone. If such a framework

is established, Kyrgyzstan should adhere to its requirements. However, if differentials continue to persist, Kyrgyzstan should ensure that its own rules provide incentives for hard currency exports as attractive as the most favorable treatment in other countries, in order to discourage the sale of such exports through other states. In early 1992, surrender requirements and the exchange rates applied to the surrendered foreign exchange varied widely and were often prohibitively punitive. The replacement of this system with a straightforward 10 percent export tax payable in hard currency represents an improvement, but should be considered an interim measure. An export tax may only be justified in a situation of exchange rate overshooting, and alternative measures to encourage exporters to remit foreign exchange within the country will have to be considered. Several aspects of trade policy may have to be reformulated if Kyrgyzstan opts for its own currency. In the meantime, a common tariff structure vis-a-vis the rest of the world should be maintained in coordination with other ruble area countries.

15.   Efforts to contain the collapse of interrepublican trade should begin with the reciprocal elimination of barriers to such trade in the context of an extension of free trade agreements with all the states in the ruble area. State trading agencies may continue to be needed in the short term to ensure adequate trade flows, particularly for bulk commodities such as food. Compulsory state orders at government mandated prices should, however, be replaced with market-based transactions, and the state agencies involved in interrepublican trade should increasingly be used to facilitate trade on an enterprise to enterprise basis through dissemination of information on markets.

Structural Reform

16.   Adjustment of enterprises to price liberalization is inhibited in Kyrgyzstan by a highly concentrated and monopolistic industrial structure that is characterized by: the ownership of commercial banks by enterprises that are their main customers; the organization of most industrial enterprises into conglomerates; an excessive degree of vertical integration; barriers to entry and exit; restrictions on labor mobility; a high level of dependence on interrepublican trade; a lack of enthusiasm and shortage of skilled personnel to enact the Government's privatization program; deficiencies in the legal framework; and a lack of entrepreneurial skills even in comparison to other states in the FSU. Combined with an unstable macroeconomic environment and the destruction of financial savings resulting from recent inflation, these factors pose formidable challenges to the emergence of a market economy.

17.   These characteristics suggest that the process of transformation into a market economy will be difficult and will require a sustained effort. It is clear that reforms in almost every area of economic activity will ultimately be needed. In particular, inadequate adjustment at the enterprise level in the presence of adverse external shocks could undermine the entire reform effort. While the authorities should thus be encouraged to proceed with a wide-ranging agenda of reform, it is also important to recognize that constraints on implementation capacity arising from technical as well as social factors will limit the speed of the transition. Since a competitive market economy will be slow to emerge, care will be needed in managing the pace at which the structures of the command economy are dismantled: In instances where a rapid dismantling cannot be replaced by a workable alternative in the short run, more gradual adjustments may be called for to moderate the collapse of output. Such strategic decisions of sequencing cannot be fully anticipated at the outset of the reform, but will need to be considered as part of an ongoing process. They should be interpreted as requirements for sustainability of the overall reform process rather than reversals of the ultimate objective of a market economy.

18.   An early priority for promoting enterprise reform is to disperse the current concentration of lending by banks to their major shareholders in order to harden the enterprise budget constraint and

improve the access to credit for non shareholders and emerging enterprises. Banks should thus be directed to reduce the share of loans provided to their large shareholders (defined as those on the bank's board or owners of at least 5 percent of the banks' shares) from the current practice, which in some banks reaches 90 percent, to 25 percent by the end of 1994 with appropriate intermediate targets. Complementary measures to strengthen other prudential regulations and bank supervision, raise minimum capital requirements for new and existing banks in parallel with inflation, and enhance bank profitability are needed. As a means of encouraging banks to comply with the new prudential regulations, NBK should consider using access to its rediscounts as leverage, ultimately limiting such access to banks that comply with the new capital and lending regulations.

19.   Interest rates should be encouraged to play a greater role in mobilizing savings and in the allocation of scarce credit. The discount rate of the NBK should be set in accordance with the rate set by the CBR while Kyrgyzstan remains in the ruble zone. The maximum mark-up on commercial bank loans using resources from the NBK should be substantially raised from its level of 3 percent in 1992 (and ultimately eliminated), and subsidized loans to special sectors should be eliminated unless the subsidies are entirely financed through the budget. Banks should be encouraged to raise deposit interest rates to levels that promote the growth of financial savings, and until the pattern of bank lending has been adequately dispersed, it may be necessary to enforce minimum lending rates on loans from banks' own resources. The recommendations on interest rate policy will only be valid once confidence in the ability to withdraw deposits from the banking system is credibly restored.

20.   In early 1991, the Government designed a three stage program for commercialization and privatization of virtually all of Kyrgyzstan's enterprises, and in January 1992 a detailed privatization program was announced. In practice, however, there have been severe problems and delays in implementing the enterprise reform program due to conflicting ownership claims and legal provisions, the opposition of vested managerial interests, concern about employment consequences, and a lack of capital, staff and resources.

21.   Priority should be given to segmenting and privatizing, as rapidly as possible, distribution, wholesale, local transport, and other trading enterprises. This will be particularly important to phase out de facto reliance on the system of state orders. To facilitate this task, the State Property Fund (SPF) must be able to initiate and follow through on privatization in the above priority sectors as well as housing, and will need more resources to accomplish this. For the smallest enterprises, particularly in retail trade and services, privatization could be further accelerated through an auction process that limits bureaucratic intervention to exceptional rather than routine cases. For medium and large enterprises, some form of mass privatization is likely to be necessary. The outcome of such a program should include an ownership structure that permits effective governance, and segmentation of enterprises into a structure that is more conducive to competition. Until such a framework for reform is developed, it is essential for the Government to exercise its ownership rights more effectively. This will include closure of plants that are clearly no longer viable and the initiation of restructuring of those enterprises that are to remain in the public sector in the medium term. This will require well-defined limits on bank credit and government transfers to such enterprises as part of the restructuring program. Large enterprises should be formally corporatized and a special effort to strengthen governance of the previously Union controlled enterprises is necessary to fill the current ownership vacuum.

22.   To encourage private sector activity, the approval process for establishing an enterprise should be simplified, bureaucratic obstacles removed and the ability of local authorities to obstruct business start-ups diminished. Access to office facilities and government controlled inputs, including

information on markets, should be made available on an equal basis to the private sector. The expansion of the commodity exchanges should thus be encouraged in conjunction with their privatization. Finally, there is a need for rationalization and harmonization of existing legislation to provide confidence in the Government's intention to guarantee the rights of private enterprises, close existing gaps in the areas of property rights, intellectual property and contract law, and strengthen the capacity to enforce the new legal regime.

23.   Adjustments in labor market legislation are needed to facilitate the process of labor reallocation and contain the fiscal burden of unemployment compensation and the wage bill of state-owned enterprises (SOEs). In particular, no special category of workers should be given protection from layoffs, officially mandated job assignments should be terminated, employers should not be charged for the training of their previous workers, and permanent residency provisions should be removed from the criteria for employment eligibility. First-time job seekers and labor market re-entrants should not be eligible for unemployment compensation.

24.   To minimize suffering and maintain the social acceptability of the reform program, it is important that adequate resources be made available for essential social needs. However, with social expenditures comprising two-thirds of consolidated fiscal expenditures in 1991 (including those of the Pension Fund), it will be impossible to maintain their level in real terms. De facto, these cuts are already occurring. In 1992, the real value of pensions and family allowances has been drastically eroded through inflation and payment delays, and the quality of educational programs has declined. In fact, infant and maternal mortality rates have already increased. There is therefore a need to restructure the system of social expenditures to improve the efficiency and equity of its deliverance, by better targeting of intended beneficiaries, and by protecting the most vulnerable.

25.   Nearly half the population of Kyrgyzstan is eligible for either pensions or allowances, and the share of family allowances in GDP at 8 percent in 1991 may be unsurpassed. Inflation has sharply eroded the real value of these benefits in 1992. A basis for restructuring such expenditures to limit the decline in benefits for the most vulnerable could include: indexing the minimum pension to a level that is necessary to maintain a reasonably healthy diet based on a basket of foods consumed predominantly by poor people; allowing pensions above this level to temporarily merge with the minimum pension; raising the retirement age for women to that of men; and taxing cash benefits. To limit spending on family allowances, allowances for children above 6 may have to be abolished or reduced substantially, coupled with a safety net provision for large families in need. The social safety net should ensure that consumption levels do not fall below the level implied by the above minimum consumption basket.

26.   Supply disruptions and the scarcity of foreign exchange have produced an alarming shortage of medical supplies. External assistance is hence urgently needed to provide medical supplies for primary health care programs and basic institutional care. To keep additional expenditures on pharmaceuticals from constraining the availability of funds for other health inputs, increased health budget support is also needed to complement any foreign exchange assistance. (The health budget amounted to only 3.4 percent of GDP in 1991.) At the same time, the retail price of drugs should be raised to discourage inefficient consumption, and, in the longer term, prices should be liberalized and the growth of private pharmacies encouraged. Greater use should be made of patient fees in both ambulatory and inpatient care, with exemptions for low income groups. Cost recovery schemes especially in higher and middle education will also be needed to protect the share of education expenditures in GDP.

Sectoral Policy Issues

27.   Recent trade disruptions and price liberalization have threatened to render a portion of agricultural production unprofitable and have set back the Government's efforts to encourage private activity in the sector. The policy challenge is to guide agricultural reforms during the transition in a manner that is sensitive to short-term concerns regarding shortages and profitability, but that does not detract from the objective of restructuring production to exploit Kyrgyzstan's comparative advantages under international prices and increased private ownership. If longer-term production prospects are favorable, output price increases to encourage supply should be the preferred policy. Given the short-term uncertainty regarding imports of critical commodities, raising procurement prices to minimize output losses also may be justified, even if a different cropping pattern might ultimately emerge. If prices are not yet liberalized, the relative prices of inputs and outputs should approach international relative prices, to promote more rational production patterns. But where there is little prospect for the profitability of specific commodities, any price support is inappropriate, and targeted income transfers may be needed to induce restructuring in desired directions. Any government intervention during the transition should, however, respect overall fiscal constraints. Given the significant macroeconomic repercussions of alternative policies, they should be coordinated by a body with access to the key policy makers and should not be managed solely by the agricultural ministries.

28.   A program for liberalizing agricultural commodity prices should be developed, while state orders should be converted to state purchases, using bidding procedures rather than bilateral negotiations, and limited to goods required by public agencies. Private activity in all aspects of agricultural production and trade activity should be explicitly permitted, and access to inputs, infrastructure and extension services for the emerging private sector should be provided on non-discriminatory terms. Finally, a program for privatization of land and its use as collateral in rural finance should be developed with due consideration to social conditions. Where land privatization is not feasible in the short term, an unrestricted program of allowing land lease rights that are tradeable and transferable should be considered.

29.   Kyrgyzstan has been a heavy consumer of energy relative to its level of industrialization and per capita income. As energy prices move to world levels, major adjustments in energy use, including substantial contraction of imported oil and gas appear inevitable. Energy pricing policy, discussed above, is pertinent not only from a fiscal standpoint but also to guide investment decisions in a non-distortive manner. The Government's strategy to increase the degree of electrification appears sound for the long term. However, given fiscal constraints and uncertain electricity demand in the short term, investment priority should be accorded to hydro projects that were due for completion in the next 1-2 years. Major new investments should not be initiated until a study of electricity demand in the new environment is available, or until hard currency export contracts have been concluded. Attracting foreign investment for oil and gas exploration and mineral extraction is also a priority, for which reforms in the legal and fiscal framework will be important.

30.   Kyrgyzstan's telecommunication infrastructure is insufficient to support the desired outward orientation of the economy. Investment in the short term should focus on high revenue generating international services and the needs of emerging business subscribers. The tariff structure will need to be revised to permit such investments on a commercial basis. Regulatory and institutional reforms are also needed to establish autonomous providing entities that can be commercialized to improve the quality of service and financial viability.

31.   The transport sector in Kyrgyzstan appears relatively well developed. Adjustments in the price and tax system to phase out user subsidies will be needed to ensure that the infrastructure is properly maintained. Creation of a competitive transport market will be facilitated through the segmentation and privatization of existing transport companies.

Medium-Term Outlook and External Financing Requirements

32.   Projections of the medium-term outlook and financing requirements are clouded by the considerable uncertainty surrounding the evolution of interrepublican trade, the terms of trade, inflation in the ruble area, and the ruble exchange rate. A discussion of the medium-term outlook is contained in Chapter 2, while the external financing implications are provided in Chapter 3. In summary, Kyrgyzstan is expected to make significant progress on macroeconomic adjustment and structural and sectoral reform along the lines discussed above. Interrepublican trade is expected to continue to contract in 1993, with prospects beyond 1993 tied to the effectiveness of efforts to construct a suitable payments mechanism. Irrespective of the overall trend, significant deficits on interrepublican trade are expected to emerge, projected at $220 million in 1993 and at least $250 millon as world energy prices are reached. Hard currency imports in 1992 may have fallen to 5 percent of their level in 1990. As the pattern of trade and production is rationalized, a full restoration to earlier import levels would not be warranted. But some recovery will be needed to maintain the functioning of critical aspects of economic activity and to limit the compression of consumption. Hard currency exports could grow rapidly in the 1990s with the adoption of an appropriate incentive framework and assuming greater macroeconomic stability, but their base is so low that large trade deficits in convertible currency are expected to re-emerge. This deficit is projected at $150 million in 1993, with prospects beyond 1993 tied to export performance and financing availability.

33.   An output decline of 12 percent is projected for 1993, reflecting continued disruptions in interrepublican trade, the need to stabilize the domestic economy, and the difficult process of restructuring that must be initiated, particularly in the industrial sector. This scenario would bring the cumulative decline in per capita output during 1991-93 to about 40 percent. A renewal of growth and employment creation by the mid-1990s will be needed to sustain the reform effort. After massive declines during 1991-93, a recovery in investment, higher productivity of such investment, and the growth of hard currency exports are expected to help generate the economic recovery. An improved incentive framework in agriculture and increased activity in the mining and metallurgical sector in response to more profitable export opportunities are expected to lead the supply response. However, in view of the extent of restructuring that is required, the multifaceted constraints to private sector activity, and the uncertainty of developments elsewhere in the FSU, a robust economic recovery is not anticipated until 1995-96.

34.   Even this scenario of economic recovery is threatened by major risks. Slower than envisaged enterprise reform and an inability to reduce inflation substantially within the ruble area (or by Kyrgyzstan separately if a new currency is introduced), could significantly delay the timetable for recovery. At the same time, the extent of economic decline already expected could threaten the ability of the authorities to pursue reform forcefully. The technical capacity to implement the far-reaching reforms envisaged may limit the speed of reform, even if the social and political consensus for reform can be maintained. Finally, external financing shortfalls could aggravate each of these risks, deepen the output decline and further delay the recovery.

35.   Significant external assistance will therefore be required, both in the form of financing and technical assistance to implement the reform agenda. While technical assistance requirements in 1993 are estimated at $35 million, TA disbursements are projected at $20 million per year, constrained in part by absorptive capacity. Including TA (as a service import), the above trade estimates, and a modest reserve accumulation, financing requirements in 1993 are projected at $400 million to $450 million. The requisite level of commitments for 1993 is only moderately higher, at $470 million to $520 million, since the bulk of the financing requirement is for balance of payments assistance. These projections exclude any debt servicing on Kyrgyzstan's portion of the FSU debt, which was taken over by Russia in the autumn of 1992. Financing requirements are projected to remain at approximately the 1993 range during 1994-96, as a widening of the interrepublican trade deficit is compensated by growth of hard currency exports.

36.   These financing requirements are large in relation to Kyrgyzstan's economy and debt servicing capacity. External financing should therefore largely be in the form of grants or highly concessional loans. Based even on optimistic assumptions regarding Kyrgyzstan's ability to generate hard currency export growth for the rest of the decade, and the ability of the Government to access foreign exchange to service debt, a financing mix exceeding 20 percent of market-based borrowing should be avoided if debt servicing capacity is to be maintained at manageable levels; i.e., the grant element in projected financing should be at least 80 percent.

PART I

The Macroeconomic Framework

Among the Commonwealth of Independent States, Kyrgyzstan was one of the earliest to start the transformation to a market economy. Prices have been liberalized for over 90 percent of all retail goods, and administered prices for other goods have been substantially increased in most cases. Privatization started in 1991, and in July 1992 Kyrgyzstan's Parliament approved an accelerated program of economic reform. However it is already apparent that the process of transition will be long and difficult, not least due to the almost total isolation from market economies and the entrenched nature of past habits. The task has been and will continue to be complicated by adverse developments in the external environment. First, there have been major disruptions in interrepublican trade and hence production. Second, the large transfers from the Union to Kyrgyzstan's budget have ended, while funds provided directly from the center to state enterprises have also ended, except for the provision of currency from the Central Bank of Russia to the National Bank of Kyrgyzstan, and the inter-central bank financing arrangements within the CIS. Third, recent and prospective increases in oil and gas relative prices will cause a major terms of trade deterioration. These factors are expected to lead to a substantial drop in the country's real income during 1992 and 1993 even if Kyrgyzstan is able to make good progress in the restructuring of its incentive systems, enterprises and institutions for the creation of a market economy. Under these circumstances, there would be a strong case for substantial support from the international community to ease the burden of adjustment and improve the prospects for successful transformation.

Part I of the report analyzes recent economic developments (Chapter 1), discusses the policy priorities during the transition and assesses the medium-term outlook (Chapter 2), and provides an analysis of external financing requirements in light of Kyrgyzstan's debt servicing capacity and the implications for the Government's aid coordination capability (Chapter 3).

CHAPTER 1

Recent Economic Developments

Background

1.01   From 1936 to the end of 1990, Kyrgyzstan was a constituent republic of the Soviet Union, known as the Soviet Socialist Republic of Kirghizia. The nationalist sentiments which contributed to the dissolution of the Soviet Union had manifested themselves in the republic during 1989 when a law was enacted making Kyrgyz the official language (although Russian remains the main language of government). In 1990, there was major ethnic violence near the border with Uzbekistan over what was regarded as an unfair distribution of land. This was followed by widespread demonstrations against the Communist Party, which was blamed for mishandling the crisis. These protests became the focus of a broader anti-government campaign by all opposition forces, which eventually forced the parliament to hold new Presidential elections. In October 1990, the Communist Party lost the Presidency to Askar Akayev, a pro-democracy physicist who was called back from the Soviet Parliament in Moscow after the first round of elections in parliament ended in deadlock. By the end of 1990, Kyrgyzstan had declared sovereignty. In 1991, during the August coup attempt in Moscow a parallel coup was attempted against Mr. Akayev in Bishkek, and was also defeated. Kyrgyzstan formally declared its independence in August 1991, and joined the Commonwealth of Independent States in December 1991.

1.02   Kyrgyzstan is bordered on the north by Kazakhstan, on the west by Uzbekistan, on the south and west by Tajikistan and on the east by China. Its area is 198,500 square kilometers, or less than 1 percent of the area of the former USSR. Only about 7 percent of the area is suitable for agricultural crops, most of which is irrigated by streams and rivers from the country's high mountain ranges. About 40 percent of the total area is used as pastures for the extensive sheep and cattle raising that constitutes the main traditional activity of the economy.

1.03   The population was 4.4 million in 1991, which represented a growth rate of 2.3 percent annually since 1979. Over half the population is Kyrgyz, a people of Turko-Mongolian origin who were originally nomadic, and who are still dominant in the rural areas. Russians account for 21 percent of the population. The other main nationality groups are Uzbek (13 percent) and Ukrainian and German (2.5 percent each). Net emigration, mainly of Russians, was about 90,000 annually in 1990 and 1991.

1.04   The country's per capita GNP in 1991 is estimated at US$1,550, or less than half of that in Russia (US$3,220), on a basis comparable to the per capita GNP data published in the World Bank Atlas. A relatively large margin of error is however associated with this estimate. Moreover, with the large drop in income estimated for 1992-93, a substantial reduction of GNP per capita is expected.

Economic Setting

1.05   Kyrgyzstan's economy is heavily dependent on developments in the Russian Federation and the other members of the CIS. As an integral part of the USSR, the country was subject to directions from the center on production, investment, trade, and virtually all other aspects of economic activity. This dependence has been only moderately reduced by political independence. The country remains in the ruble zone, and the bulk of its trade is still with other members of the CIS. Although barriers to free trade have been erected among several CIS members, Kyrgyzstan has reestablished free trading arrangements with Russia, Belarus and Kazakhstan for most goods, and in practice interrepublican borders remain largely open.

1.06   Economic developments thus continue to be strongly influenced by external factors. Within the context of a functioning ruble zone, monetary, fiscal and trade policies would need to be closely coordinated. Such coordination in turn would lead to convergence in domestic inflation and interest rates, and preclude the use of the exchange rate as a tool of economic policy. While in practice coordination has been flawed, for a country as small as Kyrgyzstan the degree of interdependence remains high, contributing to the uncertain economic outlook. The outcome of Russia's stabilization effort is still not clear; nor is the pace at which imported energy prices will reach international levels. The supply of currency from the Russian Central Bank and the extent of foreign assistance are also uncertain.

1.07   Nonetheless, Kyrgyzstan's prospects will depend increasingly on its own economic policies. This report attempts to identify those policy areas that will be of particular importance to the country's future. Developments in 1992 clearly indicate the unsustainable nature of emerging fiscal and external deficits, which makes domestic adjustment imperative. But this adjustment will have to occur against the backdrop of a failing payments system for interrepublican trade, an evaporating faith of the public in the ruble as a store of value, and the inevitable rise of barter in response to the unprecedented combination of these phenomena. Moreover, real wages have already fallen sharply and the unaccustomed threat of rising unemployment looms heavily. This chapter describes the development of Kyrgyzstan's economy prior to the current crisis and analyzes the evolution of the economy in 1992 to provide the economic underpinning on which to base the priorities for stabilization and structural and sectoral reform that are discussed in the subsequent chapters of the report.

Economic Structure

1.08   Gross domestic product in 1990 is estimated by the statistical authorities at R8.3 billion, about 38 percent higher than the net material product (NMP). Half of the difference between these two measures is accounted for by capital consumption allowances and the other half by value added in service sectors excluded from NMP. In 1990, agriculture accounted for one third of GDP and 22 percent of employment. The latter figure, however, excludes labor on private plots and may not fully incorporate vegetable and livestock production, where the private sector is of growing significance. Raw wool and manufactured woolen products accounted for about 22 percent of 1991 exports. Industry and mining accounted for 28 percent of GDP and 19 percent of employment in 1990. The main industrial activities are mining and metallurgy (gold, uranium and antimony), wool processing and textiles, agricultural machinery, electrical equipment and electronics, using facilities developed originally for defense purposes, and sugar refining that was based on raw sugar from Cuba. The country produces substantial amounts of hydroelectric power, but is a net importer of oil, gas and coal. Energy products accounted for 10 percent of 1991 imports. Another 15 percent of imports consisted of grain, flour and other food products, while raw sugar for refining and reexport accounted for about 7 percent.

1.09   External trade represents a high share of Kyrgyzstan's economic activity. The total of exports and imports accounted for nearly 80 percent of GDP in 1991. This trade is predominantly with other republics of the FSU, reflecting political and strategic objectives as well as economic considerations. About 20 percent of imports were from outside the USSR in 1991, while less than 1 percent of exports went outside. In recent years up through 1990, the country ran trade deficits averaging 18 percent of GDP. About half of this was financed by transfers from the Union, while the remainder was apparently financed by loans and investments from centralized ministries and financial agencies in the USSR directly to state enterprises in Kyrgyzstan.

Developments in 1985-1991

Production

1.10   During the second half of the 1980s, Kyrgyzstan's economic performance was somewhat better than that of the Russian Federation. Total output growth averaged 4.5 percent between 1985 and 1990, compared with only 1.2 percent in Russia. The ratio of fixed investment to GDP averaged 28 percent of GDP in Kyrgyzstan and 25 percent in Russia. During 1991, the process of economic reform started to accelerate in the region and the command economy began to erode. Economic dislocations resulting from the initial phases of price liberalization and the reduction in control of the central planning authorities led to a drop in GDP of 9 percent in Russia and of 4 percent in Kyrgyzstan.

1.11   The most important source of growth in Kyrgyzstan in the second half of the eighties was livestock production, which grew in real terms by over 6 percent annually. This increase appears to reflect efforts in the USSR to encourage output of meat and dairy products, and was associated with an increase in relative prices for agricultural goods.[1] However, there was no output growth in the main agricultural crops. This apparently reflected inadequate incentives and constraints arising from poor maintenance of the irrigation system and from supply limitations on fertilizer. In addition, a substantial amount of irrigated land was being used uneconomically for production of fodder for livestock.

1.12   Industrial production rose on average by 3.3 percent annually between 1985 and 1990. The two largest components of this sector were light industry and mechanical and electrical engineering. Both of these grew at the same rate as the total. Food processing, the third major category, expanded at a slower rate of 2.4 percent. The most dynamic sector was nonferrous metals, where output nearly doubled during this five year period; these metals include gold, mercury, antimony and uranium. However, the aggregate value of output of this sector was only 5 percent of the total in 1990.[2] Output of electric power (4 percent of 1990 gross output) rose at an average rate of 6 percent, as an expansion in hydroelectric production was utilized to increase exports to neighboring republics.

1.13   In 1991, the decline of GDP was primarily due to poor agricultural performance. Overall agricultural output dropped by 9 percent. The volume of crop production was down by 18 percent, while livestock production, which had a higher weight in the total, fell by 6 percent.[3] In industry, there was a 10 percent decline in output of the food processing sector during 1991, which paralleled the drop in agricultural output. This was offset by a moderate increase in mining, light manufacturing and engineering. Overall, industrial output remained flat in 1991, in contrast to a reduction of 8 percent in Russia. This suggests that Kyrgyzstan's industrial sector was subject to fewer disruptions in supply

---

1.   The GDP deflator for agriculture rose by 30 percent between 1983 and 1990, compared with 13 percent in the overall GDP deflator.

2.   Uranium output may be excluded from this total.

3.   It is possible that production did not decline as much as reported, and that a significant amount of (unreported) output was diverted through unofficial channels in domestic markets or to other republics where prices were higher.

during the year than elsewhere in the USSR. In current prices, value added in industry rose by more than GDP as a whole, mainly because of a sharp relative increase in prices of engineering goods and construction materials.

Prices

1.14   Data on price movements before 1988 are very limited, but all indications are that inflation was negligible prior to that year. During 1989-90, however, there were significant increases in procurement prices for most agricultural products causing the overall GDP deflator to rise by about 12 percent in that two year period. Prices increased substantially after April 1991, when Kyrgyzstan, along with the rest of the Soviet Union, relaxed controls on prices. The new rules affected only a limited set of products and included several forms of constraint to the extent of price rise. They nevertheless had a strong inflationary effect. By December 1991, consumer prices were almost 3 times higher than the December 1990 level, and wholesale prices were almost 4 times higher. The 1991 inflation closely followed Russia's experience with consumer prices, while wholesale prices rose somewhat less than in Russia.

Consumption, Investment and Saving

1.15   During 1985-89, both consumption and investment increased more rapidly than GDP, the difference financed by an increase in resources available from the Union. The external resource deficit rose from 16 percent of GDP in 1985 to 22 percent in 1989. In 1990 consumption fell moderately, and investment fell sharply. Even so, the latter remained relatively high as a share of GDP at 33.5 percent. These cuts in expenditures helped to reduce the resource deficit to 17 percent of GDP in that year. During 1991, the preliminary national accounts data show surprising developments--a drastic cut in the resource deficit to about 1 percent of GDP and a large drop in consumption--by 13 percent in real terms. As a share of GDP, consumption fell from 83 percent in 1990 to 70 percent in 1991. Between 1989 and 1991 imports showed a drop from 56 to 40 percent of GDP, while exports rose from 34 percent to 39 percent. The data imply an increase in national saving from a stable ratio of about 25 percent of GDP in the 1985-90 period to one of 41 percent in 1991. It is not clear what factors explain these startling changes in consumption, saving and trade during 1991. It is possible that in part they reflect inadequacies in the underlying statistics.

1.16   There are, however, other possible explanations. One is suggested by the fact that a majority of Kyrgyzstan's industrial production was under the control of Union enterprises. It is possible that as prospects for the dissolution of the USSR increased, the parent enterprise would seek to transfer real resources from their subsidiaries. This could be done by reducing funds for imports by the subsidiaries and by increasing exports from them to the parent company. Such measures would be consistent with the substantial decline in imports and increase in exports during 1991. Under this hypothesis, the apparent increase in national saving would in effect represent a movement of capital from Kyrgyzstan to Russia (where most of the Union enterprises had their headquarters). Another possible explanation, which would be consistent with the first, derives from the fact that Union enterprises that wanted to raise prices during 1991 had an interest in showing profits that were nominally low. They may have made abnormally large purchases from Kyrgyzstan and elsewhere to add stocks for this purpose. On the side of imports, an alternative explanation is suggested by the fact that the cut in imports relative

Table 1-1. Macroeconomic Indicators, 1985-91

Gross Domestic Product by Industrial Origin

	Bln Rbl	Share of GDP (%)[a]				Real Growth Rates (%)[b]		
	1991	1985	1989	1990	1991	1985-89	1990	1991
GDP	16.9	100.0	100.0	100.0	100.0	5.1	3.2	-3.9
Agriculture	4.8	30.1	32.9	33.7	28.6	5.6	5.5	-9.1
Industry	6.4	31.5	29.5	28.2	37.8	5.7	-0.9	0.3
Construction	1.2	10.6	10.3	10.1	6.9	4.7	1.5	-6.2
Transport	0.7	4.8	4.7	4.8	4.1	4.9	7.4	1.7
Service	3.8	23.0	2.5	23.2	22.6	3.8	6.4	-3.2

Annual Rate of Change in GDP Deflators

	1985-89	1990	1991
GDP	0.6	5.8	111.3
Agriculture	2.5	6.0	89.8
Industry	-1.3	5.4	171.7
Other	-0.5	5.3	85.1

Gross Domestic Product by Type of Expenditure

	Bln Rbl	Share of GDP (%)[a]				Real Growth Rates (%)[b]		
	1991	1985	1989	1990	1991	1985-89	1990	1991
GDP	16.9	100.0	100.0	100.0	100.0	5.1	3.2	-3.9
Consumption	12.0	80.8	82.5	83.4	70.3	5.2	-2.2	-13.0
Investment	5.2	35.4	39.6	33.5	31.0	9.5	-21.4	-6.4
Saving	6.8	25.8	24.6	25.1	41.1			
Exports	6.5	n.a.	34.1	30.0	38.8			
Imports	6.8	n.a.	56.4	47.2	40.1			
Non factor services	-0.11	1.0	0.2	0.2	---			
Resource Balance	-0.35	-16.2	-22.1	-16.9	-1.3			
Official Transfers	1.93	6.2[c]	7.1	10.9	11.4	10.0[c]	59.2	-4.6
Disposable Income	18.85	106.5	107.1	110.9	111.4	5.2	4.6	-7.4

a/ Based on data at current prices.
b/ Based on data at 1983 prices.
c/ Estimate based on 1987 transfers.

to GDP was entirely in hard currency purchases, which fell from 12 percent of GDP in 1990 to 6 percent in 1991. The hypothesis here is that an administrative decision was made in Moscow to limit hard currency imports for Kyrgyzstan because of the uncertainties during the year. The result may have been shortages of consumer goods, which led to a substantial reduction in consumption and an involuntary increase in saving.

Public Finance

1.17   During 1987-90 consolidated expenditures of the republic and local governments averaged between 36 and 38 percent of GDP. When expenditures of the social security system are included, the total share was about 45 percent.[4] Expenditures from the government budget on social security (primarily pensions and child welfare) accounted for between 8 and 9 percent of GDP, while subsidies (mainly for meat, milk, bread and housing maintenance) accounted for another 5-7 percent. General government outlays for capital formation (mainly buildings, roads and housing) averaged nearly 6 percent in 1987-90, and expenditures on government consumption about 16 percent.

1.18   Tax and nontax revenue of the general government ranged between 28 and 31 percent of GDP during 1987-90. Payments by enterprises for social security accounted for another 6-7 percent. Transfer payments from the Union to the Republic rose from 6 percent of GDP in 1987 to 11 percent in 1990 and were sufficient to generate a surplus in the government accounts during each year of this period.

1.19   In 1991, as production declined and inflation rose sharply, there was a substantial reduction in the ratio of revenue to GDP. Tax revenue dropped from 26.2 percent of GDP in 1990 to 15.7 percent (Table 1-4). This decline, which was concentrated in taxation of goods and services (Appendix Table 4-1), appears to reflect the sharp drop in consumption in 1991 as well as collection difficulties arising from revisions in the tax system -- a sales tax replaced the turnover tax in 1991 but was rescinded by year end with the introduction of a value added tax in 1992. Expenditures were also reduced. Subsidies and transfers to social security were cut back in total from 16 percent of GDP to 12 percent. The sharpest cut was in capital formation financed by the budget, which fell from nearly 6 percent in 1990 to 1.1 percent in 1991. However, transfers from the Union rose in that year to over 11 percent of GDP. The result was an overall budget surplus of 4.1 percent of GDP in 1991.

Trade and Payments

1.20   During the late 1980s and 1990, Kyrgyzstan ran deficits both in interrepublican and hard currency trade. The combined deficits were sizeable, in the range of 20 percent of GDP, and net exports were limited to wool, tobacco, nonferrous metals, and electric power. Transfer payments from the Union to the Kyrgyzstan budget offset about one half of the deficit, and the rest appears to have been financed by capital inflows into Union controlled state enterprises.[5] The exceptional trends in trade during 1991 and possible explanations were discussed above. In addition, export growth, which was limited to

---

4.   Prior to 1991, social security expenditures were made directly from the Union Social Security Fund, and payments by enterprises were make directly to this Fund. In 1991, after responsibility for Social Security was transferred to Kyrgyzstan, expenditures of the system not covered by the budget amounted to R1.4 billion.

5.   Balance of payments data do not yet include information on capital flows.

interrepublican trade, may have been inflated as a result of a terms of trade gain resulting from the nature of price liberalization, in which petroleum prices were relatively stable. Engineering exports were particularly strong and also gained from relative price increases.

Developments During 1992

Production

1.21   There are widespread indications that output and trade have dropped sharply in 1992. However, most of these indicators are partial and qualitative, and some are of doubtful reliability as a result of disruptions in statistical reporting systems associated with privatization. Realized contracts for supplies of raw materials and other inputs by state enterprises showed a shortfall well below those planned. Some of these contracts were substituted by barter arrangements with other suppliers, but there is little basis yet for judging to what extent. In agriculture, overall output in 1992 appears to have been at least maintained at the 1991 level. The grain harvest was substantially larger than in 1991 (permitting a sharp decline in grain imports), and production of other crops on balance may be about flat. Livestock production by state farms in the first 9 months of the year was reported at only two-thirds of the 1991 level. However, there has been a substantial transfer of livestock from state and collective farms to the private sector, so that on balance overall livestock production in 1992 may be only moderately lower than in 1991.

1.22   In industry, however, production declined by about 23 percent in the first three quarters relative to the same period in 1991. Early in the year, there were large accumulations of inventories of finished products because of the steep drop in effective demand. There are reportedly serious problems of obtaining inputs of raw materials and components, even allowing for growing barter arrangements. With the breakdown in interrepublican payments arrangements there has been a large increase in arrears throughout the ruble area. These problems are compounded by export restrictions that have been imposed in some of Kyrgyzstan's trading partners in the CIS -- although such restrictions were largely removed in early 1992 with the two most important partners, Russia and Kazakhstan.

1.23   In the transport and construction sectors, available indicators show a fall in the volume of activity of between 40 and 50 percent in the first three quarters of 1992. Finally, the economy was adversely affected by a series of earthquakes and mudslides in May and August. Balancing the relatively favorable performance in agriculture with the very large declines in all other sectors, real GDP is estimated to decline by 24 percent in 1992.

Prices, Wages and Employment

1.24   In January 4, 1992 Kyrgyzstan followed Russia in a second stage of price liberalization. The January action was an almost complete release of price controls. Limits were set for a few commodities on the extent of price increases, but most of the limits were 4 to 7 times the 1991 year-end prices. In consumer goods, limits were imposed for bread, milk, meat, baby foods, and a few other core items in the consumer budget. No increase was allowed for rents. Subsequently, the prices of most of these consumer items were liberalized, with only bread, milk and poultry products, vodka, rent, and transportation subject to control as of October.

1.25   With the January action consumer prices took another major jump, rising 157 percent in January, 29 percent in February, 16 percent in March and 18 percent in April. From May through August, the rate of increase dropped sharply to an average of less than 6 percent a month. In September, however, the consumer index rose by 27 percent. The latter increase was due primarily to increases in three important items -- bread (28 percent), milk (81 percent) and sugar (161 percent) resulting from reductions in subsidies and the decontrol of sugar prices. By September, the overall level of consumer prices was between 6 and 10 times the level a year earlier.[6] Increases were widespread across food and nonfood products, but there were wide variations. For example, over the year ending in September 1992, prices for bread and milk rose by 12 times, while the index for vegetables rose by only 67 percent and that for fruit by only 52 percent. Such differences presumably reflected the urban market conditions for fresh food supply that already existed at the beginning of the period, with more open price setting mechanisms and a wider variety of suppliers.

1.26   While inflation in the first three quarters was high in Kyrgyzstan, it was significantly less than in the Russian Federation for both consumer and wholesale prices. While Kyrgyzstan's consumer prices rose 7 times from December to September, the Russian index rose by about 10 times, even though the extent of liberalization was roughly the same as in Russia. The authorities believe that arbitragers came into Kyrgyzstan's markets during the first half and made large cash purchases of certain commodities for export to states where prices were higher. These market activities will tend to bring domestic prices more closely into line with those of Russia. However, price differentials can be expected to continue to persist given (rising) transport costs, remaining trade barriers, and the impact of lower wages in Kyrgyzstan on the price of non-tradeables.

---

6.   The price data for Kyrgyzstan have ambiguities for measuring changes over extended periods such as a year. The monthly data are available only as a ratio to the preceding month or as a ratio to the same month of the preceding year. A fixed-weight price index for a base-year basket of goods is not available. When an index is calculated by chaining monthly changes into an annual series, the result is a year-to-year ratio that is often very different from the year-to-year ratios calculated on the basis of the same months in the previous year.

Figure 1-1

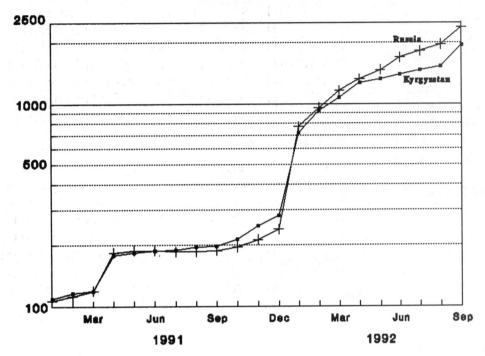

Consumer Prices
In Kyrgyzstan and Russia

Figure 1-2

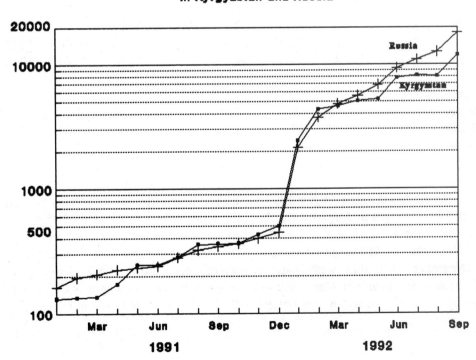

Wholesale Prices
In Kyrgyzstan and Russia

1.27   Wholesale prices rose far more in the first three quarters than consumer prices. The increases were led by fuels, which by September were 59 times their December levels. Kyrgyzstan's oil imports are virtually all in the form of refined products, such as gasoline and diesel fuel, and for some time these have been priced above ruble zone levels for crude oil. Refined products have reflected the subsidy element in the cost of their crude input content, but they have carried no additional subsidy on refining costs. Therefore, as imported crude moves closer to world prices the effects on Kyrgyzstan's refined imports should be somewhat less than proportional.

1.28   Nonfuel wholesale prices had increased by September 1992 to about 20 times their December levels, led by machinery products in both 1991 and 1992, which by September were 38 times those of a year earlier. A 48 percent rise of the wholesale price index in September was accounted for mainly by a six-fold increase in the index for cereals, which resulted from a large increase in the procurement price for grain.

Table 1-2. Price Ratios, 1992

	Relative to same month, 1991			Relative to December, 1991		
	March	June	Sept.	March	June	Sept.
Consumer Prices	8.99	7.40	9.80	3.85	4.98	6.97
Retail prices	6.24	5.16	6.52	2.67	3.40	4.62
Foods	5.02	3.97	6.48	2.53	3.00	4.80
Nonfoods	6.70	5.61	5.86	2.63	3.45	4.13
Wholesale prices	33.82	31.59	32.91	9.17	15.50	23.72
Fuels	19.07	58.57	59.76	19.62	59.34	59.09
Nonfuels	35.43	28.56	29.90	8.00	10.62	19.77
Russian prices						
Consumer	9.75	9.00	12.69	4.83	7.05	9.98
Wholesale	23.13	39.05	52.23	10.80	21.04	40.54

1.29   Wage data through August 1992 indicate a sharp reduction in real terms, following a 13 percent drop in 1991. Wages in August were about three times their nominal level of the fourth quarter of 1991, and, following a Presidential decree doubling minimum wages, most wages and benefits were doubled as of November 1. Minimum wages rates have been raised more than the average. From a level of R180 in December 1991, they were increased several times during 1992 to a level of R1600 on November 1, or nearly 9 times the December 1991 rate. Average real wages in 1992 are estimated to have declined by 35 to 40 percent, with a somewhat lesser real decline in the minimum wage.

1.30   The real wage decline was exacerbated by the currency shortage during the first half of 1992, which with wage payments almost entirely in cash, resulted in significant delays in such payments. There may have been a catchup in actual receipts of wages in the second half of 1992 as the currency shortage was considerably eased. But at 1992 inflation rates, wage receivables can lose value very rapidly, and hence the conventional measure of real wages can significantly overstate both the real income of workers and the real cost to employees.

1.31   A decline in real wages might have been one means of insulating employment from the sharp output losses experienced thus far: through late-1992 registered unemployment was still negligible. More fundamentally, however, the lack of adjustment in the labor market reflects the constraints on adjustment within the enterprise sector (discussed in Chapters 4 and 5), the characteristics of the labor market and remaining deficiencies in labor market legislation (Chapter 6).   While registered unemployment may not yet have risen, the practice of involuntary leaves of absence at reduced pay has increased. As enterprise budget constraints are hardened -- that is, the expenditure of enterprises is limited to their own resources as government subsidies are phased out and access to bank borrowing is based on commercial criteria alone -- an increase in unemployment is to be expected, reflecting not only the loss of output but also the fact that estimates of previous overstaffing in enterprises range from 20 to 30 percent.

The Outlook for Disposable Income and Expenditure

1.32   In addition to the substantial decline in real GDP, Kyrgyzstan's disposable income has been reduced by the ending of official transfers from the Union, which constituted 11.4 percent of GDP in 1991. Disposable income in 1992 has also been adversely affected by a deterioration in the country's terms of trade caused by the sharp rise in prices of energy products. This loss of income corresponds to about 7 percent of GDP.

1.33   The combined impact of these adverse developments has been a reduction in real disposable income by about 36 percent during 1992. However, it is estimated that the current account deficit in 1992 was about 11 percent of GDP in contrast with a current account surplus in 1991 which corresponded to 10 percent of GDP. This large swing in the external deficit means that resources available for domestic expenditure have dropped in 1992 by less than the drop in disposable income. Nevertheless the fall has been substantial--about 25 percent. Very tentatively, the decline in investment is estimated at about 50 percent, while consumption is estimated to be down by about 12 percent. National saving in real terms is estimated to be down by 74 percent below the exceptionally high level reached in 1991. As a share of disposable income at current prices, national saving in 1992 was about 18 percent, compared with 37 percent in 1991. The main economic aggregates are shown in Table 1-3 below, which also provides comparable data for 1990.

Table 1-3. GDP, Disposable Income, and Expenditure - 1990-92[a/]

	Constant 1991 Prices (Bln Rbl)			Real Change (Percent)		Current Prices (Bln Rbl)
	1990	1991	1992	1991	1992	1992
Gross Domestic Product	17.6	16.9	12.8	-3.9	-24.0	180.5
Terms of Trade loss	-0.2		-0.9			
Net Transfers	2.0	1.9	---	---	---	---
Disposable Income	19.4	18.8	11.9	-4.1	-36.5	180.5
Current Deficit[b/]	1.1	-1.7	1.0			19.6
Resources Available	20.5	17.1	12.9	-16.6	-24.5	200.1
Consumption	14.9	11.9	10.4	-20.1[c/]	-12.1	148.2
Capital Formation	5.6	5.2	2.5	-7.1	-52.5	51.8
National Saving	4.5	6.9	1.8	53.3	-73.9	32.3

a/   The estimates for 1992 are uncertain and intended to be illustrative only. Data for 1991 are also tentative.

b/   This is the balance of payments current account deficit after official transfers. The minus sign for 1991 signifies a surplus.

c/   The decline in consumption (the residual item in the accounts) is larger at 1991 prices than at 1983 prices, used in Table 1-1 because of differences in the deflator for the current account deficit.

Public Finance

1.34   The Government has faced an extremely difficult situation in managing its public finances for 1992. Total revenue is likely to fall to about 12 percent of GDP compared to 32 percent in 1991 as transfers from the Union cease, and tax revenue in real terms continues to contract sharply (Table 1-4). Although total expenditures have fallen from 28 percent of GDP in 1991 to about 24 percent in 1992 -- a drop of about 35 percent in real terms--the deficit for the year is nonetheless expected to rise to over 12 percent of GDP (including the cost of settling domestic inter-enterprise arrears), from a position of surplus in 1991.

1.35   The drastic price increases in January 1992 led the Government to make substantial revisions in the budget presented in December. The revised budget, which was approved in January, assumed no change in the level of real output and estimated a fourfold increase in prices. While this budget projected substantial real cuts in expenditures, it is evident that the assumptions underlying these projections have been overtaken by events -- e.g. this report assumes a GDP deflator of 14 times the level of 1991 and a decline in real GDP of 24 percent. In view of the uncertain macroeconomic situation, the Government has been revising its budget forecasts on an almost continuous basis.

Table 1-4. Government Finance[a/]

	Billion Rubles				Shares of GDP(%)		
	1990	1991	1992 Govt. Est.[b/]	1992 Staff Est.	1990	1991	1992 Staff Est.
Total Revenue and transfers	3.21	5.43	15.2	21.0	38.6	32.1	11.6
Tax Revenue	2.18	2.66	13.6	18.4	26.2	15.7	10.2
Non-tax revenue	.12	.84	1.6	2.6	1.4	5.0	1.4
Union transfers	.91	1.93	-	-	10.9	11.4	-
Total Expenditure	3.18	4.73	30.5	43.4	38.3	28.0	24.0
Current Expenditure	2.70	4.54	28.4	41.3	32.5	26.9	22.9
Wage and Salaries	.53	1.11	10.0	9.6	6.4	6.6	5.3
Other Consumption	.84	1.40	9.1	14.9	10.1	8.3	8.3
Transfers	.76	1.28	5.6	7.8	9.1	7.6	4.3
Subsidies	.57	.75	3.5	3.5	6.9	4.4	1.9
Interest	-	-	0.2	0.5	-	-	0.3
Enterprise Arrears	-	-	-	5.0	-	-	2.8
Capital Expenditure	.48	.19	2.1	2.1	5.8	1.1	1.2
Balance	0.02	0.70	-15.3	-22.4	0.4	4.1	-12.4
Financing:							
External (net)[c/]				2.4			1.3
NBK			15.3	20.0			11.1

a/   Consolidated accounts of the republic and local governments.
b/   As of October 1992.
c/   Foreign financed portion of disaster relief.

1.36   There was a substantial drop in real tax revenue during the first half of 1992 with the increases in prices, loss of output and greater reliance on barter, which made tax enforcement more difficult. But the budget was kept in approximate balance on a cash basis by a sharp cut in real wages of government employees, the effect of which was compounded by a build up of arrears on wages and pension payments.

1.37   Several factors contributed to the rapid growth of the deficit during the second half of the year, financing of which was facilitated by large infusions of currency from the Central Bank of Russia. First, such financing allowed the Government to draw down its arrears. Second, government wages in the second half of the year were increased on several occasions, most recently in November. Third, liability for the support of armed forces on its territory was transferred from Russia to Kyrgyzstan in the second half of the year. Finally, the budget was subjected to further strains for relief outlays for damage caused by earthquakes and mudslides. To help accommodate these increased expenditures, sizable reductions have been made in the real level of food subsidies and transfers for child allowances. As a share of GDP, these payments haven fallen from 12 percent in 1991 to about 6 percent in 1992. Capital expenditures financed by the budget were again limited to just over one percent of GDP. Nonetheless, the deficit in the third quarter rose to R5.5 billion and is estimated to have increased substantially in the fourth quarter.

1.38   Another burden on public finance in the fourth quarter of 1992 is the cost of settling domestic inter-enterprise arrears, estimated at R5 billion, which the government plans to borrow from the NBK for on-lending to enterprises. When these expenditures are consolidated with the budget, the estimated deficit for 1992, rises to R22.4 billion or 12.4 percent of GDP.

1.39   Only about R2.4 billion of the deficit was financed directly from abroad, for disaster relief, with the remaining R20 billion borrowed from NBK. This is clearly an unsustainable level of central bank credit to the government, corresponding to 11 percent of GDP.

Money and Credit

1.40   As a small member of the ruble zone, Kyrgyzstan has had limited control over monetary policy and inflation outcomes. In particular, the National Bank cannot control the volume of currency in circulation. In principle, interest rates and changes in monetary aggregates should have been coordinated across the ruble area. However, monetary coordination in practice has been far from complete. For example, credit to the economy in Kyrgyzstan is estimated to have experienced a steeper decline in real terms than in Russia during the first half of 1992, while increases in interest rates charged by the NBK have lagged behind the adjustments made by the Central Bank of Russia (CBR). Thus, while the CBR raised its lending rate to 80 percent in May, the NBK rate stood at 50 percent as of November.

1.41   A large uncertainty in the monetary environment concerns the growth of currency in circulation. Currency is a major medium of exchange for market transactions and wage payments, and its velocity of circulation is almost certainly much higher than for deposits. The rate of currency issue by NBK in 1992 is the result of an interaction between the requests for currency from NBK to CBR and the volume of new currency received from CBR. In the early part of the year currency issue lagged far behind the rise in prices that began in January, increasing only 22 percent in the first quarter while nominal GDP rose to more than four times its fourth quarter 1991 rate. This caused severe shortages of cash for ordinary transactions and was in itself a source of anxiety to the public. Currency issue was much larger in the second and third quarters, however, and the currency/GDP ratio appears to have risen between the first and third quarters of the year.   About R12 billion in currency was received by Kyrgyzstan from the CBR through October 1992.

1.42   The currency question is further obscured by the open borders between states in the ruble zone.   Currency can be carried into and out of Kyrgyzstan without restraint, and in the first quarter of 1992 the comparatively low prices in Kyrgyzstan evidently attracted large amounts of currency into the country for the purchase of goods.   The amount of currency inflow is unknown, however, and more broadly the stock of currency actually circulating in Kyrgyzstan is unknown.   The currency amounts that appear in the monetary survey for Kyrgyzstan are only those that have been issued through NBK.   They are part of the base for domestic credit, but they do not measure the currency component of Kyrgyzstan's actual money stock.

1.43   As a money stock component, deposits at banks are at present an inadequate substitute for currency.   Checking deposits are held primarily by enterprises and they are essentially not available to individuals as a substitute for currency in transactions.   This puts a severe burden on the currency stock.   With currency supply dominated by forces outside Kyrgyzstan's control, the present payments arrangement leaves the country highly vulnerable.   Caught between ruble zone inflation and constraints on currency issue, both the payments system and credit to domestic business will be choked off without greatly expanded use of deposits for storing assets and settling transactions.   As estimated in Table 1-5, the real value of all financial aggregates contracted sharply in the first half of 1992.   The nominal money stock rose by less than 60 percent in that period, whereas nominal GDP went up more than sixfold.   As a consequence, velocity rose over four times and the real stock of credit to the economy declined by two-thirds.   For the year as a whole, the real money stock is unlikely to rise from its level in June.   While credit to the economy increased moderately in the third quarter, increased NBK lending to the Government in the fourth quarter can be expected to limit credit to enterprises, and further reduce the real stock of credit to the non-government sector.

1.44   Reversing the contraction of financial variables and enlarging the role of deposits within the banking system will be of critical importance for promoting a market-based economic recovery. These objectives will require an easing of the cash shortage to the extent that permits the free conversion of deposits into cash, and a reduction of inflation and increase in real interest rates.   Chapter 4 discusses the main elements of recommended policy on interest rates, in addition to the steps needed to strengthen the banking system and induce it to assume a more constructive role in financial intermediation.   While an increase in real interest rates will be necessary to attract real resources into the banking system, the pace of adjustment will need to take into account the likely negative impact on the quality of the banks' portfolio and the potentially adverse impact of the latter on confidence in the banking system.   Also, interest rate increases will have little impact in attracting bank deposits if confidence in the ability to withdraw such deposits is lacking.   Notwithstanding these considerations, the NBK discount rate will have to converge rapidly to the CBR rate in the context of a functioning ruble zone.   (N.B. Even the CBR rate remains highly negative under most scenarios of expected inflation.)

1.45   Transactions through deposit payments between enterprises within Kyrgyzstan traditionally were cleared and settled overnight through an NBK facility.   However, the growth of arrears, particularly for interrepublican transactions, and the deteriorating financial position of most enterprises has placed even this system under strain.   Although information is not available, it is likely that the velocity of circulation is affected by inter-enterprise debts.   If these debts are a substitute for scarce currency, policies to foster this market, and make it more transparent, should be considered.   For instance, banks could rediscount bills of exchange, netting out positions among enterprises.   If these debts mainly reflect forced financing of loss-making enterprises, a more direct intervention of the Government in the loss-making enterprises would be appropriate, de-linking them from other enterprises in the economy.

1.46   The system for settling payments across the ruble zone, inherited from the FSU, is extremely slow by modern standards, and money received through the system may be delayed more than 5 weeks before it can be used. At 1992 inflation the transit time is expensive. To bring bank deposits more actively into money stock transactions, it will be important to reconstruct the interrepublican settlement system soon. This is an expensive task, but it is basic infrastructure for CIS conversion to market economies. In the Union the present system served principally as a bookkeeping device to track Gosplan activities, and the costs of check float were invisible. In 1992, the system is nakedly inadequate and an impediment to recovery in ruble zone trade.

Trade and Balance of Payments

1.47   Kyrgyzstan's trade in 1992 has been subjected to several shocks that have caused substantial declines in volume and a deterioration in the terms of trade. Ruble trade has been impeded by difficulties in the payments mechanism, a shortage of currency, and erosion of the state order system that used to determine the purchases and sales of enterprises throughout the FSU. In addition, most states including Kyrgyzstan imposed export barriers in early 1992 in the face of domestic shortages, compounding the contraction in trade. And in late 1992, there was additional uncertainty regarding the future of the system of bilateral payments as Russia, Kyrgyzstan's largest creditor, was reluctant to finance increased deficits through the so-called central bank correspondent account. However,

Table 1-5. Preliminary Monetary Survey End Period

	June 1991	1992
	Billions of rubles	
Net foreign assets		
Foreign exchange	0.0	-0.7
Net domestic assets	10.0	16.5
Credit to government	-0.5	-1.2
Credit to the economy	8.3	19.7
Other items, net	2.2	-2.0
Money stock	10.0	15.8
Currency outside banks	2.8	5.6
Deposits	7.2	10.2
	Percent of GDP	
Net foreign assets		
Foreign exchange	0.0	0.5
Net domestic assets	49.0	12.4
Credit to government	-2.5	-0.9
Credit to the economy	40.8	14.8
Other items, net	10.8	-1.5
Money stock	49.0	11.9
Currency outside banks	13.9	4.2
Deposits	35.1	7.7
	Monetary Velocities	
Money stock	2.0	8.4
Currency outside banks	7.3	23.7
Deposits	2.8	13.0
GDP at annual rate	20.4	133.0

negotiations with Russia to cover bilateral payments through end-1993 are ongoing. Finally, prices of energy imports are estimated to have increased by more than 50 times their 1991 levels, representing a major increase relative to the prices of other ruble traded goods.

1.48   This adjustment in relative prices is estimated to at least double the share of energy products in ruble imports from its level of 13 percent in 1991, notwithstanding a decline of about a quarter in the volume of energy imports. Trade data for the first half of the year indicate that Kyrgyzstan's exports to the ruble area fell by far more than its non-energy imports, assuming that price increases of these two categories of trade were of the same order of magnitude. However, it is not clear how comprehensive the reported data are in view of the growing role of barter trade.

Box 1-1. Interrepublican Trade and Payments

Kyrgyzstan's transition to a market economy is obstructed by a number of interrepublican trading arrangements that are carried over from Soviet practices. These arrangements block much of the flexibility that enterprise managers need during the transition into new forms of operation. Nevertheless, in the absence of an effective multilateral payments system the continuation of these arrangements may have acted to prevent an even greater decline in interrepublican trade.

CIS republics have had a bias toward maintaining balance in payments *bilaterally* with one another in the ruble zone. This bias now reflects a reluctance to become ruble creditors in a payments system that is primitive and under the control of the Central Bank of Russia (CBR). The bias has produced a number of restraints on trade, including export licensing and continuation of the practice of negotiating bilateral protocols to control interrepublican trade over the course of a year. The protocols have been unwieldy arrangements that include strong elements of barter and artificial pricing for long lists of specific commodities. To some extent they have included state commitments to deliver specific goods and have operated together with the state order system for domestic production.

Kyrgyzstan's decision to eliminate its state order system, however, presumably implies that its trade protocols with other republics will become much looser agreements. This in turn calls for increased efforts to establish a system of multilateral settlements within the CIS area that would allow direct enterprise-to-enterprise trade to expand, so that the effort to liberalize domestic transactions within Kyrgyzstan does not exacerbate the fall in its ability to conduct interrepublican trade.

The primitive nature of the present inter-republic payments system is clearly one basis for the bias toward bilateral payments balance and negotiated trade agreements. What is needed is a replacement of the present system by an efficient multilateral settlements system organized at the CIS level that clears all payments in one or two days. Such a change would be a major help in eliminating state-imposed restraints on trade. A settlements system need not in itself entail debtor-creditor relationships. It is rather a mechanical structure for expediting transactions, and setting it up is technically straightforward. It needs support from the international community, however. Improving payments procedures should be a project that is kept separate from other problems in ruble zone management and promoted very soon.

Persistent economic instability in the ruble area would accelerate the current trend for CIS members to establish separate currencies. In such an event the multilateral clearing system would become more complex to administer but could still be a major facilitator of trade between countries whose currencies are unlikely to initially be convertible. If the system can be maintained through a period when the states are developing stable forms of economic relations with one another it could ultimately be transformed into a more fully developed payments system, which might lead eventually to reunification of some of the currencies.

1.49   Kyrgyzstan's hard currency trade deficit was drastically reduced in 1992 (Table 1-6), primarily reflecting the lack of foreign currency to support the previous level of imports. This shortage appears to have pushed most hard currency trade into barter, rendering published data less meaningful. During the four years 1987-90, Kyrgyzstan's exports outside the ruble area averaged about $90 million annually. Thirty percent of the total was accounted for by nonferrous metals and 15 percent each by light engineering products and semi-finished materials -- timber, wool, hides -- and another 5 percent by high quality honey. In 1991, the dollar value of nonruble exports is reported to have dropped sharply to only $23 million, perhaps reflecting the reluctance of exporters to surrender their foreign exchange in view of the growing spread between official and market exchange rates. With the increased profitability of such exports in 1992, there have been some increases in the reported volume of such trading in the first half of the year, and there is informal evidence that actual exports are much larger than the amounts that enter the statistical system. During the first half of the year, surrender requirements for hard currency exports ranged from 20 to 90 percent at varying exchange rates, some as low as R1.75/$. These regimes could not however be enforced, and were replaced in September by a straightforward 10 percent export tax payable in hard currency, improving the prospect that such trade transactions would at least enter into the official statistics. Realized as opposed to recorded exports are hence estimated to reach $70 million in 1992.

1.50   Hard currency imports rose from $1.15 billion in 1987 to $1.7 billion in 1990, but then dropped in 1991 to $785 million and are estimated at less than $100 million in 1992. Wheat and maize accounted for about 16 percent of 1991 imports, 31 percent comprised raw sugar for refining and re-export to the FSU, while another 30 percent consisted of television components for assembly and export to the FSU. Textiles and clothing comprised 12 percent. More than half of the decline in 1992 was accounted for by the drop of TV components and raw sugar, and these do not significantly affect resources available to Kyrgyzstan. Grain imports also declined reflecting the improvement in domestic grain production. Nonetheless, a decline of other imports of some $200 million would still represent a serious cut into the resources of the country.

1.51   While the foreign exchange shortage sharply reduced the hard currency trade deficit, ruble trade shifted from a surplus in 1991 to a deficit approaching 10 percent of GDP, financed primarily by credit from the CBR and an estimated build-up in arrears. The consolidated trade deficit is estimated at R20 billion, converting nonruble trade using an average exchange rate for the year of R170/$. This rate is derived from the reported average rate for trade transactions of about R40/$ in the first half of the year and the assumption that all transactions in the second half of 1992 were enacted at the market exchange rate prevailing in Moscow. The current account deficit excluding transfers corresponds closely to the trade deficit, with the takeover by Russia of interest obligations on FSU debt in the autumn of 1992 (discussed in Chapter 3).

Table 1-6. Trade Transactions, 1989-92 (mln rbl)

	1989	1990	1991	Est. 1992	Price index, 1991 = 1.0 1992
Inter-republic trade					
Exports	2549	2446	6505	65000	14.1
Imports	3362	2863	5409	82000	17.5
Balance	-813	-417	1096	-17000	
Non-ruble trade (stated in rubles)					
Exports	51	53	41	11900	97.1
Imports	919	1043	1374	14450	97.1
Balance	-868	-990	-1333	-2550	
Total cross-border trade					
Exports	2600	2499	6546	76900	16.2
Imports	4281	3906	6783	96450	19.9
Trade balance	-1681	-1407	-237	-19550	
Percent of GDP					
Inter-republic trade					
Exports	33.5	29.4	38.5	36.0	
Imports	44.1	34.4	32.0	45.4	
Balance	-10.7	-5.0	6.5	-9.4	
Non-ruble trade					
Exports	0.7	0.6	0.2	6.6	
Imports	12.1	12.5	8.1	8.0	
Balance	-11.4	-11.9	-7.9	-1.4	
Total cross-border trade					
Exports	34.1	30.0	38.7	42.6	
Imports	56.2	46.9	40.1	53.4	
Trade balance	-22.1	-16.9	-1.4	-10.8	
MEMORANDA:					
Exchange rate (Rubles/US$)	0.63	0.60	1.75	170	
Nonruble transactions (mln US$) Trade					
Exports	81	88	23	70	
Imports	1459	1738	785	85	
Balance	-1378	-1650	-762	-15	
GDP (millions of rubles)	7620	8320	16900	180500	

CHAPTER 2

Reform Agenda and Medium-Term Outlook

2.01   Kyrgyzstan has good longer-term potential for development. It has a wide range of minerals that probably can be exploited profitably on an expanded scale -- gold, antimony, mercury, uranium and rare earth metals. Substantial expansion of hydroelectric capacity may be warranted, and the country's geology suggests unexploited potential for developing natural gas production. (Exploration for gas was not a priority in the past given the extensive deposits in neighboring republics.) There are good possibilities for raising yields of agricultural crops through better irrigation and cultivation practices and an improved incentive framework. The country's extensive snow capped mountains provide a favorable backdrop for the development of tourism, and the services sector in general will need to expand during the transition. Most importantly, high literacy rates and a relatively well developed human resource base should provide the foundation for a sustainable recovery from the current crisis.

2.02   However, it will take some time for these important assets to provide the basis for renewed growth. In the next few years developments in the economy are likely to be heavily influenced by developments elsewhere in the ruble area. In particular, the prospects for stabilization in Russia are far from clear and output among Kyrgyzstan's major trading partners is expected to continue to fall significantly in 1993. It is not clear how effectively the problem of inter-enterprise arrears across states will be addressed, or whether a payments mechanism through which to reconstruct interrepublican trade will be developed. Kyrgyzstan's terms of trade are also expected to continue to deteriorate as fuel prices in the ruble area move towards international levels. This combination of adverse external shocks can be expected to dominate the short-term macroeconomic outlook.

2.03   Hence economic policy will have to be conducted under highly adverse external circumstances. This chapter discusses: (i) the priorities for stabilization and structural reform; (ii) an economic scenario which foresees a continued and substantial decline in economic activity in 1993 with a significant recovery not envisaged to begin prior to 1995; and (iii) the major risks to the development of such a scenario.

Stabilization and Structural Adjustment

2.04   While Kyrgyzstan has already endured painful cuts in consumption, the emerging fiscal and current account deficits cannot be maintained indefinitely. Hence, a sustained period of adjustment is unavoidable. This will involve a systematic analysis of fiscal resources and expenditure priorities in light of the fundamentally altered financing outlook. An appropriate incentive framework to promote hard currency export growth will also be essential. At the same time, government action to promote adjustment in the state-owned enterprises, privatization, and development of the private sector will be needed to complement the stabilization effort and to lay the foundation for economic recovery.

Stabilization Policies

2.05   The elimination of Union transfers, which averaged 11 percent of GDP in 1990-91, would by itself have required major adjustment in government expenditures. But there has been, in addition, a sharp drop in tax and non-tax revenue as a share of GDP -- from an average of 29 percent in 1987-90 to 21 percent in 1991 and to less than 12 percent in 1992. It will be essential that this decline be reversed if Kyrgyzstan is to support the minimum of public services required in the transition to a market economy. A reasonable medium-term target for total revenue might be in the order of 18 percent of GDP. Hence action to improve revenue performance warrants the highest priority in the Government's policy agenda for the immediate future.

2.06   In 1993, however, most of the factors that contributed to the declining revenue (Chapter 1) are expected to remain in force. In particular, tax revenue from industrial enterprises should not be expected to recover in view of the extent of adjustment that is required for the sector and the likelihood that industrial output will continue to decline significantly. Thus revenue from the profit tax can be expected to decline in real terms, and, without additional action, overall revenue could well decline further as a share of GDP in 1993 given the continued decline in real income that is expected.

2.07   This prospect highlights the importance of enacting measures to improve revenue performance in other areas. Widening the tax base and strengthening tax administration will be vital. With regard to the former, greater reliance on excise taxes can be an important source of additional revenue in the short term. Reinstating the excise tax on gasoline, which was in effect for only a brief period in 1992, should again be considered. Such a tax could also be extended to other petroleum products, while existing rates for tobacco and alcohol (including vodka) could be further raised. The authorities should resist reducing the VAT rate (unless this action is jointly taken throughout the CIS and Kyrgyzstan decides to remain in the ruble zone); indeed the VAT base needs to be extended to items currently not covered, including imports from outside the CIS countries (again if properly coordinated within the CIS). In general, exemption from taxes such as for personal income and enterprise profits should be minimized, and tax rates for different categories of enterprise or sectoral activity should be equalized. Contributions to the Employment Fund should be adjusted to allow the Fund to remain self-financing. For example, raising the payroll tax paid by employers to 1.5 percent and introducing an employee contribution of 0.5 percent is estimated to allow the Fund to operate in 1993 without budgetary support.

2.08   Existing user fees should be raised on a regular basis to at least cover the economic cost of providing the public service, and incorporating also environmental costs. User charges for transportation, telecommunications, electricity, and irrigation in particular will need to be adjusted. Finally, rents, which include water, gas and heating, should be increased to at least cover operation and maintenance costs, and to provide the impetus to accelerate the Government's housing privatization effort. Adjustment in rents and municipal services would have to be implemented in accordance with affordability criteria determined largely by wage trends.

2.09   Strengthening tax administration (for which technical assistance from the IMF has already been received), particularly for the recently implemented VAT and excise taxes is of high priority, as is enhancing tax enforcement capability. The latter could be facilitated through raising penalty rates for delayed payments to reduce collection lags and arrears, coupled with more stringent punitive measures to counteract tax evasion.

2.10   Enacting these measures will contribute to the objective of raising revenue in the medium term, particularly once the economic decline is arrested. But even assuming a good beginning is made soon to strengthen revenue performance, government revenue is unlikely to exceed 14 percent of GDP in 1993 if output declines as projected (Section II). Hence further adjustment in the real level of government expenditure will be necessary if a significant reduction in inflation is to be achieved. This will be the case either in the context of a coordinated tightening of financial policies across the ruble area, or if a new currency is introduced in 1993. In the latter case, a tighter expenditure stance will be particularly important to provide confidence in the Government's ability to manage the transition to a new currency without a return to recent inflation levels. Moreover, it would be unrealistic to expect adequate progress on the structural reform agenda without a significant reduction of inflation.

2.11   Tightening government expenditure is made more difficult by the sharp cuts already experienced: the real level of expenditure is estimated to have declined by about 35 percent in 1992. Budgetary expenditure on basic health care may have to rise in real terms (and foreign assistance could be earmarked for this purpose). Expenditure on unemployment benefits will also rise as enterprise restructuring proceeds (hence the recommendation to raise contributions to the Employment Fund), while the number of pensioners is expected to grow by about 20 percent as current recipients of Union pensions (such as internal security personnel) become eligible for government pensions in 1993. Capital expenditure financed from the budget is estimated at only one percent of GDP in 1992. This share will have to rise to develop the infrastructure for a market economy, though there may not be much scope for an increase during 1993. Finally, interest payments on hard currency external debt can rapidly become a significant budgetary item, given the large external financing requirements that are estimated (Chapter 3), even if a high degree of concessionality on external borrowing is achieved.

2.12   Thus considerable effort will be required to contain government expenditure in 1993. Some decline in real wages from the November 1992 level may be inevitable, particularly if output falls significantly as anticipated. Furthermore, wage increases for public enterprises outside the direct control of the budget will need to be limited by decree, given the lack of a hard budget constraint for such enterprises. Fiscal transfers or subsidies to nonviable enterprises should be phased out in the context of a more active government role towards promoting enterprise reform (discussed below).

2.13   The cost of food subsidies on items remaining subject to price controls (bread, milk and poultry products), estimated at 2 percent of GDP in 1992, may tend to rise in 1993 as procurement prices increase. Hence, further adjustments may be necessary. In particular, price controls on poultry should be eliminated while milk prices too could be liberalized if it is possible to target subsidized milk to poor children and lactating mothers through other means (e.g. through health centers and schools). The costliest subsidy is on bread, which is also the most critical item in the consumption basket of the poor. Since the Government currently does not have the capacity to undertake means testing to target subsidies to the poor, some form of generalized subsidy may need to be retained in the short run. But this could be limited to lower quality bread that is dominant in the consumption basket of the poor to contain the fiscal cost of the subsidy.

2.14   The largest category of government expenditure is for social expenditures, namely education, health and the support of social security programs, especially family allowances and pensions. The past level of expenditure in these areas (estimated at nearly two-thirds of government expenditures in 1991 including those of the Pension Fund) cannot be supported now. The real value of such benefits has already fallen sharply but there is a need for more focused targeting to ensure that a minimum consumption basket derived from a realistically defined poverty line is available to the truly needy. This implies the need for a tightening of eligibility criteria for the majority of beneficiaries, and Chapter 7 provides indications of the priorities for the restructuring of social expenditures.

2.15   Enactment of the above measures would help to reduce the budget deficit in 1993 below its real level estimated for 1992. Once economic recovery takes hold they would facilitate further reduction of the deficit to a more sustainable level. However, the success of the stabilization effort will depend not only on the budgetary outcome but also on the credit policy of the National Bank. Particularly in the second half of the year, the latter appears to have been relaxed. Directed lending from the NBK continued at interest rates well below the rediscount rate of 50 percent, which in itself is highly negative in real terms and below the CBR rate of 80 percent.

2.16   Such a credit policy is problematic in several aspects. Extending highly subsidized loans to particular sectors or enterprises can only occur at the expense of the economy in general in a credit-constrained environment. If the Government intends to provide subsidies to particular sectors or enterprises this should be accounted for fully within the budget, in the context of an agreed fiscal target consistent with stabilization objectives. This would enhance transparency and allow the National Bank to withdraw from the process of determining credit priorities and concentrate instead on focusing its responsibilities on activities such as supervision of commercial banks and the conduct of monetary policy.

2.17   As noted in Chapter 1, the Government is considering a financial assistance package in the context of dealing with the problem of inter-enterprise arrears. Any such assistance should again be fully budgeted. Moreover, it should be explicitly linked to restructuring within the individual enterprise that is to be assisted. Otherwise enterprises would infer that a subsequent build-up of arrears could also be handled through government assistance. The critical objective of forcing enterprises to adjust to the new environment would then be missed, and the goal of stabilization again undermined.

Structural Reform

2.18   Adjustment of enterprises to the emerging market environment is at the core of the transition. As discussed in Section III below, insufficient reform at the enterprise level would pose major risks for the adjustment strategy. However, in common with other countries attempting to construct a market economy, there are technical as well as social constraints to the speed of adjustment. Several of the chapters that follow address the issue of enterprise reform from the perspectives of reforming banking regulations to harden the enterprise budget constraint and promote more rational lending patterns; privatization; promotion of competition; and reform of labor regulations and incentives. This section summarizes the key priorities for reform that will have an important bearing on the overall reform effort.

2.19   Recent and prospective shifts in relative prices and demand are likely to cause major losses in the enterprise sector. It is possible that a significant share of current production, particularly in manufacturing, may not be viable under emerging market conditions. At the same time, potentially viable firms may experience losses resulting from supply disruptions or the build-up of receivables. Since the current structure of bank and enterprise ownership is generally not conducive to promoting adequate adjustment, and the emergence of new ownership structures cannot be instantaneous, the Government will need to actively assist the process of enterprise reform.

2.20   Such a program should include several elements. There is a need to make an early and realistic division of enterprises into those that can be privatized in the short to medium term and those that will remain under state ownership. Both should be taken out of the present unclear ownership structures comprising of managers-workers-local authorities-ministries, with rapid privatization of the former and corporatization with restored de facto government ownership of the latter. As of October 1992, less than 5 percent of fixed assets had been privatized. Moreover, most of the enterprises categorized as privatized had been transformed into (closed) joint-stock companies controlled by either labor collectives or indirectly by government agencies. It is not apparent whether this transformation has had any discernable impact upon the management and performance of the "privatized" enterprises.

2.21   For enterprises slated for early privatization, the Government needs to develop an institutional framework that facilitates the privatization process while minimizing ministerial intervention and delay. The privatization of small trading and retail enterprises, shops and restaurants should be accelerated through an auction process that recognizes the need for speed and limits bureaucratic intervention to exceptional rather than routine cases. To facilitate the development of the private sector in these areas, it will be essential for the Government to focus on removing the obstacles to entry and operations for privatized or new enterprises (Chapter 5, Section I).

2.22   For medium and some large enterprises, some form of mass privatization is likely to be necessary, given inadequate domestic purchasing power and foreign interest. It is likely that the current issue of vouchers used primarily for the purchase of one's residence would need to be supplemented with vouchers specifically for enterprises, and made tradeable in the context of mass privatization.[1] While speed is important for the success of such a scheme, the objectives of privatization -- to improve enterprise performance and accelerate restructuring -- should not be lost during the process. Thus the outcome of the process should lead to an ownership structure that permits effective governance; e.g. one owner with enough shares to have the incentive and ability to exercise management control over enterprises that need restructuring. Finally, for very large enterprises where restructuring poses complex and socially difficult issues, a case-by-case method of privatization and segmentation will need to be designed, in all likelihood with foreign technical assistance. To give impetus to the Government's privatization program, the resources, training and authority of the State Property Fund will need to be enhanced.

2.23   Industrial restructuring is likely to be the most difficult part of the reform program, given the combination of declining output and large labor force retrenchment likely to take place. It is essential to make rapid progress on the resolution of ownership rights, so that owners and managers begin to take responsibility for the restructuring process, rather than relying on outside factors (including government subsidies) to direct the process for them. Privatization must be the driving force for this process, but it will take time, especially in the large-scale industrial sector. Hence, there is an urgency of moving ahead very forcefully with small-scale privatization, where more rapid progress is possible. It is vital to give managers and the collectives an unambiguous signal that the reforms are unavoidable. For this, it is crucial to proceed with corporatization and the launching of a privatization drive throughout the economy. Imposition of tighter budget constraints on enterprises, including measures to reduce the flow of inter-enterprise arrears, is necessary to start the restructuring process, as well as to control the growth of credit in the economy and achieve macroeconomic stabilization.

2.24   Even if the Government is successful in implementing rapid privatization, based on the experience of Eastern Europe and elsewhere, a significant proportion of public enterprises is likely to remain under state ownership over the next few years. For these enterprises, there is a need for further categorization into those that should be closed versus those that require restructuring to improve or regain profitability. For enterprises with no prospect of surviving the new environment, a strategy for closures

---

1.   A World Bank Technical Assistance mission on privatization and financial sector reform, scheduled for November/December 1992, is expected to provide further recommendations.

that is compatible with socially acceptable criteria needs to be devised. If nonviable enterprises are permitted to survive indefinitely, the resources available for restructuring of potentially viable enterprises and emerging firms will correspondingly be reduced. The closures should focus on plants where the emerging relative price structure has rendered technology obsolete; typically these may involve heavily energy intensive production structures for which demand within the ruble zone is not expected to recover to earlier levels.

2.25   However, there may be a case for government intervention in enterprises with positive value-added but where cash flow problems would otherwise force an excessive contraction of output and employment. This is particularly the case once the political costs of rising unemployment are incorporated. The means of subsidy or protection would have to respect budget constraints and should only be extended if: a) there is a reasonable prospect that the enterprise will eventually be able to survive without assistance; and b) if adjustment can be assured during the period that the enterprise is receiving assistance. Government intervention in this area could consist of assistance in maintaining previous channels of trade or developing new ones, trade protection (in the context of a separate currency), and subsidizing employment or wages. (Such subsidies could only be justified in the case of viable enterprises that do not have access to bank credit. By contrast, limits on public enterprise wages are called for through decree or tax measures in cases where access to bank credits is unrestrained.) Such measures for influencing enterprise behavior are only appropriate in the early phase of transition when the price system still cannot allocate resources efficiently across sectors and when the ownership structure of banks and enterprises does not induce existing enterprises to react with enough flexibility to allow efficient growth.

2.26   Privatization or corporatization by themselves will not lead to adjustment unless enterprise budget constraints are tightened. In Kyrgyzstan, the practice of banks lending primarily to enterprises that are their major shareholders is the most blatant violation of this principle, and Chapter 4 contains specific recommendations to reduce the concentration of bank lending to their owners. Complementary measures to strengthen other prudential regulations and bank supervision, and raise minimum capital requirements in parallel with inflation will be needed. The authorities will have to judge whether such adjustments can be achieved within the current institutional structure or whether new corporate structures for banks would be needed to rationalize lending patterns. As a means of encouraging banks to comply with the new prudential regulations, the National Bank could consider using access to NBK resources as leverage, ultimately limiting such access to banks that adopt the recommended lending guidelines. (As of July 1992, NBK resources accounted for more than half of the loans outstanding from commercial banks.)

2.27   Interest rates should be encouraged to play a greater role in mobilizing savings and in the allocation of credit. Complete liberalization of interest rates would be warranted once lending patterns are driven primarily by commercial rather than ownership criteria, and when confidence in the ability to withdraw deposits from the banking system has been credibly restored. In the interim, the NBK rediscount rate should be set in accordance with the CBR rate while Kyrgyzstan remains in the ruble zone, and the maximum spread that banks are allowed to charge on loans using NBK resources should be substantially raised from its level of 3 percent in 1992. It may also be necessary to enforce minimum lending rates on loans from bank's own resources until the pattern of bank lending has been adequately dispersed.

2.28   Additional legal reforms will be needed to strengthen the framework for private sector development. In particular, there is a need to address significant gaps in the areas of property rights, contract and bankruptcy laws, harmonize existing legislation to provide confidence in the Government's intention to guarantee the rights of private enterprise, and strengthen the capacity to enforce the legal regime. Technical assistance to adjust the legal system and gear institutional development to the needs of market economy will be required.

2.29   A necessary element to pursue the stabilization and structural reform agenda is the provision of an adequate social safety net to protect the poor and those most adversely affected by the reforms. However, fiscal resources are not sufficient to support Kyrgyzstan's past system of social protection. Massive cuts in the real value of social benefits have consequently been felt across the board in 1992. There is therefore an urgent need to prioritize budgetary outlays through better targeting of intended beneficiaries in order to protect the most vulnerable and to protect the human capital stock that will serve as the basis for future economic growth. If adequate resources to protect the poor are to be made available, eligibility criteria for pensions, family allowances and unemployment benefits, will have to be tightened, as discussed in Chapter 6 and 7. The minimum pension may have to be reformulated in terms of a minimum consumption basket, and it will not be possible to fully protect the real value of pensions above the minimum.

Improving Information

2.30   The economic information system developed by the USSR was geared essentially to tracking implementation of its economic plans. The system was well developed for its purposes and produced a wealth of information on many aspects of the economy and the welfare of the population. However, it was not much concerned with price relationships, which played only a marginal role in the country's incentive system, and it collected little information on the (relatively small) private sector. These latter two aspects of the economy are now becoming increasingly important, and the Government needs to strengthen efforts to collect data in these areas and to compile it in useful ways. In respect of both price data and production data, reforms are needed in the practice of making frequent changes in weights so that changes over time can be monitored more readily. Improved data on trade is another priority. The most urgent need is to develop good (and prompt) information on prices and quantities of trade, both interrepublican and external.

2.31   A second area where improved information is needed concerns the enterprise sector, both in Kyrgyzstan and in other republics. With the disappearance of the state order system, it will become of great importance for enterprises to be able to access information on alternative sources of supply and alternate markets for the output of their enterprises. This is not a task for a government agency but the kind of service typically performed by brokers and similar middlemen in a market economy. However, the governments of the CIS countries should help to promote the development of this kind of service, possibly with technical assistance from abroad.

The Outlook for 1993 and the Medium Term

2.32   Macroeconomic developments in the near future will continue to depend heavily upon developments elsewhere in the ruble area. If Kyrgyzstan remains in the ruble zone, the prospects for inflation will remain closely tied to the outcome of Russia's stabilization efforts. But even if a new currency is introduced during the course of 1993, developments will be influenced by interrepublican output and trade trends, given the still very large shares of such trade in the domestic economy. At the same time, the path of recovery from the current crisis will increasingly depend on the pace at which productive activities within Kyrgyzstan can be restructured and new activities created, to take advantage of the re-orientation in the relative price and organizational structures that the economy is currently undergoing.

Prospects in 1993

2.33   Following the estimated 24 percent decline in real GDP in 1992, a further drop of about 12 percent is projected in 1993 taking account of prospects elsewhere in the FSU and the experience of the post-reform economies of Eastern Europe. Industrial production can be expected to continue to decline substantially in view of the extent of restructuring that is required, the slow pace of restructuring experienced thus far, and continued supply disruptions reflecting the relatively greater dependence of industrial enterprises on interrepublican trade. Private sector development may also be slowed by the multifaceted constraints to such activity (Chapter 5). Moreover, given its present negligible share in production, even robust growth of the private sector could not compensate for the expected decline of the state enterprise sector. The relatively favorable performance in agriculture in 1992 is primarily attributable to a good harvest.[2] For 1993, no change in overall agricultural production is projected. Underlying this projection is the assumption that privatization of the state and collective farms progresses significantly prior to the 1993 cropping season, but that continued disruptions in traditional supply and distribution channels are inevitable.

2.34   Investment, which is estimated to have declined by about 50 percent in real terms in 1992, is projected to decline further as a share of GDP in 1993 reflecting the deteriorating financial status of most industrial enterprises and the scarcity of budgetary resources for capital spending. The unstable relative price structure in the short term would also act as a disincentive to investment. The overall decline in investment would not preclude new investments in selected areas where prospects for high profits appear favorable. These would include, inter alia, exports for hard currency for which hard currency import requirements are minimal. With the expected decline in overall investment and the increase in external financing, the share of consumption in GDP can be expected to rise, although consumption in real terms would fall still further below the 1992 level.

2.35   Trade prospects for 1993 are particularly difficult to gauge given the still unclear outcome for 1992, in turn a reflection of the growing use of barter. Hard currency exports are projected to grow to about $100 million, reflecting some diversion from interrepublican trade and the initial impact of currently planned investments such as in the leather industry. The projection of rapid growth of exports outside the CIS reflects the lagged impact of higher profitability of such trade following the elimination of the punitive surrender requirements in effect during the first half of 1992. However, whether the foreign exchange receipts from higher exports are actually retained by the Government or domestic

---

2.   Crop production is estimated to have increased while livestock output declined.

Table 2-1. Key Indicators, 1991-95

| | Estimates | | | Simulations | |
	1991	1992	1993	1994	1995
Real GDP Growth[a]/(%)	-3.9	-24	-12	-2 to 0	2 to 4
Agriculture	-9.1	0	0	2 to 3	3 to 4
Industry	0.3	-25	-18	-5 to-8	1 to 3
Shares of GDP[a]/					
Consumption (%)	70.3	81	85	83	79
Investment (%)	31.0	19	17	19	22
Terms of trade loss[b]/(%)	--	7	14	14	13
Current account/GDP (%)[a/c]/	-1.3	-8	-16	-16	-14
Government balance/GDP (%)	4.1	-12	-8	-6	-4
Reserves (excluding gold, US$m)	0	0	25	50	75

[a]/   Growth rates and shares based on constant 1991 prices.
[b]/   Represents the loss of real income from the deterioration in the terms of trade relative to 1991.
[c]/   Excludes external interest payments and transfers.

Table 2-2. Interrepublican and Foreign Currency Trade: Base Scenario (Mln US$)

	1991	1992	1993	1994	1995
Interrepublican Trade[a]/					
Exports	3,717	725	380	400	400
Imports	3,091	925	600	640	650
Trade Balance	626	-200	-220	-240	-250
Foreign Currency Trade					
Exports	23	70	100	115	130
Imports	785	85	250	250	250
Trade Balance	-762	-15	-150	-135	-120
Consolidated					
Trade Balance	-136	-215	-370	-375	-370

[a]/   For 1991 and 1992, U.S. dollar estimates are converted from quarterly ruble data using quarterly exchange rates. The implicit annual exchange rates therefore vary in relation to the quarterly pattern of flows. Third and fourth quarter 1992 trade estimates are subject to a considerable margin of error. Converting 1992 ruble trade at the estimated yearly average exchange rate (R170/$—see Para 1.51)would reduce the 1992 dollar value of trade by nearly 50 percent. The projections for 1993 and beyond assume a gradual appreciation of the ruble in real terms relative to a 1992 rate of R170/$.

banking system will depend in part on the extent to which macroeconomic stability is restored. Hard currency imports in 1992 are estimated to have fallen to only 5 percent of their 1990 peak level (though the latter was dominated by items such as raw sugar destined for elsewhere in the FSU). The extent of recovery in 1993 will depend on the availability of external financing, but allowance for imports of $250 million, the bulk of which would comprise of food and agricultural products, is considered to be prudent. The latter category of imports amounted to an estimated $500 million in 1991; the excellent harvest for grains obviated the need for imports of such magnitude in 1992, but the requirements for 1993 should be budgeted as substantially higher than in 1992.

2.36   Projecting interrepublican trade for 1993 is even more problematic given the current instability in the ruble area. Table 2-2 provides the base scenario used in the report that assumes financing for Kyrgyzstan's emerging deficits in 1993 (as well as the second half of 1992, about which information is not yet available) is forthcoming. Underlying the widening of the trade deficit expressed in dollars are the following assumptions: The price of energy imports comprising most importantly refined oil products and natural gas is projected to rise by twice the level of other traded goods reflecting the continued movement of such prices towards world levels.[3] The increase in energy relative prices would result in a decline in energy import volume by 20 percent, compared to a decline in non-energy interrepublican trade volume by about 10 percent. Energy imports would nonetheless comprise about 40 percent of interrepublican imports by 1993, up from an estimated 27 percent in 1992. Finally, a moderate real appreciation of the ruble is assumed for 1993.[4]

2.37   The above trade scenario, coupled with estimated disbursements of external technical assistance of $20 million, generates a projected current account deficit (excluding interest and transfers) of $390 million in 1993. But the large margin of error in this projection should be emphasized. This arises from the projection of hard currency exports (and in particular the uncertain availability of foreign exchange to the Government from projected export levels), the variability of agricultural output and hence import requirements, and the unstable trend of the ruble exchange rate and both prices and volumes in interrepublican trade.

Medium-Term Prospects

2.38   The economy must recover in the mid-1990s from three years of severe decline if economic reform is to continue within a democratic framework. In contrast to most countries in Eastern Europe and the FSU, Kyrgyzstan's population has grown rapidly over the past two decades -- at between 2 and 2.5 percent per annum -- implying that new entrants into the labor force will be correspondingly higher during the 1990s. On a per capita basis, the scenario envisioned already results in a decline in output of about 40 percent during 1991-93. Thus, a renewal of growth and employment creation in the not too distant future will be vital to the sustainability of the reform effort.

2.39   The basis for recovery in the medium term is expected to be a recovery of investment and the enhanced productivity of such investment relative to the past. The rising share of investment in GDP after 1993 (Table 2-1) reflects growth of investment both in infrastructure and for the expansion of hard

---

3.   The price of imported refined petroleum products would average about 70 percent of world prices in 1993 under this scenario.

4.   Relative to the year average 1992 exchange rate of R170/$. See footnote a/, Table 2-2.

currency exports. Growth of the latter, though starting from a small base, would play an increasingly important role in the recovery, and could benefit from foreign direct investment as discussed below. Hard currency export growth will also be important in generating additional borrowing and import capacity. Continued external financing to sustain minimum consumption levels for the next two to three years will also be required, as quantified in Chapter 3.

2.40   The pattern of recovery will also depend upon the evolution of economic trends elsewhere in the FSU, which as a block is expected to remain Kyrgyzstan's largest trading partner through the mid-1990s. But progress on structural reform and stabilization, as outlined in the previous section, will be a key determinant of the timing and pace of feasible recovery. In particular, restructuring of existing enterprises to enable them to compete in world markets, and closure of nonviable firms to release resources for restructuring and the creation of new enterprises will be critical for recovery to begin. A sustained recovery of investment would also be difficult without the attainment of a far greater degree of price stability than currently prevails.

2.41   Both the uncertainty of prospects in the FSU and the difficulty of the domestic reform agenda render forecasting the timing of economic recovery more difficult. Moreover, economic output is expected to continue to decline at least through the end of 1993. Hence even if a recovery were to start in early 1994, positive growth for the year as a whole may be difficult to attain, and such a result may realistically have to await till 1995. An average growth rate of 5 percent per annum during the second half of the decade is considered feasible, in view of the extent of the current decline, and assuming substantial progress in the stabilization and structural reform agenda in the interim period, and adequate external financing.

Sources of Growth

2.42   Agriculture, which accounts for some 30 percent of GDP, is expected to be a key source of growth over the medium term. While the sector faces many difficult transitional issues of adjustment, the privatization and demonopolization of state and collective farms and marketing enterprises, and exposure of farmers to international prices should result in a substantially higher level of productivity and output. This is apparent from the prevalence of relatively low yields, particularly for irrigated crops, and the seemingly uneconomic pattern of existing land use that derived from non-economic objectives of regional specialization in the FSU and the extent of variation in relative price structures vis-a-vis international relative prices. The difficult behavioral as well as social nature of adjustment requirements during the transition cannot however be downplayed. Hence, as discussed in Chapter 8, transitional policy issues are of particular relevance for the sector. In particular, policy makers must be cognizant of the disruptions in trade, scarcity of foreign exchange, and instability of relative prices as they guide the restructuring of production to exploit Kyrgyzstan's comparative advantages under international prices. Nonetheless, prospects are relatively favorable for an early supply response in agriculture if substantial progress on privatization, enhancing competition and price adjustments can be achieved in the near term. Under these circumstances, an average growth rate of at least 3 percent per annum in agriculture would appear feasible.

2.43   Other sources of potential growth in the medium term are in mining and metallurgy, hydroelectric power, oil and gas production and tourism. Sharp increases in energy relative prices and in the value of foreign exchange, make these activities potentially far more profitable in the forthcoming market environment relative to the previous era. For each of these activities, as well as the conversion of defense oriented industries to civilian use, foreign direct investment will be of critical importance as a source of scarce capital and technology. Hence, the provision of a stable and predictable legal and fiscal framework for attracting foreign investment will be a key requirement, for which expert and unbiased external advice should be a critical input.

2.44   Capital expenditure financed through the budget is estimated to have declined to one percent of GDP in 1992 and this share is likely to remain low in 1993. But government investment in key areas of infrastructure will have to increase in the medium term to lay the basis for economic recovery. The priority areas of government investment include improving the telecommunications system to permit the expansion of trade and communications outside the CIS and training in areas such as banking, management and marketing.

2.45   The changing role of the Government towards supporting rather than directing productive activities involves adjustments in the process of preparing a public investment program (PIP) that should considerably affect the nature of the Government's investment effort. Government funding of public investment should shift from direct production activities towards support for the improvement of social and physical infrastructure.[5] A number of measures are recommended to make this new orientation effective:

a)   set up a separate unit in the Ministry of Economy and Finance to prepare the PIP in collaboration with relevant sector departments;

b)   introduce and provide appropriate training for project evaluation criteria and methods in line with those generally used in market economies. It will be important to focus on the economic merits of the proposed investments and the extent to which public investment reflects development priorities and the changed role of the state;

c)   create a screening mechanism for existing investment projects to determine which projects should be retained, which should be redesigned or scaled down, and which should be abandoned and, if so, in what manner;

d)   ensure that the PIP is an integral part of the budget, and that financing from both the Government's own and from foreign sources are included;

e)   determine the size of the PIP in the context of the overall fiscal framework and as part of the economic reform program;

f)   make sure that the staff of the PIP unit liaises closely with the Aid Coordination Unit (described in Chapter 3).

---

5.   The Government has submitted a list of investment projects for the Consultative Group meeting (in December 1992). These projects have not been assessed by Bank staff. While some could be essential to implement, others may need a detailed analysis in view of uncertainties in the evaluation of relative prices.

External Trade Prospects

2.46   Kyrgyzstan's trade has been characterized by extensive inter-dependence with the FSU contrasted by negligible hard currency exports. Hard currency imports, however, amounted to more than a quarter of total imports in 1990, falling to an estimated 20 percent in 1991. Such imports in 1992 may have fallen to less than 5 percent of their 1990 level. Some recovery of hard currency imports will be needed to support consumption and maintain the functioning of critical aspects of economic activity. Thus, even with rapid growth of non-ruble exports, a significant convertible currency trade deficit is expected to re-emerge. With regard to interrepublican trade, the trend beyond 1993 will depend on whether the CIS currencies can be stabilized and payments mechanisms devised to facilitate such trade, as well as the pace of feasible substitutions between ruble and non-ruble trade. However, the underlying trend appears to be for Kyrgyzstan to sustain substantial deficits within the CIS in light of its large energy deficits.

2.47   Full restoration of trade to pre-reform levels would in any case not be warranted since trade figures in the past were inflated by large flows of intermediate products into and then out of domestic industrial activity. This was prominent in sugar and electronics, which entered as non-ruble imports -- accounting for more than half of such imports in 1991 -- and then left as ruble exports after minor domestic processing. Within the ruble zone, automotive parts, vehicles, farm equipment, and cotton also passed through the economy for small amounts of intermediate processing. The full amount of such pass-through activities may have ranged between 25 and 40 percent of trade. Some of these activities were supported by the Union for non-economic reasons and can be expected to decline permanently, particularly in light of ongoing relative price shifts.

2.48   Leaving aside the entrepot trade, medium-term *import* prospects are dominated by domestic requirements for energy, food, farm chemicals and supplies, and clothing. Oil and gas imports in 1991 amounted to about $550 million if valued at world prices. The volume of such imports will be substantially reduced as their relative price increases. In the longer term, development of increased domestic production of oil, gas, and hydroelectric power may further reduce Kyrgyzstan's dependence on such imports. But oil is used extensively in farm production and transportation, where there are limited possibilities for substitution in the next few years. Hence, annual imports of oil and gas over the medium term may amount to at least $300 million (once world prices are charged).

2.49   Demand for food, clothing, textiles, and farm supplies is unlikely to fall as rapidly as GDP in the medium term. Thus, the total import requirement can be expected to stay large relative to GDP. Imports of grain and other food materials from non-ruble markets were about $500 million in 1991 but fell by perhaps more than 90 percent in 1992 reflecting the favorable harvest, cutback in sugar imports, relative price shifts, and lack of foreign exchange. To the extent that import demand for these requirements cannot be fulfilled through interrepublican trade, hard currency imports may have to grow in the medium term and are projected to range in the $250 million to $300 million range.

2.50   Kyrgyzstan's strongest prospects for *export* expansion in the next few years may be wool products and tobacco, which are both based substantially on domestic production, and which together contributed one third of the value of total exports in 1991. There is also an industrial base in electrical engineering, which was a major net exporter in interrepublican trade. These three industries in the past exported almost entirely to the ruble zone, and their potential for non-ruble trade is unknown. Wool products and tobacco may be relatively easy to export for hard currency, while the skills developed for electrical engineering may provide the basis for convertible currency exports with the injection of foreign investment and marketing skills. An aggressive export promotion effort for these and other manufactured commodities, facilitated through technical assistance should therefore be pursued.

2.51   Other domestically-based exports may also expand over time. Exports of nonferrous ores include, importantly, uranium. However, prices in world markets for uranium are currently low with uncertain prospects. Other nonferrous ores and metals -- mercury and gold, in particular -- have potential for expansion after capital development, but this development may stretch over much of the 1990s. Kyrgyzstan has already begun to export hydroelectric power to China and negotiations are underway for the expansion of such exports. Finally, Kyrgyzstan's potential for tourism is almost totally undeveloped, but the infrastructure to support tourists from outside the ruble area will again take some time to develop. Technical assistance to formulate a strategy for the expansion of tourism may be a useful precursor to the development of such infrastructure.

2.52   Overall export prospects are clouded by uncertainties in both ruble and non-ruble trade. With barter accounting for an increasing share of both categories of trade, there is little basis for monitoring actual developments in 1992. Medium-term prospects will hinge critically on the evolution, or lack thereof, of a suitable payments mechanism for interrepublican trade. A deficit of about $250 million is however expected to emerge on interrepublican trade once all such trade is conducted at international prices. With regard to convertible currency exports, the unstable macroeconomic environment and punitive surrender requirements (for at least part of 1992) do not provide much incentive for exporters to remit their hard currency earnings voluntarily to the Government. For the longer-term, the potential for developing natural resource-based exports needs to be further explored, as does the feasibility of substitutability of goods previously destined for interrepublican trade. The base case projection is for hard currency exports to rise from $100 million in 1993 to $150 million by 1996 but the high range of uncertainty should again be emphasized.

2.53   <u>Promoting Exports</u>. Enterprises in Kyrgyzstan have had very limited experience in foreign trade, and will need assistance in identifying potential export markets and adapting production for exports to their requirements. The lack of export know-how in every area -- production, product design, marketing, etc. -- suggests that external assistance to help finance consultants and service suppliers would be fruitful. Turkey and the newly industrialized countries of East Asia may be the best source for information in this field given their successful experiences.

2.54   The system of foreign exchange surrender and taxation of foreign trade should ideally be identical across a functioning ruble zone to prevent unproductive arbitrage across countries.[6] However, if differentials continue to persist, Kyrgyzstan should ensure that its own rules provide incentives for hard currency exports as attractive as the most favorable treatment in other countries in the ruble area to prevent the sale of such exports through other states. The incentive structure should also ensure that after-tax profitability for exporting for hard currency is greater than for ruble exports, to overcome the historical legacy acting against the former category. Chapter 4 contains suggested reforms in the banking system to encourage exporters to remit their receipts within the country, while Chapters 5 and 8 respectively, contain suggestions for improving the environment for foreign investment and expanding exports in specific sectors. Finally, it should be noted that trade policy recommendations will clearly

6.   In September, Kyrgyzstan replaced surrender requirements on hard currency exports with a 10 percent export tax payable in hard currency.

have to be revisited if Kyrgyzstan opts for its own currency. In the meantime, a common tariff structure vis-a-vis the rest of the world should be adopted in coordination with other ruble zone countries.

The Major Uncertainties

2.55   The medium-term outlook is fraught with uncertainty, not least due to the lack of domestic control over currency issue, inflation and interrepublican trade. The dual objectives of stabilization and structural reform face unprecedented risks arising from: (a) the uncertain external environment; (b) political and policy slippage; (c) implementation capacity; and (d) availability of financing.

External Factors

2.56   Kyrgyzstan's macroeconomic outlook is dominated by developments elsewhere in the ruble area over which it has no control. If the stabilization effort in Russia is not successful in reducing inflation it would become increasingly difficult to construct a viable system for coordination of macroeconomic policies within the ruble area. In particular, ensuring adequate currency issue and reconstruction of a payments mechanism to conduct interrepublican trade would become more problematic. High and unpredictable inflation would further undermine the ability of Kyrgyzstan's banking system to intermediate resources. Under these circumstances, it would be in Kyrgyzstan's interest to be in a position to introduce its own currency at relatively short notice, a situation that would require prior preparation.

2.57   The persistence of macroeconomic instability would also undermine the framework in which to pursue structural reform. For example, if inflation in the ruble area does not stabilize, financial aggregates may continue to decline in real terms, undermining the ability of banks to finance the enterprise sector. At the same time, enterprise losses could mount for a variety of reasons including adverse relative price changes, collapse of prior demand, and inadequate adjustment at the enterprise level to these shocks. A vicious cycle of increased enterprise losses, insolvency in the banking system and hence, a deteriorating budgetary situation arising from the collapse of tax revenues amidst the need for greater fiscal support of the banking system, could be the result. Averting such a crisis should be a major part of the reform agenda and underscores the need for rapid adjustment at the enterprise level.

Commitment to Reform

2.58   The authorities in Kyrgyzstan have demonstrated their commitment to reform under exceedingly difficult circumstances. But the extent of economic decline already experienced and the uncertain prospects for recovery may weaken the political consensus for reform. In particular, there may be a tendency to equate the economic decline caused primarily by external factors with the enactment of domestic reform, thus slowing or reversing progress of the latter. Hence, it will be essential to explain to the population that it is the unprecedented combination of external shocks that is primarily responsible for the decline in living standards.

2.59   Inadequate adjustment at the enterprise level in the presence of adverse external shocks could undermine the entire reform effort. Moreover, if fiscal adjustment occurs merely through the build-up of arrears and without the needed adjustment of priorities, the outcomes will not be sustainable: renewed financing would merely build-up debt to unmanageable levels; alternatively, with a lack of adequate financing the level of arrears would tend to undermine the entire domestic payments system, making reform untenable. Hence, a careful and ongoing assessment of consistent domestic adjustment and external financing will continue to be needed.

Implementation Capacity

2.60   While policy design is critical, the formulation of an appropriate reform program is not sufficient; the program must be implemented. As the range of decisions broadens and the complexity of issues increases, decentralization of authority will be necessary if the pace of reforms is to be sustained. Timely and effective implementation of the structural and sectoral reform program will require a substantial strengthening of institutional capacities -- both at the center to establish priorities in the reform agenda and allocate resources to support these priorities, and in the line ministries and specialized institutions to undertake these programs. The extent of the new processes to be installed and skills to be acquired cannot be overstated. The conduct of economic activities consistent with market principles will require, for example, creating a capacity within Government to procure goods and services under conditions of competitive bidding and putting in place a system of financial control and audit to ensure proper use of funds.

2.61   The transformation of institutions into structures that are suitable for democratic processes and supportive of market-oriented activities will require fundamental adjustments in the existing institutional framework. Technical assistance from abroad can assist the transformation process -- this report identifies several areas of priority -- but it is clear that the process will be lengthy and made more difficult by the current economic decline. Training to improve the capacity to implement economic policy should therefore be of high priority. At the same time, the formulation of reform objectives should attempt to incorporate identified deficiencies in implementation capacity, to improve the realism of the reform package and the prospect that it can be fully realized.

External Financing

2.62   Whatever the macroeconomic outcome in the ruble zone, it is clear that Kyrgyzstan is faced with a massive adjustment of its fiscal and external imbalances that cannot be completed in the course of one or two years. If the external financing needed to allow a more orderly reduction of imbalances is not forthcoming, the ability to pursue the needed reforms will be disrupted, as the pace of decline in consumption becomes intolerable and the credibility of the reformers is undermined. With insufficient foreign finance, the backlash could extend beyond the economic reform agenda to also encompass the political liberalization. Chapter 3 discusses minimum external financing requirements over the medium term considered necessary to enable the reform program to be pursued fruitfully. These are estimated at $400 million in 1993, and averaging at somewhat above this level in the 1994-96 period.

CHAPTER 3

External Financing, Creditworthiness and Aid Coordination

Introduction

3.01   It is clear from the analysis of the previous chapter that Kyrgyzstan will need substantial external support during the early years of transition given the extraordinary nature of the external shocks that it faces. These shocks have caused a collapse of convertible currency imports in 1992, even as ruble imports were declining sharply. Severe consumption declines have accompanied the collapse of imports. The case for external support is, moreover, strengthened by the determined reform effort initiated by the Government notwithstanding its difficult circumstances.

3.02   The rationale for external support is hence clear. The compression of imports and consumption must be stemmed if political support for continuing the reform program is to be maintained. This requires substantial balance of payments support on a largely concessional or grant basis given the country's very limited capacity to bear foreign debt. If the international community is able to mobilize substantial financing for Kyrgyzstan, the Government in turn will have to strengthen its own capacity to coordinate such assistance. Section III of this chapter contains recommendations on the management of external resources.

Financing Requirements and Sources

3.03   Kyrgyzstan's financing requirements are clouded by the considerable uncertainty surrounding the evolution of interrepublican trade, the terms of trade, inflation, the ruble exchange rate, as well as the decision and timing regarding introduction of a new currency. Even if the Government continues to make the projected steady progress on its program of adjustment and structural reform, estimates of financing requirements will therefore have to be updated on a frequent basis.

Situation in 1992

3.04   External financing in 1992 was primarily limited to credit extended through interrepublican correspondent accounts between central banks in the FSU, an estimated build-up of inter-enterprise interrepublican arrears on a net basis, and the takeover by Russia of Kyrgyzstan's portion of the USSR external debt. The overall current account deficit (excluding interest and transfers) is estimated at $220 million, of which about $200 million equivalent may be attributable to the ruble deficit. In late 1992, the means of continued financing of Kyrgyzstan's emerging deficits within the ruble area were not clear. Kyrgyzstan's outstanding balance on its correspondent account with the Central Bank of Russia -- by far its largest creditor within the ruble area -- had reached about R8 billion (excluding receipt of currency), and Russia, at least temporarily, was reluctant to finance an increase in this balance. However, negotiations were ongoing on a new agreement with Russia to cover bilateral payments through end-1993. Kyrgyzstan's net position on the correspondent accounts with other ruble area states was approximately in balance in late 1992.

3.05   Non-ruble external financing in 1992 was limited to humanitarian assistance comprising primarily of shipments of food and medicine, valued at about $10 million, and technical assistance from official and multilateral sources estimated at $5 million. A loan agreement negotiated with the European Community (EC) for about $30 million equivalent for food purchases (on market terms) was not expected to be utilized during the course of 1992. A small amount of financing, $5 million, is however assumed to disburse in 1992 from a $75 million export credit extended by the Turkish Export-Import Bank. Thus external debt generated from new hard currency borrowing was negligible as of late 1992. Foreign exchange reserves were also negligible, and any foreign currency deposits held by enterprises in Kyrgyzstan at the Vneshekonombank in Moscow are currently frozen.

Debt Management

3.06   Kyrgyzstan's share of the FSU's external debt as of December 1991 is estimated at $760 million[1], with debt service obligations in 1992 of about $176 million, of which $69 million was subject to deferral in 1992 as agreed by the FSU's creditors.[2] However, Kyrgyzstan was one of three former Soviet republics to conclude agreements with Russia in the autumn of 1992 to transfer its share of the FSU debt, and hence any servicing obligations, to Russia in exchange for relinquishing most claims on the financial and other assets of the FSU. As a result, Kyrgyzstan approaches 1993 with practically no hard currency disbursed debt. However, the details of interrepublican financing arrangements in 1992 are not known and for the most part have not been concluded. Hence any ruble servicing obligations that may arise from Kyrgyzstan's net debtor position vis-a-vis the ruble area are not yet clear, and have not been included in the projection of financing requirements in Table 3-1.

---

1.   Starting October 1991, three inter-republican debt agreements were reached among former Soviet republics: (a) the Memorandum of Understanding on the Debt to Foreign Creditors of the Union of Soviet Socialist Republics and its Successors (MoU) of October 28, 1991; (b) the Treaty of Succession on Foreign Debt and Assets of the USSR ("Debt Allocation Treaty") of December 4, 1991; and (c) the agreement among CIS countries on debt and asset management of March 13, 1992 ("Debt Management Agreement"). Kyrgyzstan signed all three agreements, the details of which are contained in Box 3-1.

2.   In November 1991, the Group of Seven (G-7) signed a communique with the original eight signatories of the MoU whereby the official creditors agreed to a partial deferral of amortization payments on medium- and long-term debt due in 1992. This understanding was formalized in January 1992 when the Paris Club agreed to defer 100 percent of amortization payments due between December 5, 1991 and the end of 1992 on the "concerned debts" until January 1, 1993. Interest payments were not deferred and trade arrears were to be paid off in two installments in 1992. The January agreement has been reviewed by the representatives of the Paris Club. In March, it was decided to prolong the deferral of principal due (on pre-cut-off-date credits) only until the end of June 1992. On June 22, a further deferral was agreed until the end of September 1992. Similar discussions were also held with commercial bank creditors, represented by a group of major creditor institutions referred to as the Bank Advisory Committee (BAC). On December 16, 1991, March 26, 1992, and again on June 25, 1992, the BAC agreed to a rollover of principal payments due on pre-cut-off-date credits, in each case for a 90-day period. As with the case of official creditor debt, no deferral of interest payments was agreed to on those three occasions.

Box 3-1. Interrepublican Debt Agreements and Payments Situation

Interrepublican Memorandum of Understanding (MoU), October 1991. The MoU committed the signatories to the following:

- to be jointly and severally liable for the external debt of the FSU. It is generally understood that this liability is to cover all debt obligations contracted by the Government of the USSR outstanding at the date of the MoU. So far the agreement has been signed by nine republics (including Kyrgyzstan) which, according to the Debt Allocation Treaty (see below) account for about 90 percent of the debt.

- to designate the Vnesheconombank (VEB) (or any successor to be determined) as the Debt Manager with full authority to be the sole interlocutor with creditors, negotiate and enter into commitments on their behalf, and service the debt as agent on behalf of the republics.

- to conclude an agreement on the procedures and mechanism for debt service and another on the participation in the settlement of the debt -- on a joint and several basis -- of the three Baltic states.

Interrepublican Debt Allocation Treaty, December 1991. The Treaty allocated specific shares of the FSU debt to the fifteen former republics. These shares were determined primarily on the basis of the republics' shares in NMP/GDP, with Kyrgyzstan allocated slightly under 1 percent of the total debt. So far, the Treaty has been signed by eight republics (including Kyrgyzstan). The Treaty also makes some specific provisions about debt management and debt service procedures. It:

- prescribes the establishment of an Interstate Council for Foreign Debt Servicing and Utilization of Assets (IC) as a controlling body over external debts and asset management, while confirming the VEB's responsibility for external debt service as agent on behalf of the republics;

- charges the IC with reorganizing the VEB; and

- obliges the signatories to set up special accounts in the VEB for servicing the debt, to make advance payments according to an agreed schedule into these accounts, and to set up insurance funds for the special accounts with the VEB.

Interrepublican Debt Management Agreement, March 1992. On March 13, 1992, the Prime Ministers of nine republics (including Kyrgyzstan) reached agreement as follows:

- The IC, with responsibility for setting policies for and generally managing the external debts and assets of the FSU, was established with three co-chairs, two permanent ones (Russia and Ukraine), and one rotating among the other members. Voting powers are proportional to the members' shares of the debt. Policy decisions require a qualified majority of 80 percent.

- The VEB was confirmed as the sole Debt Manager, with a newly created department solely responsible for the management of existing FSU external debt.

Payments Situation. Between January and August 1992, the Interstate Council made approximately $900 million in debt service payments. Arrears on all categories of debt have begun to accumulate to a significant extent. Excluding overdue import payments, arrears stood at approximately $4.3 billion at the end of May 1992. Since the inception of the current arrangements with respect to the former USSR debt, all amounts remitted to the VEB in its capacity as Debt Manager have been by Russia. The only other source of payment in this period has been in the form of temporary drawings by the VEB on its clients' balances. Given insufficient foreign exchange to meet all external payment obligations, the stated principle of the Debt Manager has been to direct service payments to credit lines made available for the supply of food, medicine, and "other essential imports".

3.07   As discussed below, Kyrgyzstan's limited capacity to service debt suggests that external debt obligations, particularly those at market terms, should be contracted with great caution. For project financing, debt should only be contracted when it is demonstrably justified by the ensuing increase in debt servicing capacity. Regarding balance of payments loans, preference should be accorded to the most concessional sources of financing in terms of interest and maturity, while overall debt servicing costs should not be allowed to rise above 20 percent of export earnings for an extended period of time. Finally, it should be noted that during a period of macroeconomic instability as in 1992, the foreign exchange available to the Government for debt servicing may fall significantly short of overall export earnings.

3.08   Responsibility for external debt recording and management should ultimately be assigned to the National Bank, in close cooperation with the Ministry of Economy and Finance. In the short run, the entity that has the most up to date information on hard currency exports earnings and import requirements should be closely involved with external debt management and monitoring.

Financing Requirements: 1993 and Beyond

3.09   Financing requirements in 1993 are estimated to range between $400 million and $450 million. For ease of presentation, a point estimate of $420 million is used in this chapter: this figure is consistent with the trade projections in Chapter 2, where the large degree of uncertainty was emphasized. Financing requirements comprise of a non-interest current account deficit of $390 million (of which about $220 million equivalent is projected to arise from transactions within the ruble area), interest payments on new borrowing of about $5 million[3], and a build-up of foreign exchange reserves of $25 million. With the takeover of Kyrgyzstan's FSU debt, principal repayments are not projected to start prior to 1994.

3.10   The current account deficit is projected to range between $360 to $400 million a year for the 1994-96 period, as the projected increase in hard currency exports beyond 1993 approximately compensates for a widening of the interrepublican deficit. Annual debt servicing costs are projected to range from $15 to $35 million during 1994-96, consistent with the concessional nature of financing assumed. If such concessional financing were not available, debt servicing costs and hence overall financing requirements would rise commensurately. A reserve build-up averaging about $25 million per annum is also projected for the 1994-96 period. The resulting accumulation of reserves of $100 million by 1996 would not suffice to attain a desired ratio of reserves to imports (such as a level equivalent to three months of imports), if imports from the FSU are included and valued in hard currency. But it may not be realistic to assume a much faster accumulation given present financing constraints and the alternative uses of foreign exchange.[4] Such a scenario results in an annual financing requirement ranging from $400 to $460 million during 1994-96. The projections beyond 1993 will clearly have to be revised once interrepublican trade trends over the course of 1993 become more apparent, and the decision and timing regarding adoption of a new currency is clarified.

---

3.   This estimate is derived from the assumption that the bulk of financing in 1993 will be concessional in nature -- see Section II for details.

4.   If Kyrgyzstan introduces its own currency, a more rapid accumulation of reserves may be necessary.

Financing Sources

3.11   Given Kyrgyzstan's limited capacity to service debt during this decade, innovative forms of finance need to be devised to limit the accumulation of debt on market terms. The figures in Table 3-1 utilize conservative projections of grant availability relative to the need, implicitly assuming that the loans that are made available will be highly concessional in nature. Based on the simulations in the following section, a grant element of about 80 percent should be applied to the $380 million of debt creating flows projected for 1993 in Table 3-1.

3.12   <u>Foreign direct investment</u> (FDI) could ultimately play a major role in the financing pattern, but this is unlikely until there is greater clarity in the rules and regulations governing such investment, together with greater macroeconomic stability. In principle, FDI could include investment from enterprises in the FSU to their former subsidiaries in Kyrgyzstan, if this is considered necessary to maintain critical components of the production chain. FDI in convertible currency would be most likely to occur in the mining, energy and tourism sectors where medium-term prospects for hard currency earnings are relatively favorable.

Financing from Official Sources

3.13   The major portion of external financing in the medium term will have to come from official sources. The $15 million level of grants in the form of commodity assistance projected in 1993 corresponds to current estimates of planned humanitarian aid by official and multilateral agencies, primarily for food and medicine imports. But as observed above and discussed in greater detail in Section II, a large proportion of balance of payments assistance should be in the form of grants.

3.14   Technical assistance to enable Kyrgyzstan to manage and implement its ambitious reform program is needed in a wide area of activities. The Government has identified technical assistance needs in several sectors including: Enterprise reform and privatization, commercial banking, social safety issues, assistance for the Central Statistical Office, training in economics, accounting and finance, management of public investment, external debt management and coordination of external financing, legal reforms including for the mining and energy sectors, in addition to several other sector-specific requirements, most notably in agriculture. These TA requirements have been submitted to the Consultative Group for discussion in mid-December. Several of these are elaborated upon in the subsequent chapters of this report. In addition, specific TA to support the institutional mechanisms for aid management is described in Section III of this chapter. Overall TA requirements are estimated at $35 million in 1993, with $25 million for core-TA activities. However, the extent of TA that can practically be disbursed in a given year is estimated at $20 million. With commitments for TA expected to exceed this figure, prioritization and coordination of TA activities will be particularly important. Moreover, measures to enhance the capacity of Kyrgyzstan to absorb additional technical assistance productively will also be important.

3.15   Loan disbursements from multilateral agencies (excluding possible grants by institutions such as UNICEF) are projected at about $100 million (on commitments of about $115 million), comprising primarily of a possible IMF stand-by and proposed rehabilitation loan from the World Bank Group. In addition, it is possible that small amounts of project lending, such as an urgently needed telecommunications project could begin to disburse in 1993. Beyond 1993, disbursements from multilateral institutions could decline somewhat as the emphasis shifts in the World Bank from balance

Table 3-1. Financing Requirements and Sources,[a] 1992-96 (mln US$)

	Estimate 1992	Projection 1993	Simulated Annual Ranges 1994-1996
<u>**Financing Requirements**</u>	<u>395[b]</u>	<u>420[c]</u>	<u>400 to 460</u>
Current account deficit (excluding interest and transfers)	220	390	360 to 400
Interest	52	5	10 to 20
Amortization	78	0	5 to 15
Change in arrears	46	--	--
Increase in reserves	0	25	25
<u>**Financing Sources**</u>	<u>395</u>	<u>420</u>	<u>400 to 460</u>
Foreign direct investment	0	5	10 to 30
Commodity Assistance[d]	10	15	15
Technical Assistance[d]	5	20	20
Multilateral MLT loans	0	100	80 to 100
Official MLT loans	0	{240[f]	{255 to 275
Central Bank correspondent accounts (net)	22[e]		
Suppliers, buyers and export credit	5	40	20
Russian takeover of Kyrgyzstan's FSU debt	176	--	--
Errors and omissions[g]	178	--	--

<u>a</u>/   Combined estimates of ruble and non-ruble financing requirements and sources.

<u>b</u>/   Debt servicing estimates for 1992 refer entirely to Kyrgyzstan's share of the USSR debt -- see Box 3-1. In the autumn of 1992, this debt was taken over by Russia. Hence obligations beyond 1992 on FSU debt are not projected.

<u>c</u>/   The 1993 financing requirement is projected to range between $400 million and $450 million.

<u>d</u>/   Grants from official and multilateral sources.

<u>e</u>/   Excludes receipt of currency by Kyrgyzstan. Converted from quarterly ruble data using quarterly exchange rates.

<u>f</u>/   An agreement with Russia to cover bilateral payments through end-1993 was under negotiation in late 1992. In principle, official MLT loans in convertible currency could be reduced by the amount of net financing available through correspondent accounts or other sources from the ruble area.

<u>g</u>/   May in part reflect a build up of interrepublican arrears.

of payments support to project lending to improve infrastructure. Moreover, lending from multilateral institutions may have to be limited if the requisite degree of concessionality cannot be assured.

3.16   Credit from official sources at grant or highly concessional terms will have to comprise the largest source of financing. The projected need is $240 million in disbursements in 1993, rising to a range of $255 to $275 million during 1994-96. The bulk of this financing is needed for balance of payments support; hence commitments from official sources are projected at $250 million in 1993, assuming that all balance of payments commitments disburse in 1993 (Table 3-2). These figures include any financing available from within the ruble area. At the same time, the ability of Kyrgyzstan to utilize increased financing through the Central Bank correspondent accounts is not known, whereas financing through a build-up of inter-enterprise arrears across states can only be feasible for a limited duration.[5]

Table 3-2. Commitments Versus Disbursements in 1993[a] (mln US$)

	Commitments	Disbursements
Commodity Assistance	15	15
Technical Assistance	35	20
Balance of Payments	340	335
(Multilateral)	(100)	(95)
(Official)[b]	(240)	(240)
Project	25	5
(Multilateral)	(15)	(3)
(Official)	(10)	(2)
Suppliers, Buyers and Export Credits	80	40
TOTAL	495	415

[a]   Excludes foreign direct investment.
[b]   Includes any financing through Central Bank correspondent accounts from the ruble area.

Commercial Loans and Export Credits

3.17   Kyrgyzstan's most significant commitment to date of hard currency financing has been a $75 million export credit from Turkey. The projected disbursement of $40 million of credit in 1993 primarily reflects this loan, although additional sources may become available in the course of the year. However, since commercial credits tend to be expensive and of short maturity, such sources of financing should be strictly limited, on the assumption that larger inflows of concessional official and multilateral financing will be forthcoming.

---

5.   To the extent that Kyrgyzstan has repayment obligations as a result of such financing in 1992, financing requirements in Table 3-1 are understated.

Private Financing

3.18   Kyrgyzstan is not expected to have access to financing from non-guaranteed commercial sources in the medium term, and short-term trade credits are likely to be available only if officially guaranteed.

Creditworthiness

3.19   Kyrgyzstan currently has a negligible capacity to borrow in hard currency at market terms. This conclusion stems primarily from the considerable uncertainty regarding hard currency export prospects that results from several factors. First, the convertible currency export base is very low -- in 1991, it may have been as low as $23 million; while estimates vary for 1992, foreign exchange available to the Government from any such exports has been negligible. Second, the potential for diverting interrepublican exports is limited by the fact that the bulk of such exports may have limited markets outside the ruble area. Moreover, Kyrgyzstan's terms of trade deterioration vis-a-vis the CIS would suggest that its exports to the ruble area may have to decline by less than its imports in the medium term, further limiting the potential for diversion. Finally, the persistence of macroeconomic instability would make it more difficult for the Government to capture foreign exchange receipts to service external debt.

3.20   A further complication arises from the fact that projected deficits over the medium term are generated most importantly through trade with the FSU: such trade is expected to account for about two-thirds of Kyrgyzstan's consolidated trade deficit during 1993-96. Market-based hard currency borrowing to finance such deficits is inadvisable in view of the unknown timetable for ruble convertibility. At the same time, ignoring exports to the FSU may overstate creditworthiness problems, particularly if a share of Kyrgyzstan's interrepublican deficits can continue to be financed in rubles.

3.21   In view of these uncertainties, Kyrgyzstan's creditworthiness for market-based borrowing in hard currency is explored by extending the financing scenario in Table 3-1 through the year 2000. Hard currency exports, projected at $150 million by 1996 (Chapter 2), would rise to $220 million by the year 2000 assuming a 10 percent nominal growth rate. External debt projections are derived by cumulating the net debt creating flows projected in Table 3-1 (excluding voluntary or involuntary ruble financing in 1992 since the terms are unknown), and assuming that such flows are reduced to an average of $300 million per year during 1997-2000, from $365 million per year in 1994-96.

3.22   As observed in Table 3-3, these assumptions regarding net borrowing result in an untenable accumulation of debt and debt service if the borrowing is conducted at market terms (at an assumed interest cost of 7.5 percent). Even by 1996, when amortization is limited to less than 4 percent of debt outstanding, the debt service ratio (DSR) rises to 100 percent in relation to hard currency exports. By the year 2000, when principal repayments would become more significant, the DSR approaches 175 percent.

3.23   To reduce debt service costs to manageable levels there are two options: reduce the deficit, and hence financing requirements, drastically and accept a deeper decline in output in 1993 and slower economic recovery; or provide the requisite degree of concessionality in the financing. Under the second option, an 80 percent degree of concessionality is estimated to be needed on projected financing if a 20 percent DSR is to be maintained in 1996.

3.24   The above analysis may overstate the debt management problem to the extent that exports to the FSU are excluded while borrowing requirements generated from deficits with the FSU are included. If ruble financing were available over the medium term to finance Kyrgyzstan's deficits vis-a-vis the current ruble area, the degree of concessionality on hard currency borrowing could be lower. In the absence of such financing, it would be legitimate to include Kyrgyzstan's exports to the FSU into the DSR projections, either if the ruble became convertible or, in the context of emerging new currencies in the FSU, if trade transactions occur in hard currency. Valuing such exports in hard currency in the future (as well as the present) is however problematic for several reasons. In Table 3-3, a figure of $400 million is used for 1996 and 2000, based on the projections in Chapter 2. Adding these exports to the total generates DSRs of 27 percent in 1996 and 61 percent in 2000. Thus even including exports to the FSU a substantial degree of concessionality is required -- projected at 67 percent -- to maintain a 20 percent DSR by the end of the decade.

3.25   The unstable nature of current conditions highlights the large margin of error with respect to trade and financing projections. Nonetheless, until there is evidence that hard currency exports can expand faster than assumed, or that ruble financing to cover Kyrgyzstan's deficits with the ruble area will be available over the medium term, the financing that is provided should either be in the form of grants or should be highly concessional in nature as described above.

Table 3-3. Creditworthiness and Required Concessionality (mln US$)

	1996		2000	
	Excluding FSU Exports	Including FSU Exports	Excluding FSU Exports	Including FSU Exports
Exports	150	550	220	620
Debt[a]	1,480	1,480	2,680	2,680
Debt Service (100% market terms)	150	150	380	380
Debt Service Ratio (100% market terms)	100%	27%	173%	61%
Degree of concessionality required to maintain 20% debt service ratio	80%	27%	88%	67%

a/ Excludes any debt accruing from interrepublic deficits prior to 1993. Debt creating flows less amortization are projected to average $365 million in 1994-96 (Table 3-1) and $300 million in 1997-2000.

Management of Foreign Aid

3.26   Against the background of a substantial resource gap and a limited capacity to absorb debt on other than concessional terms, the Government of Kyrgyzstan is in the process of establishing an institutional capacity to manage external resources. Managing the flow of foreign resources requires dealing with a multitude of agencies, with different forms of assistance and a wide variety of financial terms, appraisal procedures and disbursement conditions. The first aid commitments have been made. As the earlier part of this chapter indicates, the external financing requirements are large, and the necessary resources must be identified, secured and disbursed quickly if the economy is to be sustained during the transition to a market economy. This section discusses the management of external resources in Kyrgyzstan, and makes recommendations on how to develop an institutional capacity to ensure their effective utilization.

3.27   The Present Situation. In creating this capacity, account needs to be taken of the existing institutional setting and the assignment of responsibilities for economic decision-making among the main actors. The Government has taken the strategic decision to combine foreign investment coordination with aid management, and to place the agency under the direct control of the highest economic authorities of the country. On July 27, 1992 this agency (the State Commission on Foreign Investments and External Assistance--GOSCOMINVEST) was established. Chaired by the President, the State Commission will comprise the Prime Minister, the Minister of Economy and Finance and other key officials responsible for the management of the economy. The main aim of the State Commission is the unification and standardization of state policy in regard to foreign investment and the effective utilization of foreign aid for economic development. Subject to the Commission's policy guidance and approval, an Executive Secretariat ("The General Board") will be responsible for aid coordination, facilitation of foreign investment and procurement and audit services.

3.28   The General Board would be headed by a Director General, and be organized into three units: the Aid Coordination Unit, the Foreign Investment Bureau, and the Procurement and Audit Advisory Service. The head of each unit would report directly to the Director General. Although staffed largely along donor lines--rather than sector lines--the General Board may have separate divisions for the Economy, Finance, Contract Law, Analysis and Projections, Accounting, and Administrative Services.

3.29   A representative of the National Bank should also be a part of GOSCOMINVEST since the NBK will manage Kyrgyzstan's foreign reserves and be responsible for debt servicing. Thus the NBK Chairman could be made part of GOSCOMINVEST, and a representative of NBK could participate in the General Board's meetings.

3.30   Aid Coordination Unit (ACU). The ACU should act as the facilitator of contacts between donors and ministries and be the focal point for coordinating relations with donors. The ACU should not have authority to set overall economic or investment priorities, nor to evaluate the economic validity of projects, but would select donors to whom they could propose a particular project. Initially in Kyrgyzstan, aid coordination was handled by the State Committee for External Economic Relations. This Committee was instrumental in initiating effective coordination of external aid and relations with donor countries and institutions, and assembled a small core of professional staff during the summer of 1992. The staff will now be available for transfer to the General Board, which can therefore become operational as soon as it is formally established. The State Committee should then be abolished, lest it duplicate the functions of the Secretariat or of other economic management organs. The ACU should be organized along donor lines, and have limited but high-quality staff: 10-15 professionals selected from the government services should be able to handle the aid programs Kyrgyzstan is likely to develop over the coming years.   It is crucial that the ACU should establish a close relationship with the other economic agencies of government, particularly the Ministry of Economy and Finance (MEF) and the National Bank. The ACU should maintain close links with the debt management units in these institutions, and the budget department in the MEF, to ensure that adequate provision is being made for debt servicing in the budget.

Box 3-2. Requirements for Good Aid Management

Good aid management depends on good economic management generally. Aid cannot be effectively managed in a vacuum. Experience from other countries shows that the following are needed.

Clear development priorities.   Policy makers need to have a clear view of development objectives and communicate them to aid managers. In other words, the Government must know what it wants to use foreign aid for. This includes striking a balance between various uses of aid, notably between balance of payments support, which benefits the economy generally, specific project aid directed towards public investment in infrastructures and the social sectors to support a market economy, and technical assistance. Failing that, donors are likely to take the initiative in designing aid programs, and their preferences may not coincide with Kyrgyzstan's priorities.

Public Investment Program (PIP).   The Government must have the capacity to turn broad development aims and strategies into concrete programs and projects, pass these through a screening process, and assemble them into a PIP. The PIP is a means for setting public investment priorities and determining resource needs. The PIP plays a key role in realizing the country's development objectives, and also serves as a basis for attracting and guiding foreign financing. Although Kyrgyzstan will be receiving assistance that remains outside the PIP (e.g. balance of payments support, food aid), the PIP will nevertheless be an important basis for formulating aid requests, particularly in the medium term.

Integration of aid into the budget. Foreign aid supplements the Government's own resources in financing public expenditures. These resources are allocated through the budget, and effective use of aid thus requires that the budgetary process functions adequately. It is particularly important that all expenditures under the PIP, including those financed by aid, are included in the budget. Aid managers need to maintain close links with those in charge of budget preparation to ensure that aid flows are included in the budget, and that adequate provision is made for the Government's own contribution to foreign aided projects and for external debt servicing.

Institutional capacity for aid management. Responsibilities for managing foreign aid need to be clearly assigned. Whatever arrangements are chosen, it should be clear (i) who is responsible for overall aid policy, (ii) who has the authority for making day-to-day decisions on aid, and (iii) what are the communication channels between aid agencies and the government. Although separate aid agencies have been set up in some countries, the usual arrangement is for the aid coordination unit to be part of the Ministry with overall responsibility for resource allocation. Separate agencies have often found it difficult to integrate their activities into the mainstream planning and budgeting process. Active management of aid requires a body with an overview of aid flows and specialist knowledge and experience of different aid agencies.

Government accounting. Aid management requires accurate government accounts to keep track of Government expenditures and aid utilization. Recording aid expenditures can be difficult when aid agencies disburse directly and care has to be taken to include such outlays in the accounts. Special arrangements are normally made for recording external debt obligations in order that interest and principal payments on foreign loans are made in time.

3.31   In addition to keeping track of financial assistance or food aid, the ACU should move quickly to coordinate Kyrgyzstan's technical assistance requirements (provision of short and long-term foreign experts, studies, training and associated equipment), to ensure that the highest priority needs are being met. In allocating technical assistance (TA), priority should be given to increasing local capacity to manage the economy and the reform process. It is important, in a newly-independent country such as Kyrgyzstan, to underline that TA carries risks as well as advantages. In the short term, there is a risk of wasting resources if the foreign advisor proves less than fully competent. In the long term, there is the opposite risk of coming to rely on competent foreign experts to actually direct the activities rather than advise the responsible local officials. It is therefore crucial to ensure that: (i) TA fits into a well-designed structure with clear objectives; and (ii) the advisor carry a specific responsibility for training local counterparts. If these requirements are met, TA can make an important contribution by providing specialized know-how and advice that is not available locally, in a way that is not influenced by internal political considerations.

3.32   Foreign Investment Bureau (FIB). The FIB would: (i) facilitate foreign investment; (ii) ensure compliance with applicable laws and regulations; and (iii) negotiate with large potential investors. The FIB should be guided by the general principle that an investment license will normally be granted without government scrutiny of the viability of the project unless either (a) a specific public interest is at stake, as specified in the applicable legislation, or (b) public moneys or public resources (or guarantees) are involved. To facilitate foreign investment, the Bureau could disseminate abroad general information about the economy and investment prospects, and could provide visiting investors with specific information about their sector of interest and arrange for useful business contacts. It can also act as "one-stop window" to provide information on laws and regulations and help secure necessary permits. Beyond such practical assistance, it is normally unnecessary and undesirable to grant foreign investors fiscal or other incentives that are not granted to domestic investors. Furthermore, the Bureau's assistance services should be made available to domestic investors as well. Concerning negotiations of large investment projects, the FIB should seek assistance from advisors with special expertise in the field in question.

3.33   Procurement and Audit Service (PAS). Procurement and audit are essential and general functions, common to the entire government. Concerning aid-financed projects, a special Project Implementation Unit will sometimes be set up to assist the implementation of the specific project--and such a unit may have its own procurement and/or audit staff. In addition, especially in the initial stages of the Government's experience with external aid, and in the context of the general move away from state orders, the PAS can provide an important advisory service. It could, for example, supply government agencies with information on international standards and, on request by a government agency or on instruction by the President, intervene to resolve problems or irregularities. The PAS should in any event maintain close contact with the Project Implementation Units in order to assure that procurement under all aid-assisted projects conforms to international standards and laws.

Technical Assistance

3.34   A program of technical assistance is recommended to support the institutional mechanisms for aid management, public investment support, and procurement and audit services. The TA program would have four components: (i) assistance to the ACU; (ii) assistance to the FIB; (iii) assistance to the PAS; and (iv) assistance to the MEF for preparing and implementing the public investment program. Assistance to the ACU would comprise one long-term advisor and short-term advisors as needed. It would also include communications and computing equipment, a study tour for staff, a regional seminar and other training to familiarize the staff with the operations of different donor institutions. Assistance to the FIB would be in the form of short-term advisory services of experts in particular fields to help the Government in negotiating large projects with foreign investors. Assistance to the PAS would include a long-term procurement advisor and short-term audit advisory services as needed, plus appropriate staff training. Assistance to the MEF in the public investment area would comprise a team to screen the "overhang" of existing projects, a long-term advisor on public investment methodology and another long-term advisor on organizational and institutional issues of public investment programming and monitoring.

The Longer-Term Dimension

3.35   The above plans of the Government appear workable and give promise to assure effective coordination and facilitation of external resource inflows. Yet, it is fundamental to keep in mind the need to develop institutional capacity in the longer term. Thus, first, the Government should guard against the risk that GOSCOMINVEST becomes a "superagency" usurping or duplicating the economic management functions of the line ministries or of the core economic agencies. Second, as indicated earlier, an equally vigorous effort is needed to streamline and strengthen the core economic management institutions--particularly the MEF which is in charge of the budget and of public investment programming and monitoring. When circumstances and internal developments will permit, responsibilities for aid management and foreign investment facilitation and appropriate regulation should devolve to the regular organs of government. Therefore, the GOSCOMINVEST should have a limited mandate of a certain number of years. But also, by that time the regular organs of government must be prepared to assume the responsibility: the reform and strengthening process is of long gestation. To provide the basis for such a process an operationally-oriented study of the needed transformation of the economic management institutions should be launched as soon as possible.

PART II

Structural Reforms

At the beginning of 1992, the Government undertook major steps towards economic liberalization. While these measures have already resulted in significant adjustments in relative prices, the response at the microeconomic level to these changes has inevitably been slower. As efforts to stabilize the economy intensify, it will be particularly important to promote factor mobility and adjustments at the enterprise level in a manner that would foster a strong supply response and strengthen the recovery from the current crisis.

Reforming the financial sector in Kyrgyzstan is of critical importance in mobilizing savings, redirecting credit to its most productive uses, and promoting adjustment at the enterprise level. A description of the financial sector and proposed reforms is provided in Chapter 4. Chapter 5 assesses existing legal and institutional constraints to the expansion of private sector activity, including foreign direct investment, and proposes adjustments to increase competition, eliminate barriers to entry, build managerial and marketing skills, and reform the legal environment. Promotion of enterprise reform through corporatization and privatization through a variety of means is a key focus of this chapter. Chapter 6 provides an overview of the labor market and analyzes policies to strengthen labor market legislation and enhance labor mobility to facilitate the process of enterprise reform.

A necessary element to pursue the agenda for structural reforms is the provision of an adequate social safety net to protect the poor and those most adversely affected by the reforms. Chapter 7 contains a description of the existing system of social protection, and assesses the adjustments that will be required, including more focused targeting of benefits, in view of reduced resource availability and the fundamental changes in the organization of economic activity that are envisaged.

CHAPTER 4

The Financial Sector

Introduction

4.01   Kyrgyzstan's banking system will have to play a central role during the economy's transition, providing credit to new enterprises and offering reasonable deposit conditions to households and private investors.   In the nonfinancial sector the transition requires major changes in business operations, with breakups of traditional state enterprises into smaller privately-owned units and creation of new firms to compete directly with existing enterprises. These changes can only occur with adequate credit to restructure state enterprises and to establish new companies. The forms of such finance are not yet clear, and they deserve attention in monetary policy as a key aspect in the next few years. It is clear, however, that credit must be available to ventures with reasonable risks at market interest rates, and that yields on deposits must be closely tied to rates that are able to attract real resources into the banking system. Traditional forms of credit rationing and administered interest rates will have to be gradually abolished if the financial markets are to be effective in facilitating a successful transition to a market economy.

4.02   To give borrowers and depositors real choices in their banking needs the banks must be independent firms that operate as financial businesses to promote their own incomes and positions, and there need to be a number of such banks in the market competing with one another. The present banking system in Kyrgyzstan does not meet such a description. The large banks that dominate the sector are still too close to the Soviet model of sectoral finance agencies, and they lack the expertise and the independence that would give them the ability to develop the market potentials in both credit and deposits. Moreover, they lack many of the banking skills and marketing viewpoints that would help their customers (and themselves) in correspondent relations with other CIS republics, and foreign markets. The interest rates required to match expected inflation are also difficult to implement against the background of the rate structure that existed previously in the Soviet Union.

4.03   These legacies from the Soviet Union leave the present banking system poorly suited to finance an emerging market economy, and major changes must thus be accomplished in the methods of banking operation. During the next few years the present system must be transformed into a more independent and active financial market, and broadened beyond domestic banking to include a variety of new financing services, particularly services related to foreign trade. In the immediate future, however the banks must be pressed hard to provide at least minimal elements of a banking system to the economy. To achieve this goal, there is an urgent need for training and regulations, to disperse the current concentration of lending to the primary owners of the banks, to shift the structure of interest rates to at least approximate those of a competitive market economy, and to promote the use of bank deposits and checks instead of cash in the payments mechanism. To promote public confidence in the banking system, the prudential supervision by the National Bank must be intensified. This chapter describes the present situation of, and the short-term measures for reforming the financial sector.

Box 4-1. The Evolution of the Banking System in the former Soviet Union

Until 1987 the Soviet Union had a monobank system in which the State Bank of the USSR (Gosbank) ensured that resources were allocated in accordance with the government's economic plan. This centralized banking system fit the needs of the centralized economic planning system. As increased autonomy was given to enterprises and cooperatives, there was a corresponding need to change the banking system.

The restructuring of the banking system began in 1987. The first stage of the restructuring involved the creation of a two-tiered banking system. Gosbank was established as the Central Bank of the Soviet Union and given responsibility for the implementation of monetary policy, the maintenance of a stable currency, the supervision of commercial banks, and the facilitation of inter-bank settlements. The non-central banking functions were allocated to the second tier of the two-tier banking system, comprising five specialized banks: the Savings Bank (Sberbank), the Foreign Trade Bank (Vneshtorgbank), the bank for construction and industry (Promstroibank), the agricultural bank (Agroprombank), and the social and small enterprise sector bank (Zhilsotsbank).

The emergence of independent and private banks in 1987 created the need for operational and accounting rules and a regulatory and supervisory system. In 1989, Gosbank created a Commercial Bank Department to perform audits and conduct regulatory and supervisory functions; Gosbank also issued prudential standards, established licensing procedures, set capital and liquidity standards, and instituted monthly and annual reporting requirements.

In 1991, three of the large specialized commercial banks—Promstroibank, Agroprombank, and Zhilsotsbank—were reconstituted as self-supporting joint-stock banks with their headquarter banks and territorial branches established as independent banks, separate from the State.

The Foreign Trade Bank, Vneshtorgbank, was renamed the Bank for Foreign Economic Affairs, Vneshekonombank, and maintained within the Soviet Union's central banking system. This bank was given responsibility for official reserves, financing foreign trade, and for managing the Union's foreign debt. By the end of 1991, Vneshekonombank's responsibilities were primarily focused on managing the Union's foreign debt. However, Vneshekonombank was then made accountable to the Central Bank of Russia.

During 1991, the Union's Savings Bank (Sberbank) was first classified as a commercial bank, then reclassified as part of the Central Bank, and later constituted as a commercial bank but with special provisions because almost all household deposits are held in the Savings Bank.

Source: Adapted from the World Bank's Country Economic Memorandum on Russia.

The Banking System

4.04   The financial sector of Kyrgyzstan consists of the National Bank of Kyrgyzstan (NBK), three large commercial banks that have been sectoral banks but that are trying to become universal, nine small commercial banks, also largely sectoral in nature, and the Savings Bank (SB).

4.05   The system emerged from the institutions that operated under the previous regime. The laws that currently govern the banking system were passed in June 1991, and consist of the "Law on State Bank" and the "Law on Banks and Banking", both of which are being revised, however. In February 1992, the State Bank was replaced by NBK, which inherited the legal rights and responsibilities of the State Bank and acts as the central bank of the Republic.

The National Bank of Kyrgyzstan

4.06   NBK is responsible for all monetary affairs and the banking sector, acts as the fiscal agent of the Government, and manages relations with other CIS and foreign central banks. It extends credit to the commercial banks, holds their reserves, and provides clearing services for interbank transactions. It reports to the Supreme Soviet and its five Board members including the Chairman are nominated by the Supreme Soviet at the recommendation of the country's President for five year terms. As of April 1992, NBK had 89 employees in nine departments: Executive office (Chairman's office, including a legal division); Economic Department (including bank licensing and supervision); Currency circulation; Foreign exchange; Accounting (including interbank clearing); Data processing; Personnel; Administration; Auditing.

4.07   A major issue that effects both NBK and the commercial banks is the supply of currency since Kyrgyzstan is totally dependent on the central bank of Russia (CBR) for the supply of rubles. The terms and conditions under which NBK can obtain cash were unclear. As of April 1992, it was assumed that in the future currency would be issued for a one-time printing charge of one percent and then recorded as NBK debt to the CBR carrying an annual interest of 20 percent (since then the interest rate has been raised several times). It was not clear what quantitative limitations would be imposed by the CBR, or how these would be determined.

4.08   During large parts of 1992, the lack of cash dominated financial activity. NBK rations cash to the banks, but with no clear criteria, making the allocations arbitrary. Commercial banks limit their clients' cash withdrawals from deposits, and enterprises often pay their employees after significant delay. The lack of cash is further intensified through hoarding by individuals and businesses, who realize that deposits cannot be cashed and refrain from depositing the cash they have. This tendency is reenforced by the very low interest rates paid on deposits. Checking account balances pay only 5 percent interest, and savings in the Savings Bank, where practically all household savings are held, pay very low nominal interest rates (10-22 percent in September 1992), not worth the risk of being unable to obtain cash when the depositor needs it. Fixed term deposits in commercial banks paid only slightly higher rates.

4.09   NBK monitors the banks' compliance with the following norms: (a) Capital to liabilities -- minimum 5 percent; (b) single borrower exposure -- maximum 50 percent of capital, exposure defined as the sum of all loans and half of guarantees provided; (c) liquidity -- short-term assets at least 30 percent of short-term deposits; (d) long-term exposure -- longer than 3 years maturity, assets not to exceed long-term (more than 3 years) liabilities plus capital; and (e) reserves -- deposited with NBK amounting to at least 15 percent of deposits.

4.10   Intercompany transactions within Kyrgyzstan are handled by the banks through bank transfers and check clearing. The clearing between the banks is done by NBK through debiting and crediting the banks' accounts in NBK, with all transactions cleared daily. Although NBK handles such clearing largely manually, the small number of banks and daily transactions make the prompt clearing feasible. However, the clearing of payments between enterprises in Kyrgyzstan and other CIS republics, accounting for the bulk of such transactions for non-service related enterprises, has become more problematic. While some enterprises received payments on time, delays and arrears were increasingly evident.

4.11   NBK assets and liabilities are recorded according to the Soviet accounting system, making it almost impossible to construct a Western style balance sheet. The accounts as of end-February 1992, are shown below:

Table 4-1. NBK Assets and Liabilities, February 29, 1992 (mln rbl)

Assets:	Cash	326
	Credit to commercial banks	3,832
	Loans to the government	700
	Other and parallel accounts	17,939
	Total Assets	**22,797**
Liabilities:	Commercial banks' deposits	690
	Other liabilities and	
	Parallel accounts	22,044
	Equity and retained profits	
	(Net worth)	63
	Total Liabilities & Net Worth	**22,797**

Most of the parallel accounts are netted out in Western accounting practice. The net difference in the parallel accounts of more than R4 billion includes credit to the state, debt to CRB and other items, but the breakdown could not be obtained. The need to adjust accounting standards and procedures to a modern system is discussed below. In interpreting the accounts as they are recorded today the only three significant numbers are the net worth, which is very small (less than $1 million at the prevailing exchange rate), the very low cash position (and lack of any foreign exchange in cash or deposits abroad), and the relatively large sum of credit to commercial banks, which finances almost half of all credit extended by the commercial banks.

Commercial Banks

4.12   The commercial banks are all joint-stock companies. Their shares are held mostly by enterprises that are their customers but also by some individuals. This situation is a result of the policy of making all banks, previously branches of Soviet Union-based sectoral banks and the commercial segment of the monobank, into independent banks. With no other potential buyers, and no organization to arrange the sale of banks' shares, the shares were offered to each bank's main customers (with heavy sectoral concentration in the sectoral banks). These owners are the major borrowers and enjoy preferential treatment in interest rates, credit availability and the supply of cash. Given the scarcity of credit and the prevailing negative real interest rates access to credit for non-owners is very limited.

4.13   The three largest banks dominate the commercial banking sector with the following approximate shares in activity: 94 percent of branches, 95 percent of total staff, 94 percent of loans outstanding, and 90 percent of deposits. (These ratios exclude the Savings Bank, discussed separately below). All three large banks have large branch networks with a presence in all the regions of the country. Kyrgyzpromstroybank and Kyrgyzstan Commercial Bank are present in all towns with 26 and 21 branches, respectively. Agroindustrial Bank (or Agroprom Bank), has a presence in the rural areas, with 46 branches and with more than 1,200 employees. All three banks are trying to become universal banks, but they all suffer from common weaknesses. Their staff are still familiarizing themselves with modern banking techniques; most transactions are processed manually; accounting is done in the old manner according to the Soviet chart of accounts; their primary customers are their main shareholders, who receive concessionary credit; there is little exposure to international banking activity, since all foreign exchange transactions were previously dealt with by the Moscow banks.

4.14   The other nine banks are relatively small, each with up to three branches. At least one has reportedly only private shareholder. The new banks are relatively dynamic and experiment in new financial services (one is preparing the introduction of credit cards, another obtained a short-term loan from a Moscow bank and lent the money to its customers at a spread). Most of them have high concentrations of loans to a specific sector, and their owners are also their main borrowers.

4.15   Practically all banks are heavily dependent on NBK loans as a source for lending.[1] NBK loans amounted to R11.0 billion on July 31, 1992, constituting 56 percent of their outstanding loans.

4.16   The commercial banks' balance sheets are also prepared in the Soviet method. An attempt to present the highlights of their accounts in Western terms is provided below:

Table 4-2. Commercial Bank Accounts: Selected Items, July 31, 1992 (mln rbl)

Bank (with number of branches)	Paid-In Capital	Total Capital	Credit Limit	Loans Outstanding	National Bank Resources
PROMSTROY (26)	172	205	4102	4842	2726
AGROPROM (46)	203	209	4190	10122	6293
KYRGYZSTAN (21)	278	401	7030	3304	1489
SATURN	29	28	560	7	20
AUTO (2)	20	25	496	173	85
KURULUSH (3)	23	17	332	460	185
MASKAT (1)	17	18	356	260	25
AHNIET	46	61	1230	205	120
DUKAN	7	5	100	232	50
ADIL	35	32	650	26	34
KYRGYZ DJER	.5	.9	18	35	-
MELBUSAES	2	2	32	.1	-
TOTAL (99)	842	1005	19086	19668	11048

Source: NBK

---

1.   As of November 1992, NBK resources were provided to commercial banks at an annual rate of 50 percent with loans for the agricultural sector set at lower levels. NBK allowed the banks a maximum mark-up of 3 percent on on-lending from its sources.

4.17   A major issue in evaluating the performance of the commercial banks is the status of their loan portfolio. All banks claim that all their outstanding loans are performing well. There are two possible explanations: (i) With high inflation and low nominal interest rates, even enterprises in difficulties have no problem paying their debt; and (ii) Most enterprises have very low financial leverage, and most of their financial requirements were previously met by equity investment of state funds, and not by bank loans. With the economic decline and relative price changes, this situation may not persist, and debt servicing may become a major problem particularly when interest rates rise.

4.18   Another major issue is the effect of inflation on loan volume and capital. Banks show nominal profits, but are rapidly losing the real value of their capital. This is evident if nominal variables are related to inflation indexes or to foreign exchange rates. For example, the total net worth of the banking system as of early August 1992 was only about $5 million at the exchange rate prevailing at that time.

The Savings Bank

4.19   The Savings Bank is a relatively large organization with 58 branches and 2,000 employees. It almost exclusively serves the household sector and as of end 1991 total deposits stood at R3 billion, more than 70 percent of the total for all commercial banks. An almost equivalent amount is on deposit in the Moscow Savings Bank. Only R0.5 billion, accumulated in the last year is not deposited in Moscow and has been lent locally, to individuals, commercial banks and to a limited extent to businesses. The SB has begun to extend very long-term loans (up to 25 years) to citizens buying their apartments through the housing privatization scheme. These loans are provided at an annual nominal interest rate of 3 percent, a rate that provides a huge subsidy to the borrowers at the current inflation rate. These loans are financed by deposits for much shorter periods. SB management did not appear to be aware of the impact of high inflation on the financial standing of their bank; the fate of the Bank is also heavily dependent on the arrangements that will be made regarding the R3 billion deposited in Moscow.

Non-Bank Financial Intermediaries

4.20   No non-bank financial intermediaries were known to be established as of April 1992. The only significant non-bank financial institute was the State Insurance Company (SIC), which holds a practical monopoly in the insurance market, and provides various types of insurance services to the country's enterprises. SIC offers the banks insurance for loans provided to risky borrowers. However, this insurance is provided only for very small loans, at a premium of 6 percent per annum, and the total volume of loans insured is very small, around R50 million. SIC is planning to further decrease its loans' insurance activity, thus making the scheme insignificant for the credit market.

Proposed Reforms

4.21   The financial activity of the NBK and commercial banks is heavily influenced by developments beyond their control. Inflation, foreign exchange rates, and the supply of cash are all externally determined, and the outlook for these parameters is highly uncertain. This uncertainty limits the freedom for reforming the financial system. Hence the following suggestions do not constitute a comprehensive reform, but rather a list of measures that can be taken in the near future, independent of developments elsewhere in the ruble area, to strengthen the financial system. If Kyrgyzstan chooses or is forced to introduce a national currency, several of these recommendations would have to be reconsidered or altered.

4.22   The following recommendations assume that the current shortage of cash will be overcome, and therefore the free conversion of deposits into cash will be possible. Otherwise, the banks will not be able to function as financial intermediaries, and their role in the economy will quickly decrease. Another assumption is that inflation rates will be within the range that allows for the functioning of the financial system, and will not reach the levels that make financial intermediation impossible.

Supervision and Licensing of Commercial Banks

4.23   NBK should substantially strengthen its capacity to supervise the commercial banks. A number of adjustments in existing regulations are needed to strengthen the financial system and increase competition. The limits on single borrowers should be adjusted downwards (to a smaller percentage of capital), and the sectorial concentration of loans should also be limited. At the same time monitoring and enforcing the banks' compliance with the regulations will need to be intensified, and will require on-site supervision. A separate supervision department in NBK has recently been established and should receive priority in staffing, training, and access to technical assistance.

4.24   The number of banks is large enough for an economy the size of Kyrgyzstan and small enough to facilitate proper supervision and training of key personnel in modern banking techniques. Therefore, NBK should not encourage the opening of new banks, unless foreign banks are interested in entering and bringing with them expertise and international connections. Minimum capital requirements were raised in June 1992 to R20-100 million, depending on the Bank's legal and ownership structure. They should be linked to inflation to maintain their real value. Moreover, from the prudential aspect an increase in capital requirements to the Basle norm of 8 percent over a period of two or three years would be desirable. If such requirements cause one or two of the smaller banks to liquidate or merge, no damage to the financial system will occur. The present law is unclear as to the discretion of NBK in approving or rejecting the requests for new bank licenses once the applicant meets the minimum requirements outlined in the law; such discretion should be made explicit, to enable NBK to reject requests for establishing new banks, for example, if the number of banks is considered large enough to facilitate competition and additional banks would create a supervision problem.

4.25   The present concentration of lending by commercial banks to their major shareholders is unhealthy for the development of a strong financial sector. It discourages competition and access to credit for non-owners, jeopardizes the financial strength of the banks, and should be reduced. It is proposed that the banks be directed to reduce the share of total loans provided to all their large shareholders (defined as owners of at least 5 percent of total shares, and any enterprise represented on the bank's board) as a group, from the current practice, which in some banks reaches 90 percent, to 25 percent by the end of 1994, with intermediate targets of 70 percent by mid-1993, and 50 percent by the end of 1993. Allowing free trade in bank shares could assist the process of dismantling the current linkage between owners and borrowers, but may be difficult to implement with no capital market mechanism in place. High inflation, which will cause a large increase in the nominal loan portfolio, will facilitate such a transformation. Once restrictions on related borrower lending are introduced, all banks will be in a similar situation, looking for new, unrelated customers; and large enterprises that currently enjoy concessionary terms from the banks they own, will enter the market for loans from other banks. This change will promote competition, and more careful evaluation of credit risks by the banks. To implement this policy, NBK should issue clear directives, supervise the banks' compliance with them, and apply sanctions against banks that keep their lending to related parties above the permitted ratio.

4.26   The objective of dismantling the owner-borrower linkage can alternatively be addressed by limiting the percentage of bank ownership permitted to any single owner (person or company). This approach will, however, create a governance problem. If related lending is strictly limited, the strong presence of ownership interests in the management of a bank has many virtues, and indeed should be encouraged. It can also be assumed that foreign investors (including foreign banks) will not invest in a bank if they cannot secure majority ownership.

Profitability of Banks

4.27   With interest rates highly negative in real terms, banks' total assets have been decreasing as a percentage of GDP, and this decline will continue until prices stabilize (or real lending rates become positive). Although the banks reportedly face few problems in collecting on their loan portfolios and show nominal profits, their real net worth is decreasing quickly. If this process continues, banks' capital will shrink to a level that will make it impossible for them to provide loans to enterprises in the amounts needed for conducting business at the new price levels, without reaching unacceptable risk assets to capital ratios. To enable the banks to make higher profits, so as to maintain the real value of their net worth, the current restrictions on the 3 percent spread allowed on loans provided from NBK resources should be increased substantially. However, due to the expected shortage of credit and the limited credit provided from NBK funds, it is not recommended that the limit to the allowed spread be completely eliminated (until the pattern of lending is more amenable to competition), since banks could then charge unreasonable spreads on some of their loans, and use the additional income to further subsidize their shareholders.

4.28   Subsidized loans to special sectors should be eliminated unless they are entirely financed through the state budget, and the one rate to be applied to NBK resources provided to the commercial banks should converge rapidly to CBR's discount rate, and in no circumstances be lower than the rate paid by NBK on its liabilities to the CBR. Interest rates on loans from resources other than NBK loans should remain free. However, the banks should be instructed to stop providing loans to their shareholders at preferential interest rates and charge equal interest on all loans to equal risk borrowers. It may be necessary to apply and enforce minimum lending rates for this purpose, to prevent banks from lending at interest rates lower than the lending rate set for loans from NBK funds.

4.29   An additional obstacle to earning reasonable profits results from the rapid changes in the amount of deposits in the commercial banks, which require them to hold large reserves in NBK, beyond the liquidity requirements. NBK should encourage the commercial banks to create an interbank money market, where banks from which deposits are withdrawn would be able to borrow from the banks in which the money was placed. Such an interbank market would reduce the need to keep large reserves with zero interest in NBK.

4.30   The following suggestions are based on the assumption that the nominal ruble market will have to follow developments in Russia, but that there is a possibility of identifying some segments in which financial intermediation can be developed independently. Particularly if inflation remains high in the ruble zone, the real levels of financial sector assets and activity will tend to decline further. These suggestions may thus be interpreted as means of maintaining the real values of financial activity at least for specific segments of the market.

4.31   One such segment is exports to hard currency markets. For this segment of economic activity Kyrgyzstan could explore the option of allowing exporters to keep the export revenue that they have to surrender to local banks in dollar-linked ruble accounts, thus avoiding the risks of devaluation.[2] The banks could then use these resources to provide dollar-linked ruble loans to other exporters in need of working capital. The banks would be obliged to sell the foreign exchange to NBK, and the dollar-linked accounts would be subject to the same reserve requirements as other deposits.

4.32   Another such segment is long-term savings. Such savings will not be attracted with the current interest rate structure. For such savings the option of indexation to the cost-of-living index (COLI) could be evaluated. If such a scheme is adopted, savings mobilized under the scheme could be used for mortgage financing (the current practice of providing long-term loans for housing at a nominal interest rate of 3 percent should be stopped anyway). The introduction of COLI savings for long-term deposits and housing finance could be pioneered by the Savings Bank, but permitted for all commercial banks.

Savings Bank

4.33   The reform of the SB is essential for the promotion of savings by the household sector. The SB should be placed on equal terms with the commercial banks in the market for household savings. Thus limits on its deposit interest rates should be removed and its special rights, such as an explicit state guarantee to depositors, should be withdrawn (and it is too early to consider a more general deposit insurance scheme). At the same time, regulations restricting commercial banks' ability to accept household deposits should be removed. Once the issue of its deposits in the Russian Savings Bank is resolved, the market segment in which it operates should be well defined. It is recommended that the SB not be allowed to engage in lending to enterprises, since it lacks the skills required for proper risk evaluation. It should operate mainly in the interbank market, providing funds to the commercial banks, which in turn should be encouraged to lend to small new private enterprises. One market in which it could operate directly is mortgage lending, a market that will become more important given the Government's efforts towards privatization in housing. If long-term cost-of-living index-linked savings are introduced and the funds used for mortgage lending are also cost-of-living index-linked, as discussed above, the Saving Bank could pioneer the introduction of new, inflation-safe financial intermediation instruments.

Accounting and Auditing

4.34   A general issue with important consequences for the banking sector relates to accounting and auditing systems. Kyrgyzstan should introduce a modern accounting system, compatible with international standards. It has opted to participate in common CIS efforts for developing such a system. Banks should be given priority in the introduction of the modern accounting system. NBK should then issue the directives to banks regarding the accounting and reporting regulations.

4.35   Once the first steps in introducing a modern accounting system are taken the issue of auditing by certified public accountants should be of high priority. For a rapid introduction of independent auditing, foreign auditing firms should be encouraged to open offices in Kyrgyzstan and local

---

2.   Such a scheme can only function once the acute cash shortage prevailing in early 1992 has ended and confidence in the ability to withdraw deposits has returned.

accountants sent for training abroad.   The requirement for audited annual statements   should be introduced gradually, with banks required to have their accounts audited first, and other sectors phased in over several years, with size (measured by assets or annual sales) serving as the main criterion.

Conclusions

4.36   The current situation calls for major financial sector reforms in order to enable the sector to play its role in the transition to market economy.   However, the total dependency of Kyrgyzstan on external developments, being in the ruble zone, the present shortage of cash, and the uncertainty as to the developments in the real sectors, prevent the adoption of a comprehensive financial sector reform at this stage.

4.37   Several important steps can nevertheless be taken.   These include:

a)   Strengthening NBK supervision capabilities, and introducing on-site supervision.

b)   Discouraging the establishment of new banks and increasing capital requirements for both new and existing banks.

c)   Gradually decreasing related-parties' borrowing to 25 percent of total loans.

d)   Enhancing banks' profitability by increasing the spreads allowed on loans from NBK funds.

e)   Establishing an interbank money market.

f)   Increasing interest rates to a level at least equal to the rate paid by NBK for funds obtained from CBR, elimination of subsidized loans unless fully covered by the state budget, and forbidding banks from lending at lower rates to related parties.

g)   Exploring the options of introducing foreign-exchange and cost-of-living-index related deposits and lending for specific segments in the economy.

h)   Introducing modern accounting and auditing systems to the financial sector in the framework of a general national program.

Box 4-2. Supporting the Modernization of the Financial Sector Through Technical Assistance

The development of an efficient, market-oriented, financial system in Kyrgyzstan will require considerable external support over a number of years. The World Bank's response has included the preparation of a "Financial Sector Development Project" funded under the Technical Cooperation Agreement signed with the Republic of Kyrgyzstan.

Bank Support for Modernizing the Financial Sector. The primary objective of the Bank's technical assistance is to help the authorities "develop and improve the quality of the relevant banking legislation, accounting standards, auditing procedures, and bank supervision, in order to insure the soundness of the commercial banking system." Apart from assistance in the area of commercial banking legislation, additional support to revise the central bank statute is being provided by the IMF. The project will support, among other activities, the drafting of legislation defining the scope of banking operations; licensing criteria and standards for new entrants; standards on lending exposure and lending to related parties; and the development of prudential regulations, as opposed to the purely economic regulations of the past; as well as a suitable bank supervisory framework.

An extremely important component of the Bank's technical assistance includes the transformation of the existing accounting system, to bring it in line with international standards. Under this sub-component, new charts of accounts will be adopted, in harmony with the standards set by a coordinating council and various working groups on accounting standards established by several republics of the CIS. As part of this work, bank auditing guidelines and procedures will be prepared, including setting up standards for licensing auditing firms. Parallel to this development, a basic and specific training program would be provided on banking operations, bank accounting and the establishment of internal controls with an emphasis on training the trainers to maximize the impact of the know-how being transferred.

The World Bank Technical Cooperation Agreement Trust Fund has allocated about $240,000 for the above project. Clearly Kyrgyzstan's medium-term needs require additional support. In particular, training commercial bankers in project and risk evaluation and in foreign exchange and trade operations is of high priority. Nonetheless, the Bank's project hopes to establish an initial framework which would attract further support from other agencies and donors.

Support from Other Agencies and Donors. In addition to the support being provided by the Bank and the IMF, several Central Banks have been assisting the National Bank of Kyrgyzstan in strengthening a number of central banking functions. The EC Commission has also signed a Technical Cooperation Program under TACIS, which aims to provide policy advice on a broader group of activities (trade, tax reform and budgetary procedures, debt management, privatization, sectorial policies, promotion of SME, food distribution, regional cooperation, and civil sector reform), but also covers some basic financial sector infrastructure like the modernization of the payments system.

The objective of developing a financial sector responsive to market forces and the needs of the emerging private sector will require continuous effort over a number of years. To that task the Bank hopes to contribute, as well as invite and promote (directly through co-financing and indirectly through our economic and sector work and investment projects) further assistance from bilateral agencies, donors and other multilateral agencies in support of financial sector reform in Kyrgyzstan.

CHAPTER 5

Private Sector Development

Introduction

5.01   Kyrgyzstan has made a strong commitment to develop a market economy and has focused on broad systemic reforms to accomplish its goals. These measures have recognized broad rights in private property and business activity, established a detailed privatization program, planned for substantial reorganization of large enterprises, simplified registration procedures for new enterprises and facilitated the growth of commodity exchanges. Unfortunately, the unstable macroeconomy and sharp declines in output and income provide a poor environment from which to initiate reform. Moreover, legal, regulatory and bureaucratic obstacles have combined with a shortage of competition to block the transmission of price and profit signals to individuals and would-be entrepreneurs. It is on this microeconomic level the impediments to private sector development pose an insidious challenge. Not surprisingly, the capacity to implement many of these measures is severely limited and there are numerous constraints including unclear property rights and resistance from those with vested interests in the status quo. As of mid-1992, private sector activity remained negligible, while the economy continues to be dominated by structures more appropriate to a centrally planned economy.

5.02   While progress has been made in a relatively short time, the following key conditions for an economically productive private sector are not in place:

   a)   a stable legal regime for property rights;

   b)   a private business environment providing simple and transparent mechanisms for market entry and exit, competitive access to credit and business facilities, and a cadre of domestic professionals having experience in modern monetary transactions; and

   c)   the minimalization of state participation in ownership and control of the productive sectors of the economy.

5.03   The severe economic decline is challenging Kyrgyzstan's capacity to carry out its ambitious programs for structural reforms and liberalization. Implementation of privatization, enterprise reform and private sector enablement legislation moved slowly in early 1992. Frequent administrative restructuring, the instability of the reforming institutions and the admitted uncertainty about how best to proceed have retarded the scope and likely speed of the reform program. However, in mid-1992 the Government moved to reinvigorate its efforts in these areas. This chapter assesses the various constraints to private sector development and proposes recommendations for the transition in the context of (i) the business environment, (ii) enterprise reform and privatization, and (iii) foreign direct investment.

The Business Environment

The Legal Framework for Market Exchange

5.04   While the Government has enacted numerous laws and decrees aimed at the development of a market economy, significant gaps remain, notably in the areas of contract law, bankruptcy, secured transactions and intellectual property (see Box 5-1).   Particularly detrimental to private sector development is the continuing confusion in ownership and property rights and the dichotomy between the law and its implementation.

5.05   Property Rights. The legal framework for a market economy typically consists of a wide array of laws and institutions by which property rights become:

    a)   clearly defined;
    b)   vested, for the most part, in private owners;
    c)   linked with and controlled by economically motivated owners;
    d)   freely transferrable by transparent administrative mechanisms and documentary instruments; and
    e)   enforced efficiently and neutrally.

Such a property rights regime is not yet in place in Kyrgyzstan. The legislative measures adopted in 1991 and early 1992 indicate clear progress but do not yet provide a stable foundation for modern private transactions. Judicial and enforcement reforms have yet to be agreed upon and when they are, actual practice is likely to be uncertain due to unfamiliarity with the new mechanisms. Perhaps more fundamentally, in the absence of experience with private property, measures passed to date are still largely abstractions.

5.06   Property Law. The basic law ("Property Law") removes the socialist limitations and discriminations against private property but does not provide the confidence upon which long-term investment can be based. The Law lacks clarity, conflicts with other laws and reflects a philosophy that property rights are essentially temporary, dependent on the discretion of state structures. The following comments on the Property Law illustrate the complexity of the problem:

    a)   *State Property*. The Property Law reserves, as the exclusive property of the Republic, "land, mineral resources, water, air space, the plant and animal world, other natural resources and historical and cultural monuments". This broad reservation of property for the Republic, without definition, casts doubt on the entire property rights regime. Of particular concern is the reservation of land for the state, which will impede mobility of capital and obstruct the privatization process.

    b)   *Limitations on Property Rights*. The Law grants owners the rights to use and dispose of their property. The exercise of such rights is specifically subordinated to the "rights and legally protected interests of citizens, legal entities and the state". The Law limits property rights by numerous and non-specific references to other laws. Since many laws favoring state interests remain valid, without a comprehensive revision of the Civil Code and other laws, these limitations cast serious doubt on the boundaries of ownership rights and on the intent of Government. The resulting uncertainty will limit investment in private property.

c)   *The Property Law as a Constraint to Private Sector Development.* The Property Law reflects the view that all property rights belong in the first instance to the state, to be handed out under such conditions as the state chooses, and that nothing is permitted in this respect except what the state specifically permits. This approach does not inspire confidence or create an ideal framework for private sector development.

Box 5-1. Additional Legislation Required

New laws or significant amendments to existing legislation are required in the following areas:

1.   Commercial Code including laws governing:

      a).   Sale of Bonds
      b).   Credit Transactions
      c).   Secured Transactions
      d).   Securities, Negotiable Instruments and Documents of Title
      e).   Real Property - including procedures for recording title to land, encumbering land and allocating property interest.

2.   Insolvency or Bankruptcy Law

3.   Accounting Standards - with particular attention to standards applicable to SOEs

4.   Intellectual Property

5.   Foreign Investment Regulations

6.   Property and Enterprise Laws

7.   Fair Trade and Antimonopoly

8.   Corporate Law - including basic requirements for corporate governance

---

5.07   <u>Intellectual Property</u>. Kyrgyzstan has not yet developed its own intellectual property rights regime. It relies on Russia's GOSPATENT for patent registrations. The International Engineers Academy is currently charged with reviewing patents but has not implemented any mechanism for protection or means for reviewing and registering private intellectual property rights. Kyrgyzstan could benefit substantially from assistance from the World Intellectual Property Organization, which has developed model laws for developing countries and relatively simple but effective mechanisms for know-how examination and registration of contracts, inventor's certificates, transfer of technology, and provisions for the protection of computer software. The absence of a basic regime for protection of intellectual property is a significant constraint to attracting foreign technology.

5.08   Business Association Laws. The right of entrepreneurial activity was recognized by the Law on Freedom of Economic Activity and Development of Entrepreneurship (January 1991). The Law on Economic Associations and Joint-Stock Companies ("Business Associations Law") recognizes cooperatives, limited and general partnerships, limited liability entities and joint-stock companies. Unfortunately the new measures have features unusual for business organization statutes. They specify certain labor provisions, thus potentially conflicting with Labor Law provisions and also contain regulations spelling out how the entities are to obtain resources. Thus the scope of the law may allow, and seems to contemplate, considerable state intervention in private enterprises' activities.

5.09   Contract Law. While some attention has been paid to the need to eliminate particular restrictions on contractual freedom that stem from the planning system, there has been little serious reform of contract law as such. The basic precepts of Kyrgyzstan's contract law are found in the Civil Code, which has been designed to serve the legislation governing relations between state enterprises and not complex, market transactions. There is a legislative project in its early stages, which is considering various models of contract laws. Such a project should be advanced considerably. However, currently and for the foreseeable future, there is no adequate legal basis for sophisticated, reliable, and therefore stable contracts between private parties or between private parties and SOEs.

5.10   Enforcement. The civil dispute resolution institutions remain basically unchanged from the former Soviet model. If the institutions for civil dispute resolution are not capable of enforcing the property and contract rights of market participants, the expansion of market activities will be limited by the tendency of market actors to do business with those whom they know and trust well. Virtually no allocation of resources has been made for the additional judicial personnel, facilities and training that will be needed as the burden on the civil dispute resolution system increases. Yet without an expeditious and neutral dispute resolution system, there is unlikely to be the degree of trust necessary for the economically meaningful exercise of property rights.

5.11   Bankruptcy. There is no comprehensive bankruptcy code. There are bankruptcy provisions in the Privatization and Destatization Act of 1991 but these do not suffice even for the limited purposes of enabling privatization and commercialization of state enterprises. The absence of a bankruptcy law creates a disincentive for creditors to lend and investors to invest. What a potential investor or creditor needs is a straightforward liquidation which provides simple information and procedures on the consequences should an enterprise fail.

Establishment of New Enterprises

5.12   According to the Antimonopoly Committee (AMC), private enterprises account for about 7 percent of GNP. Most of this is small business, including approximately 1100 cooperatives and 240 new small enterprises formed since 1990. Apparently many of the "new" enterprises are actually cooperatives which transformed themselves in late 1991 and early 1992, following the passage of enabling legislation. The AMC estimates (it does not have precise data) that there have been few truly new business start-ups in 1991 and 1992 due to a combination of the economic crisis and the fact that the local administrative authorities have made formation and registration formalities difficult to satisfy. In general, this situation restrains competition and impedes the overall reform process.

5.13   The registration of a new enterprise can take up to three months, involves a large amount of documentation and ultimately depends on the support of the local administrative committee. Transparency is not a characteristic of the process, which reflects the continuation of a system in which individual initiatives and risk taking are not encouraged and bureaucratic decisions preempt market mechanisms.

5.14   The establishment of a business remains a daunting task due to the lack of facilities and the numerous requirements for permits for almost every action. There is virtually no market for commercial office space. Enterprises must rent from the state or are given use of space by a governmental agency. Leases tend to be short term (usually not more than one year). Access to inputs is a serious problem with priorities being allocated by the state to its own enterprises. Thus, virtually everything needed to function is available only at the discretion of the state. The commodity exchanges, which account for less than five percent of internal trade, are often the only sources of supplies.

5.15   The AMC is charged with being a focal point for the encouragement of new businesses. However, to date, it has focused on gathering data and assisting the State Property Fund (SPF) in its efforts to reorganize and privatize the huge state industrial sector. As of April 1992, the AMC had only two staff to review enterprise reorganization and segmentation and to implement measures for the encouragement of new enterprises. The AMC, with a modest increase in resources could coordinate reform of administrative impediments to new enterprises and assist new enterprises to achieve at least a level playing field with state-owned enterprises (SOEs) in competition for inputs and facilities.

Access to Credit

5.16   New enterprises have little access to credit and only at relatively unfavorable terms. Competitive, commercial banking is still non-existent. The allocation of credit in Kyrgyzstan has been primarily the allocation of low cost refinance credit from the NBK and the granting of credits by commercial banks to the SOEs that are the banks' main shareholders. The result is that for small and medium sized private enterprise, there is practically no access to credit.

5.17   The commercial banks offer little or no service to their customers. Private enterprises report that the commercial banks are not yet prepared to help these firms with their day-to-day business, particularly if it involves inter-republic or foreign trade. Few have any experience with international terms of trade, letters of credit, etc. Small enterprises report inability to get credit without real estate mortgages (i.e., a lien on non-movable assets such as a building -- land remains state property and thus cannot be used to leverage for capital). Credit cannot be obtained against movable goods and virtually no other form of collateral exists, nor is there yet any legislation providing for secured transactions.

5.18   Collateral. There is still no mortgage market or even a legal basis for secured lending. The consequences are that new and privatized enterprises are at a distinct disadvantage in day-to-day transactions. Although housing is being privatized, there are no mechanisms for an owner to leverage his asset or for a lender to enforce a mortgage. Moreover, since land is not being fully privatized (its use may be inherited but not sold), the value of a mortgage on an apartment or villa will always be somewhat volatile and therefore risky. In a market economy, borrowers secure loans through personal guarantees, a generalized pledge of wealth or through a cosigner, the wealth of another; otherwise the borrower secures the promise to pay by mortgaging real property including equipment, movables, inventory and perhaps receivables. Except for personal guarantees, virtually none of the other forms of security are available in Kyrgyzstan.

Competition and Demonopolization

5.19   The rigid vertical integration of industry, with its inefficiencies has negative consequences for private sector development. Even a new, state of the art manufacturing facility established in Kyrgyzstan would be forced to create an otherwise uneconomical vertical integration because of the non-availability of external infrastructural support industries within the region. Sourcing and distribution support systems are not yet broken out and privatized. For prospective investors, the need to deal with the vertical integration and the resulting inefficiencies and shortages is a strong deterrent to investment at the outset. Competition is also impeded by the "concerns" or "associations" which are, in effect, large cartels that set prices, allocate inputs and otherwise function much as branch ministries in the old system. Most of the medium and large enterprises, including some that have been privatized or commercialized to date, remain within the de facto control of these cartels. Thus, integrated structures, fixed prices and controlled market segmentation continue to impede the growth of new enterprises and the efficiency of existing ones.

5.20   Antimonopoly Law. "The Decree on Restrictions on Monopolistic Activity" (December 1991) supplemented by Decrees of the State Economic Council and implemented by the AMC is intended to break-up monopolies, regulate existing ones and encourage new, competing enterprises. As with many of Kyrgyzstan's new institutions, however, the AMC is understaffed and lacks the technical know-how, and personnel needed to take the actions mandated in the law.

5.21   Commodity Exchanges. The Commodity Exchanges in Kyrgyzstan are serving as important institutions in the transition to a market economy. While most of the exchanges are owned primarily by SOEs, they engage in transactions outside the state order providing a very useful mechanism for private growth. The exchanges are essentially spot markets for whatever goods a particular exchange accepts. Although less than five percent of trade is reportedly conducted through the exchanges, the volume is expected to increase as reliance on state orders diminishes.

Constraints

A Lack of Economic Legality

5.22   There has been little progress in establishing economic legality, i.e., a mutually consistent set of laws in the economic sphere (especially property, contracts, tax, bankruptcy) and a belief by the population in the stability and fair enforcement of these laws. Numerous enterprise managers, small businessmen and commodity exchange brokers stated that they could not keep up with the ever-changing economic legislation and in any event had little confidence it would be uniformly and impartially enforced in an economy where the enforcer is the single largest actor. This constraint arises, anomalously, from the rapid process of legislative reform and the tendency to over-legislate. The difficulties associated with information collection and transmission, the virtual absence of a corporate culture as understood even in the formerly socialist states of Central Europe, and a continuing mistrust of market mechanisms compel the authorities to burden the economy with a ponderous regulatory structure. Risk taking and individual initiative are casualties in such an environment.

Business Information and Skills

5.23   The lack of business information, accounting standards and general business skills is a major barrier to enterprise formation and success. There is little printed material available on business practice. The educational institutions are rapidly changing their curricula but the lack of experience with free market mechanisms will continue to slow private sector development. While foreign technical assistance can move the process forward, effective transformation will require effective support from domestic experts. That cadre does not presently exist.

A Weak Economic Infrastructure and The Problems of Wholesale Trade

5.24   A particular problem is the undeveloped nature of wholesale trade. Without a competitive network of distributors, wholesalers, agents and other middlemen, an efficient market will not to emerge. These actors provide the basis for the market to take over from the state order. They are the means of transition. Without them, private farmers, retailers and other producers will remain trapped between monopolists. Yet, Kyrgyzstan's failure to prioritize this sector for reform jeopardizes the whole privatization process. Without developing such a network, the decline of the state order will be exceedingly difficult. Enterprises, both state-owned and some recently privatized, will continue to regard the state order system favorably -- it guarantees a market for output without requiring marketing or distribution efforts on the part of the enterprise and carries its own authorization for allocation of inputs.

Continued State Intervention

5.25   The state order, which guarantees to enterprises a large proportion of their output and supplies of materials necessary for production, dominates the system of resource allocation: its exact share varies by sector and industry but on average the state order has recently accounted for about 70 percent of production. Its dominance discourages enterprise managers from seeking more profitable opportunities or initiating changes in trade flows. In April 1992, the Government announced its intention to replace mandatory state orders with a voluntary state purchase system and a complete phase out of the state order by end 1992. These measures are commendable. However, in view of the constraints to regular market activity discussed, and in particular without a more rapid development of wholesale trade and the information network, it may be difficult to entirely eliminate the reliance on Government purchases in the short run.

5.26   The organization of government/industry relations is a major stumbling block to private sector development. Soft budget constraints and excessive verticality and consequent under-utilization of horizontal lines of contacts among producers are characteristic of the economy. Divergences between the vestiture of responsibility and authority have led to situations where individuals with responsibility in an enterprise or a reform agency have little real authority to control it, due to insufficient delegation of powers. Governmental preference for control and attempts to mandate change by fiat rather than by looser incentives add to the problems.

Recommendations

The Legal Framework for Private Enterprise

5.27   The establishment of economic legality -- a legal framework adequate to encourage and support private sector development requires efforts, particularly technical assistance, in the following areas:

a)   rationalization and harmonization of the existing legislative and legal reform measures;

b)   enactment of legislation and regulation for:

   i.   contracts
   ii.   the recording of individual, business and creditor property rights, including personal and intellectual property;
   iii.   bankruptcy, secured transactions, negotiable instruments; and
   iv.   real estate;

c)   dissemination of information about the reform measures including the establishment of a legal data base and regular publication of business-related legal information;

d)   training of legislative and regulatory staff members in the drafting and harmonization of laws;

e)   establishment of mechanisms for transparent enforcement of the new measures;

f)   training of a core of lawyers and judges for the new commercial arbitration courts and for bankruptcy;

g)   identification of the training needs of the concerned governmental agencies in the area of business law; and

h)   support to existing training centers and the academic institutions in teaching business law.

Competition and Demonopolization

5.28   Given the concentrated vertical structure of production, there is need for a more coordinated and seriously implemented program supporting competition. The following steps should be taken as a matter of first priority:

a)   The AMC and the SPF should be provided substantially greater resources to achieve their complementary purposes of creating a vigorous private sector.

b)   Emphasis should be placed on the segmentation of existing distribution enterprises and the encouragement of widespread wholesale trade. Trade organizations, concerns and amalgams should be segmented into as many units as economically efficient, commercialized and privatized.

c)   New middlemen, warehouses, distribution and wholesale firms should be privatized and encouraged to act as the necessary intermediaries in the relay of market signals from consumers to competing producers.

d)   Access to government controlled inputs must be made available equally to all market players. This means the creation and encouragement of a broad, private-based trading network, competitive bids for state purchases and a commercial real estate market.

e)   A credit system that sustains a supply response must be created and properly supervised. This requires, in part, a banking system without interlocking ownership interest with the enterprises that access their lines of credit.

f)   The Government should review the myriad of approval procedures and eliminate most discretionary requirements.

Business Information and Skills

5.29   Action in this area should focus on building basic commercial skills, the installation of a business orientation and the development of market oriented managerial and marketing skills. Training in basic commercial terminology and contracting is especially needed since with virtually all foreign trade previously handled in Moscow, there is very little experience in the fundamentals of trading and related financing.

5.30   Specifically, a three part program could comprise:

a)   support to the AMC to initiate (i) a program of practical commercial training in business methods, law, accounting, marketing and quality control; (ii) a business exchange and training program that would permit key managers to receive short-term training and (iii) exposure to a market environment outside Kyrgyzstan;

b)   funds for assistance to facilitate the growth of new enterprises. The funds would be utilized for the access to and use of communications and office equipment, technical advice including accounting, financial and legal advice, and training and marketing for the specific activity of new enterprises; and,

c)   reforms of the banking sector to provide access to credit to small and medium enterprises.

Enterprise Reform - Privatization and Corporatization

5.31   The enterprise sector in Kyrgyzstan will have to undergo major restructuring to respond to the ongoing adjustments in relative prices and the pattern of demand and financing that was so heavily dominated by links to the former Soviet Union. These largely negative external shocks will be compounded by falling demand domestically and the imposition of tighter financial constraints, as the emphasis shifts from fulfilling plan targets to generating profits in an increasingly private sector orientation. A massive contraction of output appears unavoidable in the short term. The establishment of new firms and the restructuring of potentially viable ones in the context of corporatization, and increasingly, privatization to enable them to compete in the emerging environment are hence priorities. Efforts to prevent an undue contraction of interrepublican trade are also needed, while the incentive framework for promoting growth of viable enterprises should be an area of policy focus.

5.32   In early 1991, the Government designed a three stage program for commercialization and privatization of virtually all of Kyrgyzstan's enterprises. The basic law, "The Privatization and Denationalization Act" of December 1991 (PDA), established a clear line of property ownership, vesting all productive property in the Republic and directing the Council of Ministers to divide the property into Republican and local property. A January 1992 Decree set forth a program for corporatization and privatization to be carried out by the State Property Fund. In practice, however, there are severe problems and delays in implementing the enterprise reform program due to de facto control by management and workers and conflicting legal provisions which are the residuals of earlier Union reforms.

Industrial Enterprises: Structure and Recent Performance

5.33   The industrial sector[1] comprised slightly under 30 percent of GDP in the late 1980s, rising to 38 percent in 1991 as a result of a significant improvement in its terms of trade[2], and accounted for 20 percent of the labor force (29 percent including construction). The most important industries include mechanical and electrical engineering (vehicle assembly, washing machines, electrical appliances, etc.), light industry (mainly textiles), and food processing. These together accounted for about three quarters of industrial production and about 80 percent of industrial exports in 1991. Other significant industries are chemicals, leather goods, and construction materials.

5.34   The number of industrial enterprises is subject to some uncertainty given the lack of information on previously Union controlled industries (which may have accounted for 70 percent of industrial output), many of them defense related, and the current fluid situation within state-owned enterprises (SOEs). Overall there may be more than 7,500 separable industrial units, of which about

---

1.   Including manufacturing, mining and energy. The latter two sectors comprised about 6 percent of GDP in 1991 and are discussed in Chapter 7. It should be noted that data on the industrial sector are particularly weak because of the lack of information on Union controlled and defense related industries.

2.   Industry's share in constant 1983 prices is estimated at 33.7 percent in 1991.

3,000 are classified as medium and large units organized in about 500 conglomerates.[3] About three quarters of industrial output is produced in the vicinity of Bishkek.

5.35   Key characteristics of the industrial structure are its vertical integration and heavy dependence on trade with enterprises elsewhere in the ruble area.   Hence the breakdown in interrepublican trade and payments arrangements is particularly detrimental for the industrial sector. Industrial exports outside the USSR amounted to only $15 million in 1991.

5.36   Industrial output grew by over 5 percent annually during 1985-89, declined by 1 percent in 1990 and was flat in 1991. Increased output in mining and engineering products in 1991, the latter benefiting from substantial relative price increases, appear to have produced a better output performance than elsewhere in the USSR, where output declines were generally significant.

5.37   In 1992, industrial output has been adversely affected by the collapse of interrepublican trade, increased relative prices of oil and gas imports, the sharp decline in real terms of credit from the banking system, and the drop in consumer purchasing power. Output during the first nine months of the year is estimated to have declined by 23 percent. Arrears and a shortage of financing have reached the point where the majority of transactions may be undertaken through barter.

5.38   There is little evidence that adjustment at the enterprise level has been initiated at anything like the scale that will ultimately be required. Several factors are slowing the process of restructuring. First, the lack of real owners--advocates for capital--has resulted in de facto takeovers by managers, workers, Ministries and Concerns all competing for control but none with ultimate responsibility. Widespread erosion of assets is reported. Second, through the pattern of bank ownership enterprises within conglomerates have preferred access to credit, though given the extent of overall decline in credit availability a tightening of credit for even such enterprises must also have occurred. Third, the predominant trend at least through early 1992 was for transfer of state assets to workers' collectives, which in many cases own up to 70 percent of the shares of their enterprise. Such an ownership pattern is not conducive to the labor shedding that might have been expected to accompany the output declines. While labor shedding has been relatively rare, labor reallocation has occurred by way of labor movements among enterprises within a conglomerate, redeployment within enterprises, shortened workweeks and leave of absence with reduced pay. Finally, the technical and financial capacity to undertake restructuring or modernization is also lacking.

5.39   Industrial restructuring is needed not only to respond to relative price adjustments, but also to correct the distortions introduced when priorities were established to suit the needs of the Union. While machine building and electro-technical activities were over-emphasized, mining and metallurgy were neglected despite the fact that Kyrgyzstan has considerable mining potential. Non-ferrous mining, electrical power generating and light industry appear to be the sectors with the most potential according to the authorities. Wool textiles are important as 50 percent of the washed wool is now exported in raw form due to lack of wool processing activities. Electronics is another area of potential promise based on the extensive defense industries that were established in the past.

---

3.   Using a broader definition, the SPF considers that there are no more than 320 medium and large industries, each of which has anywhere from 1 to 10 enterprises within it. The number fluctuates on a regular basis. The SPF counts 1200 small enterprises but again, each of those may include 1 to 3 enterprises.

The State Property Fund

5.40   The State Property Fund (SPF), created in February 1992, is responsible for privatization and corporatization and designated as owner of all state property, with the authority to exercise all ownership rights of the Republic. In practice, however, supervision of large Republic enterprises has been delegated to the relevant ministry or concern (an administrative body under the council of ministers indistinguishable in duties and budget from a ministry). In December 1991, legal ownership passed to the Fund's predecessor and in February to the Fund itself. As a practical matter, most of these industries have been autonomous for the past two years with ownership rights shifting.

5.41   There is considerable confusion in the exercise of property rights notwithstanding the PDA. In practice, the SPF exercises its rights only after an enterprise has applied for privatization or corporatization and these are continually undermined by competing claims. Ownership rights in Republic property are, in fact, exercised in a shifting, imprecise way among managers, workers, local governmental structures, collectives, ministries, concerns, and other State Committees. Under existing law, the SPF acts passively -- generally in response to the initiative of an enterprise, collective or local authority and thus cannot control its own privatization timetable or proceed in a sector in the most economically efficient manner. The result is that the enterprise reform program, despite ambitious Government plans, will proceed slower than planned and may be undermined.

5.42   Considerable progress has been made in defining SPF's priorities, building staff and implementing the growing body of privatization and enterprise reorganization legislation. There is a staff of 80 in Bishkek and about 140 in the regional offices. The division of state property into Republican and Local property is almost complete. The SPF has begun the creation of an enterprise data base to remedy the lack of information which continues to hinder program implementation. Nonetheless, there is a shortage of skilled personnel and equipment for the substantial tasks assigned to the SPF. These limitations are likely to impair the Government's plans for enterprise reform in 1992. Additional staff, training, modest reorganization and computer and office equipment are thus needed as soon as possible.

The Enterprise Reform Program

Privatization

5.43   The Government's program foresees privatization to occur in three phases. Phase I (1991-1992) is to focus on establishing (a) the locus of ownership of all state property, (b) an administrative framework for delegation of ownership rights, and (c) the privatization of small and medium industrial and agricultural enterprises and most small shops, trade and service establishments. Phase II (1993-1994) is intended to focus on the privatization of medium and large scale enterprises and Phase III (1994-1996) is to complete the process. Initial privatization targets for 1992 are provided in Table 5-1. These targets have subsequently been extended to end 1993, by which time 35 percent of state property is due to have been privatized.

5.44   Exempt from privatization is a list of institutions and enterprises in the areas of health, education, sports, energy, communications, publishing houses, rail and air transport, and /certain research institutes. Defence industries are slated for privatization to the extent they can be converted to civilian use.

5.45   At virtually any time, a workers' collective or controlling group within an enterprise can submit to the SPF a plan for privatization. Upon receipt of the plan, the SPF organizes and chairs a Privatization Commission, which is composed of representatives of the workers' group, a banker, a representative of the local Soviet, an auditor and other persons that the SPF deems appropriate. The Commission determines the new capital structure, the value and a timetable for transformation of the enterprise. Current guidelines call for allocation of 30 percent of the shares to workers, 45 percent to purchasers of the enterprise's production, such as retail outlets, with the balance to be held by the SPF for eventual distribution to the population.

5.46   All assets are to be valued on the basis of "residual value" multiplied by a factor for inflation. Residual value is established by reducing the initial book value by a depreciation factor which is determined according to standard, former Union accounting rules. The inflation factor is determined by the SPF based, in part, on existing market prices. If the enterprise is to be purchased by its own workers, then the social assets of the enterprise (day care, vacation property, etc.) are gifted over and a discount of thirty percent is taken off the value of fixed assets. The balance plus the value of financial assets is the sales price. The workers then pay a minimum of 25 percent of the sales price of their share with the balance due over a period of up to three years.

5.47   If the workers of an enterprise do not wish to become shareholders and if the enterprise is within the categories authorized for privatization, the SPF can initiate the privatization of the enterprise by either the auction or tender method. Each method is governed by extensive regulation but both involve the same valuation process. The essential difference between the two is that the auction is straightforward and results in a sale based on the highest bidder. In the tender case, the SPF sells the enterprise to the buyer which, in the opinion of the SPF, makes the most economically and socially attractive offer, not necessarily the highest price.[4]

5.48   In March 1992, the SPF modified its earlier policy of encouraging labor collectives to obtain a controlling interest in their enterprises. While considerable deference and a 30 percent discount in price is still given collectives, the SPF now recognizes the difficulties (equity, management and incentive problems) of collective ownership.[5] The SPF now intends to make all efforts to either retain or direct to other parties strategic blocks of shares to permit more widespread ownership and non-collective directed management. Furthermore, the SPF also intends to make efforts to move toward the distribution of shares to individuals rather than to collectives to enhance the mobility of capital. However, the current inadequacy of capital markets is a major drawback in promoting the tradeability of shares.

Corporatization

5.49   In an effort to de-link the enterprises from the ministries, break up the large amalgams and concerns, clarify their ownership and establish economically motivated management, the SPF in cooperation with the AMC has recently begun to construct a program of corporatizing the large

---

4.   It is not yet clear what role a ministry or concern would play in a tender sale where the concern or ministry was the delegate of the SPF for management of the enterprise. Apparently, a ministry or concern can request the initiation of a privatization and take a substantial role in that process.

5.   These were described in the Aide Memoire of the Bank Mission to Kyrghyzstan in February, 1992.

enterprises and breaking up their related concerns. As a first step, a portfolio analysis of several major concerns has been initiated to determine where such a reorganization can be most effective. The concern of food processors and the concern "Alatow" (producing electrical goods and employing a total of about 30,000) have been identified for immediate analysis and restructuring. These efforts are to be encouraged as major steps toward clarification of property rights and improved governance, but the task requires additional resources and technical assistance to bear fruition.

5.50   The Government has not determined what percentage, if any, of shares would be held by a government agency or what that agency should be (a Ministry, a special fund or the SPF itself). Nor is it clear whether the SPF is to have the right to initiate corporatization. On the one hand, giving the SPF the responsibility to initiate and manage corporatization would saddle it with an enormous task for which it is currently unprepared. On the other hand, a strategy of speed requires the SPF to have the right to control timing decisions and undertake action. Widespread self-initiation of corporatization would be preferable with the right of the SPF to compel corporatization, perhaps with technical assistance. Hungary's experience is instructive. While Hungary's State Property Agency (SPA) has had the right to compel corporatization since 1990, it has not exercised this right insistently or systematically. After more that two years of delay, the Hungarian Parliament recently considered new legislation which would force corporatization of all SOEs by a definite date. Similarly, Poland's emphasis on enterprise self-initiation has been a major contributor to blockage of the reform process due to the slow pace of SOE initiations.

5.51   Little consideration has been give to the disposition of the SOEs' social assets, employment, development plans and potential investment. Other issues related to break-ups, spin-offs, and asset transfers need to be addressed. Debt and other liability issues (e.g. environmental clean up) need to be worked into the SPF and AMC's programs. Finally, little consideration has been given to protecting the banking system (already under-capitalized) from undertaking loans to loss-making enterprises in the transition.

Table 5-1. PRIVATIZATION TARGETS FOR 1992ª/

MINISTRIES AND DEPARTMENTS	ENTERPRISES TO BE PRIVATIZED		
	Number of Enterprises	Value Millions of Rubles (1974 Prices)	Share of Total Assets in Sector (percentage)
1. State Energy Holding Company "KUBAT"	10	2500.0	100
a) First Quarter	10		
b) The Year	10		
2. Ministry of Industry (TOTAL)	90	1964.2	51.7
a) By Sub-Sector/Concern			
1) Machine Building	15	1144.3	60.2
2) State Concern "Kyrgyzlegprom	34	657.6	71.8
3) State Concern "Kench"	41	162.3	98.4
b) By Calendar Quarters(cumulative)			
1) One Quarter	27	548.2	14.4
2) Two Quarters	51	956.1	25.1
3) Three Quarters	73	1322.9	34.8
4) Four Quarters (TOTAL)	90	1964.2	51.7
3. Industrial Enterprises of (TOTAL) Ministry of Agriculture	113	939.5	54.3
a) By Sub-Sector			
1) Processing Branches	39	686.9	50.0
2) Production-Technical Services	74	252.6	84.0
b) By Calendar Quarters (cumulative)			
1) One Quarter	22	123.5	7.2
2) Two Quarters	55	471.8	27.5
3) Three Quarters	79	579.8	33.8
4) Four Quarters (TOTAL)	113	939.5	54.3
4. Agricultural Enterprises of the Ministry of Agriculture (collective and state farms)	159	1402.0	28.0
5. Leading Construction Organizations (TOTAL)	147	468.8	53.6
a) By Concern/Corporation			
1) "Kyrgyzkurulsh"	81	263.4	100.0
2) "Azat" Corporation	20	52.5	100.0
3) "Kyrgyzailurulush"	38	108.6	33.4
4) "Kyrgyzsuukurulush"	8	44.3	17.0
b) By Calendar Quarters (cumulative)			
1) One Quarter	42	115.2	13.2
2) Two Quarter	64	167.8	19.2
3) Three Quarters	83	208.25	23.9
4) Four Quarters (TOTAL)	147	468.8	53.6
6. Concern "Kyrgyzkurulushmaterialy" (TOTAL)	12	54.2	22.8
a) By Calendar Quarters (cumulative)			
1) One Quarter	1	5.4	2.3
2) Two Quarters	3	14.5	6.1
3) Three Quarters	7	34.9	14.7
4) Four Quarters (TOTAL)	12	54.2	22.8

Table 5-1 (cont.)

MINISTRIES AND DEPARTMENTS	Number of Enterprises	Value Millions of Rubles (1974 Prices)	Share of Total Assets (percentage)
7. Ministry of Trade (TOTAL)	1823	358.0	99.2
a) By Sector			
1) Retail Trade	1315	226.1	99.7
2) (Public) Food Services	499	44.7	94.8
3) Wholesale Trade	9	87.2	100.0
b) By Calendar Quarters (cumulative)			
1) One Quarters	427	147.3	40.8
2) Two Quarters	1017	241.5	66.9
3) Three Quarters	1823	358.0	99.2
4) Four Quarters (TOTAL)	1823	358.0	99.2
8. Kyrgyzbytsoyuz (TOTAL)	7600	166.6	100.0
a) By Calendar Quarters (cumulative)			
1) One Quarters	760	16.6	10.0
2) Two Quarters	4180	91.6	55.0
3) Three Quarters	7600	166.6	100.0
4) Four Quarters (TOTAL)	7600	166.6	100.0
9. Ministry of Transport and Highways (TOTAL)	26	78.3	21.2
a) By Calendar Quarters (cumulative)			
1) One Quarter	-	-	-
2) Two Quarters	9	18.6	5.0
3) Three Quarters	18	48.6	13.2
4) Four Quarters (TOTAL)	26	78.3	21.2

SOURCE: State Property Fund
a/ These targets subsequently were extended to end 1993.

Results

5.52   As of April 1, 1992, 232 enterprises had been "transformed" (Table 5-2), representing about one-third the goal in retail trade and much less in other sectors. Somewhat under 5 percent of state property had been privatized between January 1, 1991 and mid-October, 1992. However, most of the medium and large enterprises considered "private" continue to have majority state equity and control. In view of staffing and institutional constraints and the resistance to privatization by local authorities and large groups in agriculture and industry, even the revised privatization plan appears ambitious.

Industry[6]

Heavy Industry

5.53   The category of heavy industry includes electronics, certain energy and machinery enterprises, including defense operations. Mining and basic energy enterprises power are excluded. The SPF counts 70 enterprises in this category, all of which were formerly Union controlled. Within these

---

6.   Agricultural privatization issues are addressed in Chapter 7.

70, there are 15 enterprises employing between 6,000 and 25,000 workers, and there are numerous small enterprises and spin-offs. Of the 70, 32 were due to be privatized in 1992, but there had been no privatizations through mid-1992.

5.54   As of July 1, 1992 the SPF had received only 9 applications for privatization. Most of the targeted enterprises have been operating autonomously and with little interest in segmentation, corporatization or privatization. The SPF has the authority to seize the initiative but not the manpower or the know-how to deal with the huge amalgams. The ministries concerned would prefer to create a few holding companies, state-owned and ministry-controlled, which in turn would own each of the enterprises. The anti-monopoly committee (AMC) and the SPF oppose this approach, resulting in a standoff for the time being.

Light Industry

5.55   The situation in light industry is similar to that for heavy industry. The SPF estimates this category to consist of 74 enterprises (actually clusters of 5-10 enterprises in the same line of manufacturing), although the precise number is unknown. Of these 74, 40 are under the association "Kinch" (the old Ministry of Light Industry) and are primarily medium and large enterprises; the remaining 34 are under the Association "Legprom" (the old Ministry of Local Industry) and are primarily small enterprises. The privatization plan calls for privatizing 80 percent of Legprom's enterprises and most of Kinch's in 1992.

5.56   Of the 74 enterprises, 6 were considered privatized and 6 were in the process as of April 1992. As in the case of heavy industry, it is highly unlikely that the 1992 privatization plan targets can be met.

5.57   With no standard deal documents, each Privatization Commission appears compelled to reinvent the wheel. Considerable time is thus consumed on technical issues in the process -- contracts for labor, management sale agreements, disposition of social assets, etc.

5.58   Adding to the Commission's tasks is the requirement of the AMC to break up enterprises that are monopolies. Of the 144 heavy and light industry enterprise clusters, the AMC has identified approximately 60 monopolies requiring particular review and segmentation before or at the time of privatization. The difficulties are compounded by the fact that most output is intended as inputs for goods produced elsewhere in the CIS for which demand is now highly uncertain.

Food Processing

5.59   In this sector, the SPF estimates there are about 200 enterprises though new enterprises were forming rapidly. Of the 200, the plan for 1992 is to privatize 50 percent of the production enterprises and 80 percent of service enterprises. Of the 200, 70 are small (less than 200 employees); 80 are medium (200-1000); and 50 are large.

5.60   The SPF intends to concentrate on corporatizing the milk and vegetable processing enterprises in 1992. The intention is to grant 50 percent of the shares of these enterprises to suppliers of the materials -- the collectives, farms, etc. This is proposed to circumvent the distribution and wholesale trade monopolies which currently are inefficient (it is estimated these entities are responsible for the loss of one-third of agricultural production each year due to inefficient or negligent transport and storage).

5.61 The agreement or contract of privatization requires a privatized firm to produce and sell to the state at least the quantities "of last year's needs". In 1991 the state order in this industry was about 60 percent of total production.

5.62 As of July 1, 1992 the SPF had received only 9 applications for privatization. Most of the targeted enterprises have been operating autonomously and with little interest in segmentation, corporatization or privatization. The SPF has the authority to seize the initiative but not the manpower or the know-how to deal with the huge amalgams. The ministries concerned would prefer to create a few holding companies, state-owned and ministry-controlled, which in turn would own each of the enterprises. The AMC and SPF oppose this approach, resulting in a standoff for the time being.

Table 5-2. Privatization: Progress, Structure and Proceeds

A. Privatization as of April 1, 1992

      107 - Small Retail Trade
       70 - Small Communal Services (tailors, laundries, etc.)
       44 - Medium Enterprises
       11 - Large Enterprises

      232

      Small = less than 100 employees (most less than 15)
      Medium =   100 - 500 employees
      Large = 500+ employees

B. Proposed Capital Structure in Enterprises to be Privatized

      25%+   - State Property Fund
      25-49% - Workers' Collectives or Individuals, Suppliers
      25-75% - Foreign Investor or Combination of
                 Individuals, Foreigners, and Workers'
                 Collective.

C. Privatization Proceeds

A minimum of 32 percent of the sales price of an enterprise is paid at sale. The SPF receives 7 percent. The remaining 25 percent and the balance outstanding (to be paid over a period not to exceed 3 years under terms set by the relevant Privatization Commission) are to be distributed, on receipt, as follows:

- 43% - to general budget
- 25% - to Fund for the Support of National Entrepreneurship
- 10-20% - to Non-Budget Funds
- Balance - to Special Fund for Enterprise Guaranties of Liability (payment of debts and subsidies to losing enterprises.

The first R50 million of monies received by the Fund for the Support of National Entrepreneurship is to be directed to a special project called Askar which is concentrating on youth projects. Funds received over R50 million are to be used to finance privatization. Monies received through June 1992 for privatization total R100 million, of which the Fund for the Support of Entrepreneurship had received R15 million.

Source: SPF

Housing

5.63   The Government plans to privatize 80 percent of all housing in 1992 and 1993. Credits in the form of coupons or credits to special bank accounts to individuals are to be issued based on their income, years of employment and certain other criteria, with the intention that the bulk of existing housing would be privatized at little or no cost to residents.

5.64   The program has progressed slowly for several reasons:

a)   The credits have not yet been allocated and the SPF is still developing mechanisms for this purpose.

b)   The bureaucratic process for applying for privatization is cumbersome and involves considerable discretion by the local authorities as to the adequacy of documentation; and

c)   Rents are still highly subsidized by the state, though they were increased in June 1992. The expectation may be that ownership of housing will result in higher costs through property taxes and other fees.

5.65   Land on which housing is built remains in the ownership of the Republic and managed by the local authority. Rent for land is minimal but long-term leases apparently are not available. Establishment of contracts for long-term or perpetual use are being considered in a legislative project.

Box 5-2. Lessons from Eastern Europe

Several lessons on privatization can be drawn from the countries of Central and Eastern Europe (CEE) for Kyrgyzstan.

Small-scale privatization must be begun immediately. In all other CEE countries, small-scale privatization has been a key signal for transformation. Not only can the privatization of smaller enterprises be accomplished relatively quickly, but the failure to embark upon small-scale privatization before other stages of privatization can form a bottleneck to reform. Poland's privatization of over 50,000 retail businesses in two years has been successful in relieving the bottlenecks in distribution of both retail and wholesale goods; privatization of transportation, distribution and retail networks are priorities in Kyrgyzstan as well.

Privatization will be a long, drawn-out process; deadlines will be missed. Privatization cannot proceed alone. A number of obstacles will undoubtedly slow privatization—among them issues of liability (ranging from inter-enterprise arrears to environmental liability), the development of the financial sector, the development of a social safety net, labor mobility, monopoly and institutional capacity. Of these, however, the immediate constraint on the pace of privatization is the lack of administrative capacity. Technical assistance and foreign expertise such as that provided by the World Bank can help, but adequate staffing, training and funding for agencies such as the SPF will also be needed.

Large-scale privatization will be problematic. The experience with large-scale privatization in CEE so far can only point to its problematic nature. Most countries have encountered a number of difficulties in tackling large-scale privatization. The successful examples of large-scale privatizations in Poland, Czechoslovakia, and Hungary have been few, and those have been facilitated by the presence of a foreign partner. Moreover, Kyrgyzstan faces the additional difficulty of gaining effective control over its previously Union-managed industrial enterprises prior to privatization. Large-scale privatization in Kyrgyzstan is hence likely to prove at least as intractable as in CEE.

Lack of clarity on environmental liability can be a barrier to investment. A recent World Bank survey of 1,000 major Western corporations indicated that lack of clear rules on environmental liability was as important a barrier to foreign investment in the newly privatized firms as commercial or political risks. Countries therefore need to develop procedures both for reaching compliance with environmental laws on current pollution and for assigning liability for the results of past neglect. For the latter, it will generally be appropriate for the State, as previous owner, to assume much of the obligations.

Constraints to Enterprise Reform

5.66   The authorities in Kyrgyzstan are committed to moving as fast as they can on enterprise reform. But as elsewhere in the CIS, the capacity of the implementing institutions is severely limited.

5.67   The following issues are likely to remain for some time as obstacles to rapid enterprise reform:

a)   the conflicting ownership and management claims of managers, concerns and ministries, workers' collectives, suppliers and segments of the population employed in sectors not subject to enterprise reform;

b)   the lack of capital, capital markets, other sources of funding for buyers;

c)   the lack of demand for corporatization and privatization, particularly if a hard budget constraint is imposed;

d)   the severe lack of competitive sourcing and distribution networks to provide materials, supplies, capital, marketing and sales;

e)   the opposition of vested managerial interests, particularly in the formerly Union-managed large enterprises, to alternate governance plans and segmentation of vertically integrated manufacturing facilities;

f)   the general lack of a client/consumer-oriented business environment;

g)   the lack of staff and resources at the SPF and AMC.

Recommendations

5.68   The foregoing discussion makes it clear that rapid enterprise reform faces serious institutional and financial constraints. Nonetheless, without sufficient progress in this area, the adjustment at the enterprise level that is essential for the success of the transition will not occur. Hence there is an urgent need to revitalize the program of privatization and enterprise reform. Box 5-3 identifies areas where the World Bank is planning to support the objectives of enterprise reform and privatization through technical assistance. It is already clear that considerable additional support will be required to implement the recommended policies in this area.

5.69   For large enterprises, mostly in heavy industry, where progress has been slowest, there is a need to reassess how best to implement a realistic program. The elements of such a program should include an ownership structure that permits effective governance, closure of those enterprises and lines of production that will not be viable and whose continued operation would retard the reform process, and segmentation of enterprises into a structure that is more conducive to competition. Until such a framework for reform can be developed, it is essential for the Government to exercise its ownership rights more effectively, whether by strengthening the SPF sufficiently to enable it to perform this function, or by ensuring that Government policy is fully implemented through the responsible ministries. In either case, a special effort to reorganize, corporatize and strengthen governance of the previously Union controlled enterprises is necessary to eliminate the current ownership and efficient management vacuum that is inconsistent with adjustment.

5.70   The following steps should be given priority:

a)   segmenting, corporatizing and privatizing, as rapidly as possible, distribution, wholesale, local transport, and other trading enterprises. To accomplish this task, the SPF must be able to initiate and follow through on privatization in these sectors, rather than merely responding to the initiatives from individual enterprises.

b)   The SPF should also develop standardized deal documents and guidelines to accelerate the work of individual Privatization Commissions.

c)   To enable the SPF to perform its role, increased resources, training and technical assistance will be required in addition to possible adjustments in existing laws, decrees and the SPF's internal guidelines to establish consistency with the legal framework for property rights.

d)   To accelerate small scale privatization, particularly in retail trade and services, a reformed system of auctions should be devised.

5.71   In addition the following steps should be taken to enhance the efficiency and credibility of the enterprise reform program:

a)   The program should provide broader indicative targets. The current targets are both highly optimistic and too deterministic. The continued publication of such specific targets could undermine public and official support;

b)   The program should provide for maximum flexibility in the mechanisms of corporatization and privatization;

c)   Revisions of the program will be necessary to provide for increased direct individual ownership of enterprises as opposed to ownership of enterprises by collectives;

d)   Uniform guidelines used for both Republican property and Local property privatization are needed;

e)   Guidelines for corporate governance are necessary, especially for large SOEs not likely to be privatized in the near term.

f)   Privatization of housing should be reviewed to remove the disincentives discussed. In particular, the program will only function if rents are increased substantially, and liberalized as private ownership becomes predominant;

g)   The issue of land privatization and water rights should be revisited to balance traditional concerns with the need for economic efficiency and mobility. In particular, there should be a conclusive determination of the legal ownership rights to land for any parcel which is attached to an enterprise, dwelling, farm or building being privatized. A new water rights law should be considered.

h)   Guidelines for the sharing of known and potential costs of remediation of past pollution between the State and the prospective new owners should be established. Lack of clarity with regard to environmental liability for past pollution could delay the conclusion of privatization contracts.

Box 5-3. Technical Assistance for Enterprise Reform and Privatization

The objective of World Bank supported TA to the SPF and the AMC is to help draft and review relevant policies, strategies and implementation mechanisms aimed at (i) creating an administrative, legal and regulatory environment conducive to a market economy based on the exercise of private property rights; and (ii) transforming state-owned enterprises into commercially operating and ultimately predominantly privately-owned entities.

The scope of the TA would involve the provision of assistance until the end of 1993 to the SPF and the AMC through the placement of 4 long-term advisors in Bishkek and several short-term interventions through specialist missions as well as the possible training of local staff outside Kyrgyzstan. Special attention would be focused on enterprise governance and operation. The TA would concentrate on three areas of activity: (i) the privatization program; (ii) enterprise reform; and (iii) private sector encouragement. The first intervention would be a legal mission to review the SPF's overall program focusing on its strategy and its legal basis, procedures and methods. Harmony and consistency among these measures needs to be established. Further review and related drafting is also required to establish consistency between the SPF's legal regime and the overall legal framework for a private sector. Special attention would be paid to the Property, Enterprise, Leasing and Companies Law. Information would be developed for the drafting of a Commercial Code and a Bankruptcy Law. As soon as possible after the initial intervention, long-term advisors would be assigned including a senior advisor and legal, mass privatization and antimonopoly advisors. Specialist missions would concentrate on areas such as compilation of data bases, subsector studies, mass privatization/voucher programs, small enterprise privatization, public relations, antimonopoly law, enterprise evaluation, training, corporatization, private sector development, and commercial law drafting. Basic office equipment such as facsimile machines, PCs, photocopiers and printers would be provided as early as possible.

The Bank has budgeted $2.6 million for the TA of which $300,000 would come from previously established Trust Fund resources and US$ 2.3 million from the Bank's proposed Rehabilitation Loan. Activity started in August 1992 and is to be completed by the end of 1993. It will be coordinated by the SPF and the AMC. The output of the TA would include detailed written comments and advice in the field on the programs, day to day assistance and advice in implementation by the long-term advisors, and written recommendations for draft legislation. This program represents a first step. Considerable additional (grant) resources will be required to assist the Government in a sufficient manner.

Mining and Petroleum Legislation. To promote private sector involvement in the mining and oil and gas sectors, suitable legislation needs to be developed, particularly for foreign investment. Complementary to the TA activities in the preparation of the foreign investment law, TA is proposed for advisors and foreign experts who can assist in the preparation of mining and petroleum sector legislation. A TA budget of US$ 250,000 is proposed for legislation development for each of these two sectors.

Foreign Direct Investment

5.72   There has been little real foreign direct investment (FDI) activity in the past year, other than some negotiations in the hydroelectric sector.[7] Macroeconomic instability in the ruble zone may be the principal constraint to FDI. This section contains a discussion of other constraints, which can be addressed more directly by the Government.

Foreign Investment Law

5.73   In June 1991, a Law on Foreign Investment set forth the guidelines for establishing a local entity with foreign shareholding as well as a 100 percent foreign owned entity. The law guarantees that foreign investors are to be treated no less favorably than local citizens. Indeed, given the variability in foreign exchange surrender requirements and conversion rates in effect at the time, Government

7.   Information is not available regarding possible investment by parent enterprises in the FSU in their former subsidiaries in Kyrghyzstan.

officials were considering more favorable rules for entities with foreign participation, although the issue had not been resolved. Table 5-3 contains the additional incentives provided for in the law. Entities with foreign ownership may participate in any activity, except military production and certain agricultural forms of ownership.

Table 5-3. Investor Benefits (As Set Forth in Law on Foreign Investments June 1991)

INVESTMENT	BENEFIT
A. Income Tax	
20%+ of capital contributed in hard currency or a minimum of US$300,000 or its equivalent.	Tax exempt for 10 years on 25% of income.
30%+ of capital contributed in hard currency or a minimum of US$800,000 or its equivalent.	Tax exempt for the first 5 years on 30% of income and for subsequent 5 years on 50% of its income.
If activity of investment is listed in the Law's Supplement.	Tax exempt for the first 5 years on 100% of income and for subsequent 5 years on 60% of income.
B. There is no tax on remittance of profits by foreign investors whose income is subject to tax but a tax of 5% is levied on remittal of income exempt from income tax.	
C. Customs Tax 1. No tax on in-kind contributions to capital. 2. Customs tax for imported and exported materials and commodities subject to decisions of Cabinet of Ministers.	

5.74   The new investment law requires disputes to be settled in local courts although, the possibilities of arbitration in Kyrgyzstan under international rules would be acceptable. However, such arbitration, to be effective, must be enforceable in local courts and, to date, these courts are unfamiliar with such proceedings. Kyrgyzstan has not yet signed the New York Convention for the Enforcement of Arbitral Awards.

Constraints

5.75   A review of the Investment Law reveals a number of unresolved issues and ambiguities. Two provisions may be serious barriers to FDI: (a) uncertainty regarding export license and foreign exchange surrender requirements and (b) the repeated references in the Law to the application of all domestic economic regulations to foreign investment. If these provisions are taken literally, they presumably subject the investor to the state orders applicable to local entities and may well deny the venture the necessary freedom to control its own inputs and outputs. More generally, the Law leaves a number of crucial areas wide open and key questions unanswered. It lacks the clarity and predictability provided by the kind of comprehensive legislative and regulatory schemes that are successful in attracting multinational investment and technology transfer.

5.76   There are no organizations in Kyrgyzstan equipped to deal on a business basis with foreign investors.[8] The Ministry of Finance's staff is limited and only a few have had actual business

---

8. The functions of the recently created Committee on Foreign Investment will have go be clarified.

experience dealing with foreigners. Foreign firms report that each negotiation is overly cumbersome.

5.77   For the time being, the essential prerequisites for negotiating investment agreements are not present in Kyrgyzstan. Representations and warranties about the conditions of a local enterprise, expected by most multinational market investors, are not available. Core financial information was either not required or not relevant under the traditional socialist model in Kyrgyzstan. There are no reliable operating results since many of the enterprise managers did not know or track costs or keep profit and loss statements. Nor do there seem to be reliable inventory records. Similarly, the amount of receivables and payables recorded on a firm's books may not be accurate or collectable because bad debt reserves are either unreliable or not used. Environmental liabilities are essentially unknown since there are not yet laws or regulations. In sum, traditional market due diligence in the Kyrgyz context is ultimately a matter of subjective conjecture. Consequently, the amount of comfort that can be achieved through advance work done by an investment promotion agency may be critical to the success of a foreign investment program.

5.78   The limited capacity of the Ministry of Finance to deal with foreign firms and the lack of clarity in the rules of the game imposed on foreign firms will probably give rise to two series of negative consequences for foreign investment. First, given the plethora of legislative and administrative changes taking place, the majority of foreign companies with foreign equity will be forced to secure the services of local people to be responsible for managing their relations with the Government. Such practices result in increased costs and act as a deterrent to investment by firms whose entrepreneurial culture is different from Kyrgyzstan's. Second, negotiations with the Government will necessarily be multi-partied with no clear line of authority apparent to the foreign party.

Recommendations

5.79   A "bottom-up" approach to FDI that would build a capacity to deal with foreign investors and promote foreign investment is required. The focus should be on actual cases and concrete proposals developed for adapting the financial and business infrastructures of the locality. Significant advance work should be conducted prior to making introductions or arranging trade missions. Such advance work would concentrate on a feasible mechanism for providing hard currency profits to the investors, assure the proposed projects are as well documented as possible and maintain the respective interests of the local and foreign parties.

5.80   Streamlining of governmental procedures and enhanced regulatory transparency and the creation of a one-step investment promotion agency will be important for attracting foreign investment. The Government should also make use of standard international economic regulatory frameworks and documents that have evolved and been successfully employed in resource rich countries such as Saudi Arabia, Venezuela, Chile and others.

CHAPTER 6

The Labor Market

Introduction

6.01   Under the Soviet regime, the labor market was plagued by numerous rigidities including: administrative assignment of jobs and informal pressures to hire; job security; the obligation to work; non-existence of a legal private sector; rigid working hours; constrained geographic mobility; ineffective internal labor markets; centrally imposed, egalitarian wage distribution; and generous fringe benefits.

6.02   The primary goal of labor market policies during the transition should be to facilitate the needed adjustment by encouraging the efficient reallocation of labor and by spreading the costs equitably among the different segments of the population. Current labor market policies represent a first step in that direction. Their orientation -- of leaving primary responsibility for finding a job to the individual, and letting the state provide a conducive environment for generation of jobs together with a social safety net -- is commendable. Some tangible progress has been achieved, such as easing the pressure on enterprises to hire workers and offering unemployment benefits to the unemployed.

6.03   Thus far, however, labor market adjustment has not materialized to the extent that will become necessary: the large-scale displacement of workers that ultimately will be needed has not yet started; relative pay differences among workers have not significantly increased; and there has been almost no (registered) unemployment. Moreover, in some areas current labor market policies continue to resemble the interventionist policies of the past. This chapter provides an overview of the labor market and summarizes its recent trends, discusses the major shortcomings of current labor market policies and practices -- deficiencies in labor market legislation, weaknesses in unemployment compensation, immobility of labor, and problems facing employment services -- and concludes with recommendations.

An Overview of the Labor Market

6.04   The following major features of the labor market can be identified: a predominance of state sector employment; significant hidden unemployment; underdeveloped service sector; pay egalitarianism and distorted interindustry wage structure; reversal of trends in productivity and real wages; relatively high labor turnover and low geographical mobility; and high female labor force participation.

6.05   Predominance of state sector employment. In 1991, the state sector provided the majority of jobs -- 87 percent although since 1986 state employment has stagnated. The majority of non-state employment was in private agriculture, which accounted for 11 percent of total employment, though only small plots surrounding homes were allowed to be held privately. The share of employment in cooperatives was less than two percent, and private non-agricultural employment was negligible (Table 6-1).

6.06   Hidden unemployment. Government officials and enterprise managers estimate hidden unemployment (overstaffing) to range from 20 to 30 percent due to a number of factors. First, under soft budget constraints firms hoarded labor so as to improve their ability to fulfill the production targets set by the center. Second, once employed, workers had no fear of losing their jobs as they could be dismissed only for seriously breaching work discipline. Such virtually complete job security reduced the ability of the firm to adjust its workforce effectively. Finally, firms were forced to hire workers through both administrative job assignments as well as informal pressures by Party officials.

6.07   Open unemployment. As in other socialist economies, open unemployment was officially not recognized under the Soviet regime. With the consequent lack of official statistics, estimates are based on population surveys as well as information on school graduates, seasonally employed workers, and quit rates. The statistical office of Kyrgyzstan estimates open unemployment in 1991 at 158,800, or an unemployment rate of 8.3 percent: 46,500 were workers searching for a job (35,000 for the first time); 46,000 were seasonally unemployed workers (that is, those seasonally employed did not work in total for 46,000 person-years in 1991); and 66,300 were "discouraged workers" (not actively look for a job). The last category does not conform to ILO standards and the same may be true for those counted as seasonally unemployed. Thus, an estimate of unemployment in 1991 excluding both seasonal and discouraged workers, would be 2.4 percent; excluding only the latter this figure would double to 4.8 percent.

6.08   Sectoral Composition. The distribution of employment across major sectors has remained essentially unchanged since 1980, with about one third employed in agriculture, 29 percent in industry and 37 percent in services (Table 6-2). The high concentration in agriculture reflects the importance of the sector in the economy. But the share in services is relatively low, certainly by OECD standards, but also compared to many socialist countries including the USSR in the last decade.

Table 6-1. Labor Force, 1980-1991 (in thousands)

	1980	1985	1986	1987	1988	1989	1990	1991
State Sector Employment	1163.0	1315.0	1341.0	1342.0	1338.0	1345.0	1350.0	1343.0
Percent of women	46.6	46.6	47.0	46.6	46.8	46.8	47.6	47.7
Cooperatives		...	...	2.4	10.0	27.6	33.0	28.2
Percent of women	...	...	...	25.0	25.0	24.3	22.1	25.2
Kolkhozy	172.0	192.0	188.0	181.0	183.0	175.0	178.0	185.0
Percent of women	45.0	...	...	...	...	40.1	40.4	...
Private Agricult.	88.3	106.9	122.0	175.2	182.4	188.2	183.8	189.6
Percent of women	35.1	...	...	...	...	43.3	42.4	...
Private Non-Agriculture	0.4	0.3	0.2	1.6	2.9	2.4	3.1	3.8
Percent of women	75.0	66.7	50.0	62.5	62.1	66.7	80.6	73.7
Total Employment	1423.7	1614.2	1651.2	1702.2	1716.3	1738.2	1747.9	1749.6
Percent of women	45.7	...	...	...	...	45.4	45.9	...
Unemployed of which[a]	154.6	134.8	141.2	107.9	119.9	129.3	134.5	158.8
"Discouraged workers"	75.9	61.7	67.8	54.8	68.4	73.2	73.5	66.3
Searching for a job	14.5	12.0	11.8	11.0	10.0	10.0	11.0	11.5
Seasonally unemployed	64.0	60.2	60.3	41.0	40.0	40.0	43.5	46.0
Unemployed graduates	0.2	0.9	1.3	1.1	1.5	6.1	6.5	35.0
Percent of women	64.1	64.1	64.3	64.0	64.5	64.6	64.5	64.7
Total Labor Force	1578.3	1749.0	1792.4	1810.1	1836.2	1867.5	1882.4	1908.4
Percent of women	47.5	...	...	...	...	46.8	47.2	...
Memorandum items:								
Share of State Employment								
(Including Kolkhozy)	93.8	93.4	92.6	89.5	88.6	87.4	87.4	87.3
Unemployment Rate[a]	9.8	7.7	7.9	6.0	6.5	6.9	7.1	8.3
Working Age Population	1847.0	2037.0	2068.0	2097.0	2127.0	2165.0	2198.0	2216.0
Participation Rate	85.5	85.9	86.7	86.3	86.3	86.3	85.6	86.1
Participation Rate - Women	82.7	...	...	...	...	82.9	82.9	...
Participation Rate - Men	88.1	...	...	...	...	89.4	88.3	...

Source: Statistical Office of Kyrgyzstan

[a] Estimates of unemployment may be biased upward (see paragraph 6.07). Participation rate is defined as the percent of the labor force in the working age population (age 16-54 for women, 16-59 for men). Under private agriculture, persons officially labelled "employed in auxiliary activities" are included.

Table 6-2. Structure of Employment by Sector (percent shares)

Sectors	1980	1985	1991	USSR 1985
Agriculture	33.2	33.9	34.0	20.2
Industry	29.2	28.5	28.8	35.2
Manufacturing & Mining	(21.7)	(20.8)	(19.8)	
Construction	(7.5)	(7.7)	(9.0)	
Services	37.6	37.6	37.2	44.6
Transportation & Communications	(7.9)	(7.8)	(5.6)	
Trade, Catering & Tourism	(7.5)	(7.2)	(6.8)	
Crafts, Housing, Public Utility	(2.6)	(2.7)	(2.7)	
Financial Services	(0.5)	(0.4)	(0.4)	
Education & Culture	(11.0)	(11.2)	(12.8)	
Public Health & Social Welfare	(5.4)	(5.5)	(6.2)	
Administration	(2.7)	(2.8)	(2.5)	

Source: Statistical Office of Kyrgyzstan.

Table 6-3. Interindustry Wage Structure[a] (percentage of the national average)

Sectors	1980	1986	1990
Kyrgyzstan (rubles per month)	148	166	219
Agriculture	85	91	90
Manufacturing & Mining	115	117	121
Construction	121	124	125
Transport	119	116	109
Communications	95	88	97
Trade, Catering & Tourism	85	82	89
Housing & Public Utilities	84	84	82
Financial Services	98	100	146
Education & Culture	87	89	73
Public Health & Social Welfare	80	73	76
Administration	97	97	136

Source: Statistical Office of Kyrgyzstan.
a/ State sector only.

Table 6-4. Productivity and Wages, 1980-1991[a]

Year	Productivity	Avg. Nominal Wage	Avg. Real Wage[b]
1980	100.0	147.9	100.0
1981	102.1	150.3	100.2
1982	101.3	152.2	98.6
1983	108.1	154.6	99.5
1984	110.0	158.0	102.5
1985	106.3	162.6	105.2
1986	105.1	166.4	106.6
1987	102.8	171.4	108.7
1988	115.7	183.6	116.5
1989	119.8	197.5	122.9
1990	125.6	219.2	131.3
1991	119.0	330.0	114.2

Source: Statistical Office of Kyrgyzstan, staff estimates.
a/ Productivity relates to the so-called material sphere (social services are excluded). Wages refer to the state and cooperative employment.
b/ Deflated by index of retail prices. For 1991, the consumer price index is used.

6.09   Interindustry wage structure. As elsewhere in the USSR, Kyrgyzstan used a so-called tariff system to base relative pay scales on such factors as required education, physical strains and working conditions. Under this system, jobs were classified into different skill grades to which economywide wage rates were centrally assigned. To stimulate productivity, various bonus schemes were superimposed on base wages tying rewards to either individual or to collective productivity.

6.10   Such wage determination produced two major contrasts relative to market economies. First, the pay structure was egalitarian. Second, the sectoral structure of wages worked in favor of blue collar workers -- for instance, wages of workers in education and culture were only 60 percent of those in manufacturing in 1990. The sectoral wage structure was fairly stable during 1980-90 -- with the exception of administration and particularly financial services, which improved their relative wages after 1986.

6.11   Real wages and productivity. The generally increasing trend of both productivity (measured as output per worker) and real wages through 1990 turned into an abrupt decline in 1991, especially pronounced for real wages (Table 6-4).

6.12   Labor turnover and geographical mobility. The labor turnover rate has been relatively high at 21.1 percent in 1990 and 22.4 percent in 1991, though its interpretation may be different from Western economies given the high degree of vertical integration of industry. By contrast, geographic mobility has been extremely low.

6.13   High female labor force participation. While the male labor force participation rate in Kyrgyzstan has been comparable to that in most OECD countries, the female participation rate has been much higher. In 1989, the female participation rate was 82.9 percent, which puts Kyrgyzstan in the range of rates in Scandinavia and most East European countries. The participation rate for Kyrgyzstan may however be biased upward due to a fairly restrictive definition of working age population.

Recent Trends and Shortcomings

Slow Labor Reallocation

6.14   Even though labor market legislation introduced in 1991 allows for flexible adjustment of employment (except for certain categories of workers -- see below), the needed reallocation of labor among enterprises and sectors had failed to materialize as of mid-1992. While some of the labor reallocation may take place smoothly (that is, as voluntary job changing that does not result in unemployment), reallocation in the present crisis is bound to call for extensive lay-offs, and to produce substantial unemployment, which has not yet occurred. In 1991, only 4,600 workers were laid off, less than 0.25 percent of the labor force. The first registered unemployed emerged in the third quarter of 1991; at the end of that quarter there were 128. The number had risen to 459 by the end of March 1992 and to 800 in July 1992.

6.15   In spite of considerable open unemployment, the number of unemployed that were recognized as such by Employment Offices and qualified for unemployment compensation has been surprisingly low for several reasons. First, the relatively unrestrictive conditions for unemployment compensation set by the Employment Law (see below) were complemented by a requirement that, in order to qualify for unemployment compensation, all workers must have worked at least 36 out of the last 52 weeks. That requirement eliminated all first-time job seekers and most re-entrants into the labor market. Second, many of the job seekers have become ineligible for compensation after rejecting job offers. Third, the information on availability of unemployment compensation may not have been effectively disseminated particularly in rural areas.

6.16   Signs of tightening of the labor market are becoming more evident, however. The number of vacancies reported by enterprises decreased from about 15,000 in both 1990 and 1991, to 3,300 at the end of the first quarter of 1992. Moreover, those that could not obtain a job after having finished schooling rapidly rose in 1991 (to 35,000, from 6,500 in 1990). Lastly, in January 1992, enterprises gave advance notification of layoffs to 10,600 workers and were planning to lay off 20,000 more workers in 1992.

6.17   In view of the above, government projections of unemployment for 1992 may be exaggerated. The projections anticipate the inflow of 171,000 into unemployment in 1992 (or about 9 percent of the labor force): 48,000 of them being discharged by enterprises; 63,000 graduates -- first-time job seekers; 44,000 quitting an existing job and searching for a new job; and 16,000 re-entrants into the labor market. According to the same projections, 42,000 of the unemployed would enter vocational training, 27,000 would participate in public works, 2,000 would emigrate, and the rest -- 100,000 -- would be supported by unemployment compensation. The whole program would cost R343 million (in projections dated March 1992), out of which training costs would account for R142 million, public works (only partly financed from the Employment Fund) for R3.1 million, and unemployment compensation for

R198 million. At the current one percent payroll contribution rate as the source of financing of the Employment Fund, the program would create a deficit of R214 million. To close the gap, the contribution rate would have to be raised to at least 2.5 percent. While the above unemployment estimates for 1992 may be too high, the adjustments required in government and the public enterprises are likely to push the unemployment rate to at least these levels in the next few years.

Deficiencies in Labor Market Legislation

6.18   Inconsistent unemployment benefits. Unemployment benefits, together with the formal notion of unemployment, were only introduced in Kyrgyzstan in 1991 with the new Employment Law. An unemployed person is defined as a person who does not have a job due to reasons beyond his or her control, is searching for a job, and has not turned down a job offer extended by the Employment Office. In addition to unemployment compensation, unemployment benefits include training, training allowance, and unemployment assistance for those with children aged 14 or less (10 percent of unemployment compensation). Unemployment compensation is offered to laid off workers, those that have finished employment training, and certain other categories.[1] For laid off workers, unemployment compensation is 50 percent of their past base earnings for 26 weeks (it cannot be less than the minimum wage, nor larger than the average wage in the economy). For others who qualify, unemployment compensation amounts to 75 to 100 percent of the minimum wage, for a duration of 13 to 26 weeks.

6.19   The present unemployment compensation system may be overly generous in two ways, both of them undermining the affordability of the system. First, the system is open-ended: by allowing labor market re-entrants and those who finished employment training to qualify for unemployment compensation, the period of receiving such compensation is not limited. Second, the system extends assistance to the family members of the unemployed. Together these provisions not only jeopardize affordability, but also dampen work incentives.

6.20   Damaging protection of job security. The Employment Law generally introduces quite flexible redundancy regulations -- the employer has to give two months of advance notice to workers to be dismissed, and pay a severance pay of up to three months' wages to the laid-off worker. But the law does not apply to all workers: persons within one year of the pensionable age, single mothers, mothers with children younger than three years, and workers younger than 18 years cannot be laid off. Such constraints can only be incorporated, however, by damaging the efficiency of production -- for example, through laying off more productive workers, by postponing the adjustment and dampening work incentives. The social objectives of the above exceptions are more appropriately addressed through other means, such as a more comprehensive cash benefit system.

6.21   Lack of special treatment of mass layoffs. Redundancy legislation does not separately treat mass layoffs. Such a distinction would be useful, as mass layoffs are especially difficult to deal with and require concerted action of employers, workers, and employment offices. It may also be desirable that the employer consult with trade unions to prepare a social plan for any planned mass layoff.

6.22   Counterproductive job guarantees. The Employment Law stipulates that the government guarantee work for some groups of workers -- youth, single mothers and mothers with many children, parents of small and handicapped children, workers close to pensionable age, veterans, invalids, re-

---

1.   The tightening of restrictions subsequent to the Law has produced some ambiguity on eligibility.

entrants into the labor force, released prisoners and those that have finished a mandatory health treatment program. This guarantee is achieved through assigning such workers to both state and other enterprises. The number of assigned workers cannot exceed five percent of the workforce per year. If enterprises do not want to accept these workers, they must pay a fine equivalent to the yearly pay of the refused workers (payable to the Employment Fund).

6.23   As with the job security program, such a job guarantee program may appear just and humane. But it is economically counterproductive. As the experience of socially conscious countries, for example, in Western Europe indicates, it may be appropriate for governments to assist vulnerable groups of the population, such as the poor and disabled. Such help, however, should not consist of job assignments, but rather of income support and investment in human capital, and, possibly, of wage subsidies for first-time job seekers, long-term unemployed, and invalids, for example.

6.24   Inappropriate charges to employers for training of unemployed workers. A previous employer is currently charged for the training of an unemployed worker, if that worker has not been trained within the last two years of being employed. Such a charge is inappropriate for several reasons. First, it increases the price of labor and thus dampens its demand. Second, it induces enterprises to refrain from layoffs and thus delays needed adjustment. Third, enterprises may try to circumvent paying the full cost of training by instead offering lower quality or useless training to satisfy the law, and then lay off workers. Finally, it generates rent-seeking -- lobbying of government officials to waive the payment for training.

Weaknesses in Compensation

6.25   Absence of incomes policies. In the formation of wages, the pendulum has swung too far in the direction of complete freedom in setting the wage bill by state enterprises. In monopolistic markets and until financial discipline is strengthened, state enterprises may, in the absence of any constraints on wage payments, increase their wages well above increases in productivity thereby over-utilizing scarce resources and contributing to a lack of competitiveness.

6.26   Pressures to keep current intrafirm earnings differentials. Though enterprises are formally free to determine workers' pay, enterprises have been urged to maintain relative differences as set by the old tariff system of compensation. Such pressures hinder the reallocation of labor and thus keep labor in less productive uses. Moreover, the direct participation of workers in decision-making about pay is not necessarily conductive to an efficiency-based compensation system.

6.27   Generous fringe benefits. The present system offers many types of fringe benefits. Workers are entitled to a pension, paid vacation, and paid maternity and sick leave (the normal benefits in a market economy). There are, however, other types of fringe benefits which are typically not found in a market economy.   The latter are financed from the so-called social development fund of the enterprise and include provision of housing, payment of mortgage and consumer credits, obtaining lots for building a "dacha," paid excursions and traveling for non-business purposes, and free meals. These benefits introduce inefficiency into wage setting. Moreover, many workers would prefer to be paid in cash and decide for themselves how much and what goods to buy.

Immobility of Labor

6.28   Labor mobility is not only hindered by egalitarianism in workers' earnings, but is also constrained geographically by the "propiska" system -- the system of internal passports. A worker may only be employed in the area of his propiska, which stops many rural residents from taking jobs in the cities. Not only is this system unjust, it is also inefficient -- it precludes selection from a larger pool of candidates and thus hinders competition. Moreover, the inefficient housing market (and the resulting extremely low housing turnover rate) is another barrier to geographic mobility.

Employment Services

6.29   Employment services have until recently only provided placement and labor market information. With the increase of the scope of their services (to include counseling, administration of unemployment services and training) and the number of their clients they may be faced by the lack of both staff and resources. As of April 1992, there were 532 staff members of the employment services, with 61 local offices -- 14 of them in urban, and 47 of them in rural areas. Moreover, many of the current practices of the employment services regarding information exchange, placement, and job counseling will have to be overhauled, to provide the services needed in a market economy.

Recommendations

6.30   It is important to recognize and commend the government's efforts to introduce flexible labor market legislation. The overall objective of labor market legislation should be to facilitate the adjustments that will be needed during the transition. Since adjustments in the labor market appear thus far to be lagging output developments, the thrust of the recommendations are directed towards ensuring that deficiencies in labor market legislation are not responsible for delaying or distorting the process of enterprise reform. However, if unemployment were to rise to socially unacceptable levels or if viable firms were threatened with excessive employment contraction, alternative forms of intervention might become appropriate as discussed in Chapter 2. To assist the government in thinking about appropriate legislation and programs, the following recommendations are offered:

a)   If unemployment rises rapidly in the coming years as expected, unemployment compensation will become a major fiscal burden. Hence first-time job seekers and labor market re-entrants should not be offered unemployment compensation, nor should the basis of eligibility be employment training. The current duration and replacement rates of unemployment compensation are appropriate. However, there may be a need to create another instrument as part of the safety net for those not covered by unemployment benefits, including those laid off for more than six months. The contribution to the Employment Fund should be shared between the worker and the employer, as is the general practice in Western Europe.

b)   To ensure efficient production, no special category of workers should be given protection from layoffs. Moreover, separate treatment of mass layoffs in the Employment Law may be considered, to help ensure that in such cases employers, workers, and employment offices will coordinate their actions.

c)   For the sake of efficiency and to prevent undue costs imposed on employers, job assignments should be ceased; therefore, it would be desirable to reconsider current job guarantees by employment offices. Instead, the government may wish to introduce wage subsidies (for first-time job seekers, long-term unemployed, and invalids).

d)   Employers should not be charged for the training of their previous workers, if those workers undergo training while unemployed.

e)   It is essential to limit real labor costs in state-owned enterprises that do not yet face a hard budget constraint, for example, because of their preferred access to bank credit. Tax based incentives and penalties for limiting the growth of the wage bill could be designed for this purpose.

f)   To produce the flexible wage structure needed to stimulate labor reallocation, the government should stop urging enterprises to adhere to the intrafirm pay differences as dictated by the old tariff system of compensation. Pay differentials should reflect the supply of and demand for particular skills. To avoid the negative effects of egalitarian pay structures, moreover, workers' participation in decision-making about pay should be limited, or in line with their general participation in corporate decision-making.

g)   The provision of excessive fringe benefits should be discouraged. In particular, the provision of some benefits -- such as housing -- should not be linked to employment.

h)   To foster geographic mobility of labor, "propiska" (permanent residence) considerations should be removed from the criteria for job eligibility and the provision of health services.

i)   To ensure adequate income support for the unemployed and effective re-employment programs, the government should prepare to increase the resources available to employment services. These services should be adapted to the needs of a market economy.

CHAPTER 7

The Framework for Social Protection

Introduction

7.01   Kyrgyzstan's past system of social expenditures succeeded in maintaining a society that, relative to its income level, had low levels of poverty, an equitable income distribution and a well educated population that was showing some important gains in health status over the past decade. However, the principal social expenditures -- pensions, allowances for families with children, education and health -- comprised about 55 percent of on-budget government expenditures of all levels of government combined in 1991, and close to 65 percent if the budget of the Pension Fund is consolidated with those of the republic and local governments. These expenditures amounted to over 25 percent of GDP in 1991, up from 22 percent in 1990. With government expenditures expected to decline by about 40 percent in real terms and government obligations for unemployment compensation expected to rise, it is clear that severe cuts in expenditures for social protection are unavoidable. In early 1992, significant delays in the payment of pensions and family allowances had already been experienced, while the effectiveness of health and education programs were also in decline.

7.02   There is therefore an urgent need to prioritize budgetary outlays to protect the most vulnerable and to protect the human capital stock that will serve as the basis for future economic growth. The corollary of this approach is that it will be impossible to maintain living standards as in the past for most beneficiaries of government social expenditures during the early phase of transition. This chapter confronts this reality by assessing the major categories of existing social expenditures -- pensions and allowances, health and education -- to provide a basis for adjusting to fiscal stringencies while protecting identified priorities.

Pensions and Allowances

The Current Structure of Benefits

7.03   Kyrgyzstan faces a dilemma as a result of excessive commitments for social security and social welfare transfer payments in the forms of pensions and allowances for families with children. These payments combined rose from 10 percent of GDP in 1990 to 15 percent in 1991, with almost the entire increase in real terms the result of rising family allowances. The rise in expenditures on these programs has been caused not only by increases in cash payments to offset rising food prices, but also by increases in some of the main allowances for children. Prior to independence, from 1985 to 1990, the share of allowances in total pensions and allowances was slightly over one third, but it rose to more than 50 percent in 1991.

7.04   Pension Fund. Pensions and nearly all of the existing allowances are paid by the Pension Fund, which started operations in 1991 and receives the bulk of its income from large taxes on enterprise payrolls.[1] Most employers pay a fee for social insurance equal to 37 percent of their payroll, but for

---

1.   Prior to 1991 pensions were paid from the Union Social Security Fund to which enterprises contributed directly.

cooperatives and state farms the fee is 26 percent.[2] The Fund also receives over a third of its resources from the republic's budget to cover two of the major allowances for children plus any shortfalls in the Fund's budget. In the first two months of 1992, payments to the Pension Fund (mainly for these allowances) comprised nearly 45 percent of the total expenditures of the republic's budget.

7.05   Pensions. Under existing legislation the minimum pension is linked to the minimum wage. Thus, the minimum pension was raised in parallel with the minimum wage to R1,600 in November 1992 from its level of R350 in the first half of the year. Pensions above the minimum vary in most cases with past earnings, while higher than average pensions are paid to war veterans and a small number of outstanding citizens.

7.06   In January 1992, about 580,000 pensioners (55 percent of them women) received pensions averaging R393 per month. Of the total, about 25 percent were below retirement age, which is 55 for women and 60 for men, or after 40 and 45 years of work, respectively. About 15-20 percent of the people on pensions continue to work. Workers in certain occupations have been allowed to retire early: Some 53,000 of the early retirees are on either partial or complete disability, while around 100,000 pensioners are survivors in families that have lost their main breadwinner.

7.07   Allowances. Family allowances are all linked to the minimum wage as follows: Children up to 1.5 years of age are eligible for the full minimum wage as are children of war veterans and a few other special categories; allowances for single mothers and widows or widowers with children, and for children up to age 18 not receiving parental support are equal to half the minimum wage; and those for children from 1.5 through 16 are 40 percent of the minimum wage. These allowances for children are subject to a means test: up to early 1992 families in which earnings per person exceeded four times the minimum wage were not eligible; this threshold has progressively been reduced to three and then two times the minimum wage. However, family incomes in Kyrgyzstan are almost all below these thresholds. Counting children, over 1.6 million people receive allowances and a total of nearly 2.2 million -- nearly half the population -- receive either pensions or allowances. Expenditures in 1991 on allowances for children relative to GDP may be the highest in the world. No country had family allowances as high as five percent in 1986, and only one developing market economy had allowances over one percent (Argentina with 1.3); yet in 1991 these allowances were nearly 8 percent of GDP in Kyrgyzstan.

7.08   Information and indexation. Local authorities generally have reliable information as to which families are especially poor and which people belong to vulnerable groups of the population, in particular danger of suffering from dire poverty and malnutrition. This is partly because the state maintained significant information on each citizen and is the main employer; however, the ability to identify people in these categories is likely to decline, so that increased efforts may be needed to determine the needs of the vulnerable. By contrast, available information is unsatisfactory at present, with regard to the changes in the cost of living for the very low income population. Food costs have been indexed based on a monthly basket of foods heavy in expensive animal products and generous in other foods and total calories. By late March 1992, the basket cost around R612, or 75 percent more

---

2.   Out of these contributions 86 percent goes to the Pension Fund while the remaining 14 percent goes to labor unions to cover the cost of sick leave, rest and recreation leave, etc. Another one percent of the payroll goes to the Employment Fund which pays unemployment benefits. In addition, each employee is required to pay one percent of his/her wage to the Pension Fund.

than the minimum wage at the time. Thus while the latter is meant to be indexed to such a basket, in practice this has not been possible.

Table 7-1. Monthly Basket of Food Used to Measure Cost of Living

Meat	6.08 kg.
Milk products	26.92 liters[a/]
Fish	1.07 kg.
Eggs	18
Bread	11.00 kg.
Potatoes	5.67 kg.
Vegetables and melons	11.25 kg.
Fruit	6.17 kg.
Sugar and confectioneries	2.80 kg.
Vegetable oil	1.09 kg
(Calories per day 2,847)	

Source: Ministry of Labor and Social Protection
a/ Fresh milk equivalent

Policy Issues and Recommendations

7.09   The real value of payments for pensions and allowances in 1991 cannot be sustained under current circumstances. These levels have de facto fallen in 1992 through late payment of existing obligations and the decline in the real minimum wage to which most of the benefits are linked. It would be more appropriate to target the beneficiaries of these programs more carefully while preventing individuals and families from falling into extreme poverty. In addition, the benefit system should not have undue disincentive effects and should be capable of cheap and effective administration. The following recommendations are intended to assist the government in re-designing the system:

a)   Expenditures on pensions and allowances will have to be reduced by at least one third in real terms relative to their 1991 level to reduce their share of total government expenditures. The rapid increase in family allowances in 1991 will have to be reversed at least partially to attain this goal.

b)   It is very important not to let the real value of the minimum pension fall below a level that is necessary to maintain a reasonably healthy diet -- yet not to raise it much above this level, considering the budgetary costs and the impact on incentives to workers whose wages are low. This minimum level should be defended vigorously against inflation. Since existing cost-of-living indexes and indexation procedures are not a reliable indicator of what is required, there is a pressing need to change over to a more suitable index in which the basket of foods would be heavily weighted toward foods eaten predominantly by poor people yet sufficient to sustain reasonable health.

c)   Defending the real level of pensions above the minimum is less important and, in a period of rapid inflation and budgetary stringency, may not be achievable. Thus the level of all or most pensions could be allowed temporarily to merge with the minimum pension. The differentials could then be restored as soon as the budgetary situation permits.

d)   The retirement age for women, who had a life expectancy of 72.6 in 1990 (versus 64.2 for men) should be raised to 60, the current retirement age for men.

e)   The least justified commitments particularly in regard to their magnitude, appear to be the principal allowances for families with children; on aggregate, these allowances should be reduced by at least half. Alternative means for achieving such a cutback could be assessed once the objective is endorsed. One way to proceed would be to cut most allowances for children in half except the one for children 6 through 16, which would be abolished or reduced by considerably more than half. A safety net provision for families with a large number of children could then be installed. Actions such as these could be combined with more rigorous means testing.

f)   Active consideration should be given to including pensions and allowances, as well as other cash benefits such as unemployment benefits, as taxable income subject to the individual income tax. The present system favoring pensions and allowances increases the incentive to leave low-wage jobs or not work at all.

g)   High payroll taxes on employers raise the costs of employment thus discouraging new hiring and reducing competitiveness. In market economies, payroll taxes on employers for social insurance are typically below 10 percent of payroll, although in some countries they do reach as high as 25 percent. Moreover, in a large majority of market economies, employees pay as much or nearly as much as their employers. Within three or four years if not sooner, Kyrgyzstan will have to reduce sharply its high payroll fees on employers; thus it would be unwise to expand these taxes now. However, employees' Pension Fund contributions, now only one percent of wages, could be increased to perhaps 4 percent and a sizeable Pension Fund contribution -- perhaps 8 percent of net earnings -- could reasonably be imposed on self-employed people. Meanwhile, a start ought to be made in reducing the fees paid by employers. Taken together these changes should be at least revenue neutral until the budget deficit has been reduced to a sustainable level.

h)   In the longer run, private pensions should be allowed and encouraged, to supplement pensions provided by the government through its Pension Fund. This could also help to keep down spending by the government on pensions. Creation of these private group pensions will, however, have to await the attainment of greater macroeconomic stability and the enactment of the requisite legal and institutional framework permitting suitable investments for the new funds.

Health Sector

Health Status

7.10   Over the last ten years Kyrgyzstan has achieved gains in the health status of children, but there is evidence that the current economic crisis and disruption of the supply of pharmaceuticals and other medical materials are causing a reversal in this trend. From 1980 to 1990 the infant mortality rate fell from 43 to 30 per thousand live births. While this rate is still among the highest in the former Soviet Republics, it is relatively low when compared to other countries of similar per capita income. The gains in the health status of children from 1980 to 1990 came from programs of immunization, prenatal care, and health and nutritional monitoring that are moderately strong in most areas of the country, with the exception of remote rural regions. More recently, infant mortality rates have increased from 27.3 in the first quarter of 1991 to 31.5 in the first quarter of 1992. Toddler (age 1 to 2) mortality rates have increased similarly. Maternal mortality has increased from 43 per 100,000 births in 1988 to 62 in 1989-90. These current declines in health status demonstrate that basic primary health care programs need to be defended on a priority basis as the health sector comes under increasing pressure during the restructuring of the economy.

Table 7-2. Demographic and Health Indicators

	1970	1980	1987	1988	1989	1990	1991
Infant Mortality[a/]	45.4	43.3	37.8	36.8	32.2	29.9	29.6
Maternal Mortality[b/]			43.0	42.6	62.0	62.0	
Total Fertility Rate			4.2	4.0	3.8	3.7	
Birth Rate	30.5	29.6	32.6	31.2	30.4	29.3	29.1
Death Rate	7.4	8.4	7.3	7.4	7.2	7.0	6.9
Life Expectancy:							
Men			64.9	64.2	64.3	64.2	
Women			71.1	71.8	72.4	72.6	

a/ per 1,000 live births
b/ per 100,000 births

7.11   Malnutrition is systematically reported as an important problem, mainly because Ministry of Health officials believe that many children and pregnant women are undernourished. There is no evidence, however, that protein energy malnutrition is highly prevalent among children under five years old or that anemia is common in pregnant women. The low birth weight rate, defined as the proportion of children weighing 2,500 grams or less at birth, is a sensitive indicator of maternal malnutrition and anemia. The low birth weight in Kyrgyzstan is six percent, a level comparable with many developed countries. The standards and definitions that scholars and health officials in Kyrgyzstan use to measure protein energy malnutrition are somewhat different form those recommended by the World Health Organization, and probably explain in part the exaggeration of the problem. The current economic crisis may lead to problems of malnutrition in some poor remote rural areas where agricultural production is not sufficient to meet the local food needs. The most important variable that can trigger problems of malnutrition would be the rate of infectious diseases in children (measles, diarrhea and acute respiratory infections), which for the time being show low to moderate levels. A separate also unmeasured problem is that of obesity among the adult population, especially women.   The crude mortality rate for cardiovascular disease (especially ischemic heart and cerebrovascular disease) is very high and is higher in women than in men, suggesting that obesity and probably high consumption of animal fat are highly prevalent risk factors.

7.12   Adult health has not improved over the last ten to fifteen years. Notwithstanding the gains in child health status, life expectancy at birth has remained stable. Age specific mortality rates increased steadily from 1986 to 1990 across all five year age cohorts from age 20 and up. The gross mortality rate for cancer has increased slightly over the last decade while the rate for circulatory diseases has fallen. Since 1970 lung cancer rates have increased by 40 percent and stomach cancer rates have fallen by 50 percent. A subsequent analysis of disease specific mortality rates by age cohort is needed to establish details of the changes in adult health.

Table 7-3. Death Rates by Cause
(per 100,000 population)

Disease Category	1980	1985	1990
Infectious and Parasitic	59	53	28
Cancer	73	75	78
Circulatory	316	339	286
Respiratory	121	107	123
Injuries	110	83	92
Total	840	810	700

7.13   Several behavioral risk factors indicate emerging problems. Tobacco use is noted as growing by MOH officials. The diet provides an important risk factor for cardiovascular disease. Meat, cooking oils and dairy products comprise more than 30 percent of dietary calories. Excessive abortions are an additional risk factor for women of reproductive ages. Abortions, although less of a problem than elsewhere in the CIS, are 50 percent of the number of births (1991). This is a high rate compared to most West European countries and reflects the low quality of available alternative methods of contraception and the need for better information and education. Finally, environmental problems are less pronounced than in other CIS countries because of the lack of industrialization, but mining dust poses a hazard to miners. Kyrgyzstan has among the highest rates of brucellosis among the CIS countries.

The Health Care System

7.14   Health services are centrally coordinated through the MOH and organized into a hierarchical referral system. Locally, within districts, services are organized around secondary hospitals of, typically, 550 beds with satellite systems of ambulatory care facilities (polyclinics) and a number of smaller hospitals of 40 to 80 beds. The smaller hospitals, which are intended to provide primary care, are the base for 3 to 4 community outreach workers who provide preventive care such as immunization, early identification of primary patients and referral.

7.15   Facilities and Curative Services. The former health system was driven by service norms such as beds per thousand, medical doctors per thousand or numbers of hospitals and polyclinics. These norms formed the basis on which performance was judged for the purposes of both planning and budgeting. The result is an excessively high hospital capacity but low quality of services. For a total population of 4.4 million in 1990 there were 265 hospitals and 36,980 beds. The number of beds per thousand population, 8.4, is comparable to or higher than that found in many West European countries.

Many of the small hospitals are of the "minimum" allowable standard before independence, with no more than 4 to 4.5 square meters per bed (a more acceptable minimum is 7 square meters). Some of the smallest hospitals have low occupancy and lack radiology services, adequate heating or water.

Table 7-4. Hospital Use, 1990

Type	Beds	Beds per 1000 Popul.	Occu-pancy Rate	Average Length of Stay
Tertiary	4375	1.0	0.87	16.1
Secondary	7130	1.6	0.86	13.3
Country-side	23675	5.3	0.75	11.9
Specialty	1800	0.4	0.69	16.5
Total	36980	8.3	0.79	12.7
Total without Specialty	35180	7.9	0.79	12.6

7.16   Occupancy rates in larger hospitals are higher, averaging nearly 87 percent in the central tertiary hospitals and 86 percent for the district secondary hospitals. Although the average lengths of stay are not long in comparison to other CIS countries they are moderately long in comparison with current practice in OECD countries, suggesting possible inefficient use. For 1991, the average length of stay was 13 days in all hospitals, and 16.1 in tertiary hospitals. There is heavy use of outpatient facilities and wide coverage with polyclinic services. Polyclinics have an average catchment area of less than 10,000.

7.17   Quality of services is limited by condition of equipment and facilities and, in some cases by poor medical practices. There is an unusually large number of injections given to children during the first 5 years of life. Hepatitis A is endemic and there have been epidemics of Hepatitis E. Disposable syringes are not readily available and sterilization of syringes and equipment is sometimes faulty. Tuberculosis is still treated in some areas using long-term therapies that have proven less cost effective than short-term outpatient therapies used in other countries. Acute respiratory illness in children is a major problem. Respiratory diseases cause over 45% of deaths in the first year of life and need to be more adequately treated at the entry level. The quality of services for both outpatient and inpatient care has been severely hampered within the last two years by a shortage of supplies and reduced funding.

7.18   Prevention. The administrative attention and resource flows to prevention have been modest. With the important exception of prenatal care and child health programs, prevention is not well integrated with curative services. Family planning and chronic disease programs remain detached and neglected.

7.19   Prenatal care and child health programs provided through clinic services reach 65 percent of the population. The remaining 35 percent of children live in areas that do not have ready access to health clinics. The intention is that children in these areas are provided immunization and nutritional monitoring services by feldshars and visiting nurses, but the variation in mortality rates across districts throws doubt on the efficacy of this coverage. In areas with good clinical coverage, maternity care after detection of pregnancy consists of a polyclinic visit once per month until delivery to monitor fetal progress and to participate in maternal training programs. Eighty percent of children are fully immunized. The quality of vaccines and the reliability of the vaccine distribution system (cold chain) has deteriorated alarmingly over the last two years.

7.20   There is a clear need for stronger nutrition programs. Eighty percent of mothers are anemic and must receive supplementary iron during pregnancy. Breast feeding is practiced for 4 months by 61 percent of mothers and 6 months by 47 percent. The Ministry of Health recognizes that nutritional and health gains could be made by increasing breast feeding. Forty to sixty percent of infants are provided supplementary food through "milk kitchens", although recently there has been difficulty in obtaining adequate food supplies for the kitchens. The effect of the kitchens is not clear, however. UNICEF suggests that the milk kitchens together with the high female labor force participation rate and insufficient motivation of mothers by the medical community are impeding breast feeding.

7.21   In spite of the good coverage and integration of prenatal care and early childhood programs, family planning programs are not well developed. The moderately high rate of abortions and high total fertility rate are measures of the failure to mount effective family planning programs. Difficulties with family planning programs involve both the low quality and quantity of contraceptive supplies and inadequate family planning education. Some of the problem with quality and acceptance of IUDs and pills may be perceived rather than actual, and indicate that better follow- up and support are needed for clients. Family planning education and information programs are not well developed either for the young or for married couples in mid-fertility ages.

7.22   Chronic disease primary prevention programs are also not well developed. As is the case with family planning, opportunities for adolescent education on the dangers of smoking and alcohol are missed. There are also no programs in factories and clinics. Cervical cancer rates, although starting from a low base, have increased by 70 percent over the last twenty years, but there are no regular programs of cervical cancer screening. The MOH would like to develop a national strategy to deal with chronic diseases and attempted to introduce a chronic disease program in 1991, but because of financial problems the program was abandoned.

7.23   Health Personnel. The number of physicians per 10,000 population increased dramatically from 25 in 1980 to 34 in 1991. This compares with 15 in the United Kingdom. This high ratio of doctors per capita is not efficiently used for the benefit of health status. In spite of the high number of doctors, the geographic distribution favors urban areas and there are an insufficient number of trained personnel, doctors or nurses, in rural areas. Medical personnel are poorly paid, well below the national average. This and poor working conditions contribute to low morale.

7.24   Doctor and nurse training is of poor quality and is in need of reform. The MOH intends to reduce the number of students admitted annually to the medical school and to alter the training schedule to include a longer post graduate internship and residency with an emphasis on quality. Higher standards should also be set for nurse training, although low pay and lack of resources make it difficult to increase the status and quality of nurses and nurse training.

7.25   Pharmaceuticals and Medical Supplies. The disruption of trade among East European and CIS countries has created severe shortages of pharmaceuticals and medical supplies. Even before the recent disruption, however, uneven quality of drugs and sporadic shortages of drugs were recurring problems. Earlier pharmaceutical contracts, previously made in rubles, are not being carried out, and there have been difficulties in agreeing on terms for new contracts for 1992. Humanitarian assistance has filled only part of the gap in pharmaceutical and equipment needs. Most of the assistance has been in commodities, some of which are inappropriate or not of high priority. Continuity of supplies and difficulties with incompatible drug registration and definitions are also important constraints on effective humanitarian assistance. Direct foreign exchange assistance would allow a higher health benefit per unit value of assistance, yet this is also hampered by Kyrgyzstan's limited experience in international pharmaceutical procurement.

Table 7-5. Health Personnel (per 10,000 population)

	1980	1985	1990	1991
Physicians	25.9	30.3	33.5	34.0
Dentists	1.5	2.2	2.8	4.5
Nurses	42.2	52.7	64.1	65.8
Pharmacists	3.5	4.0	3.9	3.8
Other	27.8	27.4	28.2	26.0

7.26   Kyrgyzstan does not produce medical equipment although it does have a plant that reconditions selected large equipment, such as X ray machines. Equipment imports for 1991 totaled R36 million, of which R4.1 million were from convertible currency countries.

7.27   Kyrgyzstan also does not produce any modern pharmaceuticals for human consumption. About two thirds of the R70 million worth of pharmaceuticals imported in 1991 were produced in the USSR. The remainder were imported, through an allocation from Moscow, from convertible currency countries. The convertible currency imports were valued at approximately $35 million.[3]

7.28   It is difficult to convert the entire ruble value of pharmaceutical imports into an equivalent dollar amount on the basis of information available because of the distorting effects of the regulated prices in the ruble area and the artificial exchange rate. Approximately, however, the total value of pharmaceutical consumption appears to have been about $25 per capita, which is moderately high given Kyrgyzstan's income level. UNICEF has made an estimate of the value of priority pharmaceuticals needed to keep primary health care functioning. They estimate the annual cost of supplies for primary

Table 7-6. Trade in Modern Pharmaceuticals (mln rbl)

	1990	1991
Trade in Convertible Currency Area:[a]		
Exports	0.0	0.0
Imports	20.1	22.9
Trade in Ruble Area:		
Exports	0.0	0.0
Imports	43.9	47.0
Total Trade:		
Exports	0.0	0.0
Imports	64.0	69.9
Trade Balance	-64.0	-69.9

a/ converted using 1 US$ = 0.6 rubles.

---

3.   It is not clear whether an appropriate conversion rate was used.

health care, including basic institutional needs and preventive care, to be $3 million, or less than $1 per capita.[4]

7.29   The MOH is interested in developing the pharmaceutical and medical supply industries. Although there is no modern pharmaceutical capacity, about R10 million worth of herbal medicines are produced annually in Kyrgyzstan. Veterinary medicines are also produced. The MOH has identified factory space for the development of a pharmaceutical plant but has not studied the question further. They have also contemplated a syringe plant but note that Uzbekistan and Kazakhstan already have capacity for this and want to coordinate their effort.

7.30   The distribution of pharmaceuticals is a state monopoly. Drugs are provided free of charge to hospital inpatients. Outpatient prescription drugs are sold through retail pharmacies. There are 428 pharmacies which, with an average of 10,000 people each, provide a moderately good coverage of the population. Hospitals distribute about one third of all drugs (by ruble value) with the remaining two thirds sold through pharmacies. Prices for drugs, at both the wholesale and retail levels, are kept artificially low and do not reflect the costs of production, imports, or distribution. The artificially low prices have led perennially to over-prescription and misuse and there have been episodic shortages of individual drugs even prior to the current acute shortages.

7.31   Health Finance. Health care is primarily financed from the government budget. Additionally, there are some private expenditures on drugs and other health care goods. Out of the total expenditures on health care in 1990, 11 percent came from the central budget, 76 percent from the local budget, and 12 percent from private expenditures. The government contribution represented about 3.9 percent of GDP and the private contribution about 0.8 percent of private household consumption. Total health expenditures, public and private, equal about 4.4 percent of GDP. By comparison, the percentage of GDP spent on health in 1987 was an average of 7.3 for OECD countries. The very low percentage spent on health in Kyrgyzstan is partly attributable to the low wages in the health sector and low controlled prices of supplies, but it is also due to a low real level of expenditure in the health sector.

7.32   Under central planning the real level of resources available had been fairly constant until recently. However, the actual value of real expenditures in 1991 declined, because unanticipated price increases were not fully compensated by budget supplements, but expenditure data giving a measure of the decline are not yet available. The fall in resources has been accompanied by lower quality of services, supply shortages, postponed maintenance, and lower real wages.

7.33   In 1990 and 1991 about 10 percent of central and local state health expenditures were for drugs and medical supplies and 5 percent for equipment, the preponderance of which were produced outside of Kyrgyzstan and imported at controlled prices. About 50 percent of total expenditures were used for salaries and the remaining 40 percent for a variety of items such as food, laundry, uniforms and utilities that are primarily of local origin. The percentage of total expenditures allocated to drugs and medical supplies can be expected to grow in the future. Based on the experience of other countries, as an increasing proportion of drugs and supplies begins to reflect world prices the percentage of total health expenditures allocated to drugs and supplies will rise to 30 percent or more. This process has already begun in 1992, with an increase in the drugs share to 21 percent and a fall in wages to 26 percent. In

---

4.   The Government's own list of essential pharmaceuticals is more extensive and amounts to considerably more than this figure.

Table 7.7: Recurrent Health Expenditures by Source, 1988-1992 (mln rbl)

Source of Revenue	1988	1989	1990	1991	1992 Budget[a]
Central Budget	29.4	32.6	41.8	74.3	374.2
Local Budget	204.9	224.6	280.2	495.2	1908.7
Total Budgetary	234.3	257.2	322.0	569.5	2282.9
Enterprises	1.1	1.4	1.3	2.1	30.0
Total Governmental	235.4	258.6	323.3	571.6	2312.9
Total State as % of GDP	3.4	3.4	3.9	3.4	NA
Private Expenditures: Fee for Services	7.8	9.1	10.0	NA	25.6
Optics	1.3	1.4	1.4	NA	2.2
Drugs	26.3	28.3	33.2	NA	98.7
Total Private	35.4	38.8	44.6	NA	126.5
Total (State + Private)	270.8	297.4	367.9	NA	2439.4

a/ As of March 1992

addition to the increased foreign exchange burden, if the level of services is to remain constant the share of health expenditures in GDP will have to increase and substantial domestic growth will have to occur or the real wage in health will have to decrease further. Health workers are, however, already among the lowest paid state employees.

7.34   In a search for new sources of funds and incentives for improved health services, the Government is considering a possible restructuring of the health sector. A bill in parliamentary committee, possibly to be considered in early summer of 1992, would provide for the creation of an insurance fund to be financed partly through employer payments and partly through the government budget. The insurance fund would pay for services provided at controlled reimbursement rates through quasi-competitive clinics and secondary providers.

Table 7-8. Recurrent Government Health Expenditures by Line Item Percent

Item	1990	1991	1992 Budget
Wages	51	46	26
Food	9	10	22
Drugs	12	8	21
Equipment	5	5	1
Capital Repairs	5	5	1
Other Expenditures	18	26	29
Total Recurrent	100	100	100

Source: Ministry of Finance

7.35   The functioning of the proposed system is illustrated by Figure 7.1. An estimated 45 to 55 percent of the insurance fund would be derived from payments, in actuality a form of tax on enterprises, farmers and the self-employed. The enterprise payment would be a percentage of wages, perhaps 8 to 13 percent, and payments from farmers and self-employed would be based on their income or revenues. The remaining 45 to 55 percent of the insurance fund would come from the government budget to cover medical care for pensioners, unemployed, the poor, and children. Finally, training, investment for institutional improvements or expansion, and public health would be funded from the general government budget.

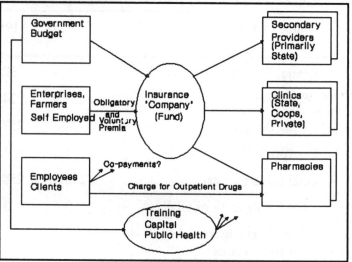

Figure 7-1. Flow of Funds in the Proposed Health Financing System

7.36   Supplementary voluntary insurance premia could be paid by enterprises or individuals to obtain additional care not covered by the insurance fund. It is not clear whether co-payments would be required from patients. Because of the tradition of free medical care, the introduction of co-payments could be resisted politically. It is probable, however, that charges for outpatient drugs obtained through pharmacies will continue.

7.37   Many details of the proposed system have not been worked out. The institutional arrangements for collecting premia, the setting of charges from service providers, billing arrangements, and quality assurance will provide special institutional problems. Help with implementation is being sought, or tentatively offered, from several bilateral sources.

Issues and Recommendations

7.38   <u>Pharmaceuticals</u>. Pharmaceutical shortages are the most pressing problem facing the health sector. The problem has both a short run aspect, related to the collapse of previous trade relationships within the former USSR and CMEA, and a long run aspect, related to the failure of the centrally planned production and distribution of pharmaceuticals to provide market clearing quantities of drugs at the managed prices. There is no obvious solution to the short run problem except direct international aid and foreign exchange assistance. The UNICEF estimate of $3 million to provide pharmaceuticals and supplies for basic care is a minimum level of support for the system. Even that level of support will mean that complementary inputs for higher level institutional care will be lacking.

7.39   Efficient pharmaceutical procurement is needed to complement any donor foreign exchange assistance for pharmaceuticals. Because prior to 1992 arrangements for imports were made through Moscow, Kyrgyzstan has not previously participated in the international market for pharmaceuticals. International pharmaceutical markets are especially complex and Bank studies and projects in several other countries have demonstrated the savings possible from efficient procurement.

UNICEF or another international organization with procurement capacity should be asked to collaborate with the Kyrgyzstan Pharmacy in pharmaceutical procurement.

7.40   Although foreign exchange is the most pressing constraint on pharmaceuticals, the real value of the health budget is also a constraint. The importance of the constraint is demonstrated by the forced increase in the share of the budget allocated to pharmaceuticals, from 8 percent in 1991 to 21 percent in 1992, as internal pharmaceutical prices start to reflect global prices. In the absence of any increase in the real value of the budget, the increased share used for pharmaceuticals will force a reduction in the allocation to other essential items such as maintenance and wages. Any additional availability of foreign exchange for pharmaceuticals should be at least matched by a comparable increase in the real value of the health budget.

7.41   Longer run adjustments in pharmaceuticals will require liberalization of trade, prices and distribution. Price liberalization should be undertaken so that retail prices reflect true wholesale, transportation and sales costs. The government should consider privatizing pharmaceutical retail sales. Pharmacists should be allowed to add additional, non drug items, such as cosmetics and toiletry items, to enhance sales. Privatization of pharmacies could be done first on a pilot basis in selected districts. Whether or not existing state pharmacies are converted to private status, the independent growth of private pharmacies should not be inhibited.

7.42   Health Service Mix. The stringent budget for health requires the selection of priority programs for support. Infant and maternal health programs, short-term therapy for tuberculosis, and basic care for respiratory diseases should continue to be supported as a first priority. Particular attention should be directed to improve the availability and quality of contraceptives and provide better access and motivation for contraception to allow couples safer and more effective control over their fertility.

7.43   In the longer term, the curative care bias of the health system is a major issue. The lack of growth of life expectancy over the last two decades and high risk behavior of the adult population provide evidence of the need for vigorous efforts to mount effective prevention programs. Impediments to this lie not only with inadequate financing for prevention but, more fundamentally, with a lack of program strategy, lack of integration of preventive programs within the health care system, inadequate training of medical staff, and insufficient national leadership and commitment in this area.

7.44   A recommended start for a revamped program of prevention would be the development of a national strategy for prevention. With regard to some crucial elements of such a strategy, WHO has formal programs of assistance for the development of (a) National Cancer Strategies, and (b) National Tobacco Control Programs; other international agencies can provide effective assistance for the development of a family planning strategy. Additional concerns are the environment, diet, alcohol and accidents. All of these elements of a program need to be tied together through an encompassing and coherent national strategy for prevention that provides coordination with primary health care, education and industry.

7.45   Health Service Efficiency. The low level of financial resources available for health care creates a special need for the system to function efficiently. Unfortunately, the past emphasis on a high ratio of beds and medical doctors per capita has led to a dispersal of limited resources over an unnecessarily large number of facilities that is constraining the efficiency of health care services. Low occupancy rates in smaller facilities, and moderately high lengths of stay in all levels of facilities are indicators of inefficiency. In addition, poor physical condition of facilities and lack of equipment compromise quality.

7.46   Existing resources could be used more effectively if the MOH would accelerate the closing of small hospitals within the next one to three years, converting some to ambulatory clinics or other social uses. A reduced number of hospitals and hospital beds, together with a shorter length of stay, will allow a better concentration of resources to achieve a higher quality of services. Finally, the government's efforts to reduce the number of doctors trained and increase the quality of training and pre-graduation clinical experience are strongly supported. Medical training should promote a shorter length of stay, better use of pharmaceuticals, and greater emphasis on preventive care for all age groups.

7.47   As part of the effort to increase the efficiency of hospital resource use, the length of stay should be reduced. Reducing the length of stay involves several complex changes that will require an organized program, supported by appropriate financing incentives. The burden of caring for long term chronic disease patients should be increasingly shifted to other social programs and non-hospital institutions. The lengths of time between admission, diagnosis and treatment should be reduced by improved scheduling. Greater emphasis should be placed on rehabilitation at home. Perhaps most importantly, medical training should be altered to reflect modern treatment practices that rely on shorter hospital stays and recovery at home.

7.48   <u>Health Financing</u>. The government needs to undertake a more careful examination of the practical problems involved in implementing the proposed health financing system. The health financing system being considered has a number of features that, under more favorable institutional and economic conditions, would be desirable. The design of the system could allow a clear separation between finance and provision of care. The use of competitive providers could increase the efficiency and quality of services. The arrangements for disadvantaged groups could contribute to greater equity in the distribution of care.

7.49   Unfortunately, the system being contemplated requires the development of supporting institutions, including a functioning banking system, capital markets, a stable currency, and contract and property law, if it is to be implemented successfully. These institutions do not exist and it may be several years before they are sufficiently developed to facilitate the contemplated changes in the structure of the health financing system.

7.50   An additional issue with the proposed system involves the extent to which a payroll tax should be used as a source of funds. The current experience in OECD countries suggests that the public budget is a more equitable and also a more efficient (in the sense of not affecting employer labor market decisions) source of funds. It would contribute to equity and the stability of the system to continue to finance the greater part of health care from the public budget. Given the separation of financing and provision of care under the proposed reforms, this would not preclude the use of competitive providers.

7.51   It is recommended that the adoption of the proposed insurance law be postponed until the experience of reform in other countries can be studied and technical assistance in designing an appropriate system is obtained. It is also recommend that the appropriate design and rate adoption of reforms be tied to changes in other sectors. Health financing reform should lag, not lead, other changes in the structure of the economy.

7.52   In the interim, greater use should be made of patient fees. The share of private spending on health care is very low and there is scope for significant use of fees for both inpatient and outpatient care. Based on consumption patterns in other countries, 3 to 5 percent of household income could be sustained using fees and co-payments for insured services for both ambulatory and inpatient care. A system of charges could be adopted providing for full cost of optional amenities and modest payments for inpatient bed days, inpatient drugs, and outpatient visits. Exemptions should be made for the unemployed and low income groups.

Education and Vocational Training

Status and Recent Trends

7.53   A generally strong education system and a satisfactory supply of educated and trained people are among Kyrgyzstan's most valuable assets. However, the quality of education is now impaired as a result of severe shortages of textbooks, notebooks and other supplies. These shortages are aggravated by the lack of any domestic procurement organization.

7.54   Higher education, specialized middle education, and vocational training are experiencing shocks associated with the impending creation of a market economy. Jobs can no longer be guaranteed to graduates; prospective earnings and numbers of people likely to be offered jobs in each field have become highly uncertain; returns from education have fallen as real wages fall, though wage differentials can be expected to grow in a market economy; first-year enrollments in many fields have dropped dramatically; and new courses and career specialties are needed. The new political situation is responsible for other shifts such as surging demand for training in Kyrgyz language and literature, plunging demand for Russian language and literature, and apparent readiness to close down higher education in physical culture and sports.

Combined enrollments as of November 1991 was 1.1 million, as follows (in thousands):

	Day Enrollment	Total Enrollment
General education	948.3	961.3
Vocational training	27.9	50.5
Specialized middle education	32.1	42.7
Higher education	40.5	<u>58.3</u>
Total		1112.8

7.55   In required general education, about 61 percent of the pupils are taught at present in the Kyrgyz language, 26 percent in Russian, 12 percent in Uzbek and a small number in Tajik. The Kyrgyz schools on average are much smaller than the others and more scattered. Textbooks for all but the Kyrgyz schools are bought in other republics.

Expenditure Trends

7.56   Most of cost of general education is borne by local governments at the oblast, rayon and locality levels. Responsibility for the other types of education is divided: The Ministry of National Education operates 10 of 12 institutions of higher education and 15 of 48 institutions of specialized middle education; several other ministries and departments have their own training institutions; and the State Committee for Training runs the 115 establishments for vocational training (trade schools).

7.57   The share of education in GDP declined to about 7 percent in 1991 from nearly 8 percent in 1990; it is estimated that spending on required general education per school-age child declined in real terms by about 20 percent in 1991 and must have fallen further in the first half of 1992. Teacher salaries have also fallen in real terms. In February 1992, teachers at lower grade levels earned an average of R556 and by the end of March average full-time pay in education and training was barely over half the average pay of an industrial worker. Draconian cuts in real expenditure are occurring for investment, purchases of school supplies and repairs.

7.58   In response to the budget squeeze the share of education and training expenditures going to wages and salaries fell from about half in 1990 to less than one third in the 1992 budget projected in January (Table 7-9). While the share of the food budget (mainly school lunches) rose sharply, funding apparently has not been sufficient to prevent a decline in quality.

7.59   Some further budgetary savings are now being projected in education, primarily through fees and user charges. These have already been introduced in most day-care centers and kindergartens, some evening classes, and one or two higher institutions, such as the music academy. Cost savings are also expected from the recent action of making the tenth and eleventh years of schooling optional partly to ease local budgets, and from closing selected institutions, as well as cost savings of a sort from declining enrollments.

Priorities and proposals

7.60   The Ministry of National Education is preparing farsighted proposals such as satellite television broadcasts to upgrade education in the mountainous republic and regular use of computers at every level of schooling. Currently, however, the Ministry considers the highest priority to be paper and printing supplies to publish new textbooks in Kyrgyz. One purpose is to transform the political, social and ideological content of schooling and bring books up to date. However, any action related to the language of instruction and business is politically sensitive. Textbooks in each language are distributed free of charge but must be returned to the school at the end of the year. They are used by a succession of young people and become battered long before they are retired, normally after four years. Printing and paper costs have soared while printing facilities are run down and inadequate.

Table 7-9. Expenditures on Education and Training (except Preschool and On-the-Job Training in Enterprises) 1990 to 1992 (Percent Shares)

Category	1990	1991	1992 Budget[a/]	Share from Local Government Budget, 1992
Wages and salaries	49.4	45.4	31.8	85
Fees on payroll	3.4	10.7	12.1	85
Food	4.0	7.5	18.6	82
Stipends for students	6.4	9.1	6.7	30
Purchase of supplies and equipment	4.4	3.0	1.0	62
Capital investment	12.5	3.5	2.4	80
Major repairs	4.3	3.9	1.3	77
Other expenditures	15.7	16.7	26.1	71
Total	100.0	100.0	100.0	77
Memo item: Value in million rubles	644	1111	4231	

Source: Ministry of Economy and Finance.
a/ Including both Central and Local Government.

Vocational Training

7.61   Training and retraining are expected to be important as one way of countering unemployment. Training in a wide variety of occupational specialties takes place in specialized middle schools. In the vocational training establishments, training is provided in 185 occupations, and at least 25,000 trainees finish successfully each year. The vocational training schools mainly train for large industrial enterprises, construction and transport. In the future, however, they will increasingly need to train for the service sectors and the unemployed.

Recommendations

7.62   a)   The share of education in GDP should be protected to at least the 7 percent level reached in 1991.

        b)   School supplies and teaching materials should be given high priority and greatly increased shares of the budget. Much more money is required for these purposes to reverse the recent fall in the quality of schooling.

        c)   Until and unless private firms fully take over the procurement of school supplies, the Ministry of National Education ought to take the lead in launching a suitable organization for this purpose, preferably in the form of an enterprise that could eventually be privatized.

d)   Textbooks in the Kyrgyz language for schools now teaching in that language are indeed required, and a strong start ought to be made quickly in publishing suitable new textbooks. However, in such a small country, widespread fluency in Russian and English, and perhaps in other foreign languages as well, will be essential for many reasons, not least to strengthen the supply of engineers, applied scientists and other technical people essential for development. The issue of languages in the schools calls for a multi-language answer.

e)   Energetic actions are needed particularly in higher and specialized middle education to introduce new courses and career specialties much needed in a market economy, such as business, management, accounting, commercial and contract law, marketing, finance and banking. A vocational training course has been started in entrepreneurship, but here, other new courses would also be useful. Courses that now exist would almost certainly benefit from Western and East Asian experience not only in regard to methods of training, but also in regard to the occupational specialties most needed as the economy is transformed.

f)   To increase pressures to introduce relevant new courses to meet the demand, educational institutions' budgets ought to be changed systematically in proportion to their enrollments, and they should have ample notice in advance that this will happen.

g)   More use needs to be made of cost recovery, especially in higher education and optional middle education. While students in some much needed specialties such as applied science and engineering should probably be kept on free tuition and stipends, those in many other fields should almost certainly be shifted to a system of tuition fees, scholarships and loans. And while free school lunches are justified in some settings, in others it is probably desirable to begin to charge all except the poorest students for school lunches.

h)   It is highly desirable to allow at least the optional purchase of textbooks as well as notebooks, paper and other school supplies, not so much for cost recovery as to improve students' school performance.

PART III

Sectoral Reforms

A vigorous supply response in key productive sectors will be needed to promote economic recovery. Corresponding improvements in infrastructure are required to support the adjustments in the real economy, and more broadly, the emerging requirements of a market economy. Part III of this report focuses on those sectors that will be particularly important in the generation of economic recovery, and for which policy adjustments are most pressing. The structure and reform issues in agriculture, energy, mining and metallurgy are addressed in Chapter 8, while Chapter 9 provides an assessment of key issues in infrastructure related to telecommunications, transport and the environment.

CHAPTER 8

The Productive Sectors

Agriculture

Overview

8.01   Kyrgyzstan's agriculture has been organized with the state controlling most productive assets under a system of state and collective farms, with marketing through state orders, fixed prices and a state marketing system. However, reform was initiated in 1991 and now about 11,000 private farms (privatized from 83 state and collective farms) control 10 percent of the arable land. Farm privatization was suspended during the 1992 cropping season but is now resuming with a target to privatize 144 of the remaining 464 state and collective farms before the 1993 season begins. The structure of production reflects the regional specialization developed in the former USSR to promote interdependence among the republics. Recent disruptions in interrepublican trade and terms of trade deterioration from the initial phase of price liberalization (reflecting prior subsidization of inputs) caused severe shocks that are expected to require important changes in patterns of production in order to ensure the viability of the sector. The policy challenge is to guide the transition in a manner that is sensitive to short-term concerns regarding shortages and profitability, but that does not detract from the objective of restructuring production to exploit Kyrgyzstan's comparative advantages under international prices within the framework of a market-oriented economy and private ownership.

8.02   Agriculture in the Economy. Agriculture has accounted for about one third of GDP in recent years and a similar share in employment if labor in private plots is included. Its share in GDP fell to 28 percent in 1991, reflecting last year's 9 percent decline in agricultural output and a terms of trade deterioration (see paras 8.05, 8.06 and 8.08). The proportion of the average consumer basket spent on food increased from 30 percent in 1980 to 36 percent in 1991 and is reported to be up to 50 percent or more in 1992.

8.03   Processing and distribution is the weakest link in the sector. The facilities remain highly centralized and state controlled. And the low priority on improving the food processing and distribution industries has resulted in old, outdated or poorly maintained equipment and technologies. Standards and quality control are not considered priorities. The retail outlets of state stores are small and poorly equipped, with no effort devoted to promote sales and now with few goods to offer. Private markets are marginally better supplied, but are also poorly equipped and maintained. Losses are high and many products are of poor quality. The very limited capacity in food processing restricts the availability of many products to the growing season.

8.04   The institutional framework currently in place is not geared for the requirements of a market economy. Ministries have been heavily involved in production activities and have very limited capacity to take a new role in guiding the sector during a transition period. It is evident that one of the fundamental requirements for the successful implementation of an economic reform program will be a program to restructure the existing administration towards a more regulatory role. This will require a major effort by the government to appropriately reorder and refocus its administrative structure and to redefine the roles of the various ministries and committees. It must also support staff training and allocate adequate financial resources, particularly during the transition period when the implementation of reforms will depend heavily on a functioning public sector.

8.05   Crop Production. The volume of crop output remained roughly constant from 1985 through 1990, but dropped by 16 percent in 1991. Preliminary data indicate a production increase over the 1985-1990 average in 1992. Increases in crop procurement prices during 1991 were substantially larger than those for livestock products so that the value of crop output at current prices rose from 37 percent of total agricultural output in 1990 to 47 percent in 1991. The arable land area covers 1.4 million ha, of which 1.07 million is irrigated. In 1992 about 47 percent of the sown area was allocated to fodder production, basically unchanged since 1986. About 46 percent of the area was allocated to grain production, of which 43 percent is wheat, 45 percent barley and about 10 percent corn. Average grain yields in irrigated areas are close to 3 MT/ha. Technical crops were produced on about 5 percent of the arable land in 1992, or 59,000 ha, of which cotton accounted for 36 percent and tobacco 35 percent. Potatoes, fruit and vegetables are produced on the remaining 6 percent of arable land. Fodder output declined slightly between the late 1980s and 1991-92. Over the same period, grain output fell by about 5 percent to 1.6 million MT despite a slight increase in the area under production. Cotton output has fluctuated substantially in recent years and was 23 percent lower in 1991 compared to the record harvest of 81,000 tons in 1990. Tobacco production also showed a drop of about 22 percent in 1991 but is expected to recover to late 1980s levels in 1992. (Annex Table 6-2).

8.06   Livestock Production. The livestock sector accounted for almost two thirds of the value of agricultural output until 1990, declining to 53 percent in 1991 as a result of the relative price increases for crop output. Production of mutton, beef, milk and wool (together more than 80 percent of livestock output) increased until 1989 as part of the USSR production strategy. But, in the 1990s the apparent production trend has been down. During the first quarter of 1992, state sector production of meats declined by 21 percent, milk by 28 percent and eggs by 11 percent; reflecting the rapid distribution of livestock to private owners.[1] Livestock productivity in the state sector also has stagnated and is now about half of West European levels. Average milk yields of 2,300 liters/cow and feed conversion ratios of 8-10:1 are indicative of the problems. Contributing factors have been serious shortages of protein feed and animal vaccines. Adjustments underway would reduce the livestock sector to a sustainable level and improve its overall performance. A program to reduce the size of the sector began in 1989, and livestock numbers have since decreased at an accelerated pace, mainly due to a lack of profitability and increasing shortages of feed. Between 1989 and 1991, the population of sheep declined form 10.5 to 9.5 million, and of pigs from 0.44 to 0.35 million, while the cattle herd remained fairly stable at 1.1 million. Most of the country's 8 million ha of natural grazing land is in a degraded status, pastures and grasslands are not well maintained, fodder output is declining, and there is significant scope to improve the quantity and quality of roughage produced. However, given resource endowments, in particular substantial grazing lands that are appropriate for small ruminants, the current emphasis on intensive livestock production needs to be reassessed in the context of forthcoming market conditions.

8.07   Outlook. The structure of state and collective farms and, to a lesser extent, agribusiness enterprises has begun to undergo a fundamental reform process. Different forms of ownership are emerging and have to compete in an unstable environment. The agricultural sector is expected to

---

1.   It is unclear to what extent the state sector productions declines have been compensated by private production, or if the reluctance of state and collective farms to deliver products to state outlets at controlled prices magnified the estimation of declines.

experience contraction in the short term, primarily reflecting input shortages and a terms of trade deterioration. As input prices approach international levels, greater efficiency in input use will become necessary. Output prices also have begun to adjust to market conditions as government intervention is reduced significantly, except in a few critical commodities. As a consequence, there will be major shifts in the structure and composition of both crop and livestock sectors. Kyrgyzstan's comparative advantages will most likely be in extensive, rather than intensive livestock production, as well as in a range of high value technical crops in the irrigated areas. Livestock numbers will have to be further reduced to an ecologically and economically sustainable level.

Core Issues of Reform

8.08   Incentive Structure. During 1990, the Government's procurement prices for grain were doubled while prices for other crops were increased only moderately. In March 1991, prices for other crops were increased on average by about 250 percent, while the price of grain increased only slightly -- perhaps in an effort to hold down the consumer price of bread. In early 1992, state procurement prices were again raised substantially -- by 5-8 times for most crops and livestock products. However, state prices for farm equipment and inputs increased by a factor of 12-25, resulting in a substantial terms of trade deterioration. With the previous year's harvest having largely been sold at the old prices, farmers have had few crops to barter and are hence unable to invest in machinery and equipment, and effective demand for even the most basic inputs such as fertilizer and pesticides has been reduced to a minimum.

8.09   Although prices for agricultural products were ostensibly freed in 1992, about one-half of production is still purchased through the state order system at negotiated prices determined by administrators on both sides of the table and fixed for periods ranging from 10 days to a year, depending on the product. The leverage of the state and collective farms in this negotiation process is dubious, particularly since they depend on the state for input deliveries. Although the state order system is to be eliminated at end-1992, the state will remain the major buyer of many products and will retain substantial control through its ownership of storage and processing facilities.

8.10   After the initial program of partial price liberalization, in April the Government committed to an Emergency Program of policies in several subsectors to maintain for 2-3 years central allocation of inputs and output, and controls over production, trade, processing and pricing. Associated with increased prices for deliveries at or above the contracted amounts, are rights to subsidized inputs and equipment as well as access to scarce products such as sugar and cooking oil. The Program also contains incentives for grain, milk and meat production in the form of increased prices and subsidized energy. Wheat procurement prices result in a consumer subsidy of nearly two percent of GDP. However, such prices remain a fraction of world prices converted using the market exchange rate.[2] It is difficult to assess how these prices would compare with international prices due to the difficulty of selecting the appropriate exchange rate and the lack of information on transport costs to Kyrgyzstan.

8.11   Government intervention in production and pricing embodied in the Emergency Program responds to the dual concerns of loss of profitability and an uncertain outlook for imports such as wheat. However, there are several difficulties with the adopted approach. The combination of input subsidies and procurement prices needed to induce greater output is not compatible with available fiscal resources

---

2.   The Government's procurement price for the lowest grade of soft wheat was set at R10,000 per MT for the 1992 season. The prices for the highest grades of soft and durum wheat were R24,680 and R29,790 per MT respectively.

unless prices at the retail level are substantially raised. Special input subsidies perpetuate the distorted incentive structure in agriculture, do not promote efficiency in input use, and are likely to maintain production that is inefficient. Finally, as a strategy, an "Emergency Program" that commits to maintaining the various controls for a period extending over several years conveys the wrong signal, if the Government's intention is to continue to explore solutions to transitional problems within a market oriented framework.

8.12   Private Sector Development. In late 1990, the authorities embarked on a program of restructuring and privatizing state and collective farms. Loss-making farms in particular were encouraged to reorganize their ownership and management structure. Initially, the program met with limited success, with only two state farms comprising 600 families privatized by November 1991. To speed up the process, a decree was issued in November 1991 to facilitate and further encourage privatization. By July 1992, some 83 state and collective farms were restructured, resulting in about 11,000 private farms, cooperatives and small collectives, and covering about 10 percent of arable land. Three percent of the cattle, 12 percent of sheep, 5 percent of horses and less than 1 percent of the poultry and pig stock had also been transferred to private farms or cooperatives. (Higher shares of livestock were already in private hands.)[3]

8.13   Land privatization in early 1992 led to serious disputes regarding ethnic issues of land distribution. Coupled with the growing discontent over high input prices and shortages in input availability for private farmers, this resulted in growing opposition to the privatization program. As a consequence of the increasing pressure, particularly from state and collective farm representatives, and in order not to risk further disruptions to the spring cropping effort, the privatization program was temporarily suspended as of March 20, 1992. As harvest draws to a close the program is being reactivated, with about one-third of the remaining state and collective farms scheduled for privatization before the 1993 crop season begins.

8.14   To compound the privatization problems, the Emergency Program also involves the preferential allocation of critical resources (inputs, credit, spare parts) to state and collective farms during the next 2-3 years. This development will jeopardize the successful evolution of private farms, which are already at the mercy of the state sector with regard to input supplies and spare parts. They have virtually no access to credit and support services and have to sell their products mainly to state monopolies for processing. Privatization in agroprocessing, marketing and storage has been insignificant to date and is expected to proceed slowly. Privatization of wholesale trade in the food sector is also at an early stage. Wholesale purchases of inputs, rather than their allocation through a set plan, is a prerequisite for a market oriented sector. So far, only very limited and small scale private retail sales and distribution entities are in place. The Government has indicated that the privatization program will be continued, but that there will be a critical assessment of the performance of the private sector,[4] and

---

3.   About 40 percent of Kyrgyzstan's vegetables and half of its potatoes are produced on private plots. In addition, over half of milk cows and poultry, and one third of sheep are privately held.

4.   While much of private output is accounted for in government statistics because marketing is through official channels, labor spent on the intensive production on these private lands and plots is not accounted for officially. Hence, labor productivity in agriculture is exaggerated in the official statistics. It is also rumored that substantial amounts of inputs are diverted to these private plots. Substantial reorganization of data collection and presentation would therefore be necessary to assess the precise role of private production in agriculture.

a testing of whether the problems related to land distribution can be resolved. In particular, the Government plans to implement land privatization on a pilot basis in the Naryn and Talas provinces.

8.15   Agricultural Marketing and Processing. The State dominates the food processing and distribution sectors. There is considerable inefficiency and fundamental changes are needed to reduce product losses, improve product quality and increase the variety of food for consumers. These changes should entail a program for the state to reduce its role in these sectors and for the private sector to gradually assume a dominant role in food and input marketing, agricultural services and agroindustry. This program must be designed and implemented in such a manner as to have a minimum adverse impact on food supply.

8.16   A critical marketing issue relates to the system of state contract purchases with negotiated prices that will replace state orders on January 1, 1993. With a cost plus pricing framework the state order system has encouraged inefficient production and, by tying input supplies to participation in the system, distortions and inefficiencies in input marketing. The new contract purchase system should greatly improve marketing efficiency, but only if effective markets, with competition, evolve quickly and state marketing coercion through linkages with provision of subsidized in puts in also ended. A related problem is managers who are ill equipped to deal with the decision making processes and risk management tools of a market economy; collective ownership of plants does not appear to promote such behavior either. The regulatory environment and routine financial procedures are also not conducive to responsible management. Financial statements are not kept in conformity with accepted accounting practices which would make privatization, joint ventures with foreign companies or attracting foreign investors difficult. Finally, the breakdown of prior trading and payments mechanisms has led to heavy reliance on inefficient barter exchanges.

Further Policy Issues

8.17   Trade. Excluding energy imports, and using the prevailing domestic prices in the former USSR, the agricultural and agroindustrial sectors exhibited an overall trade surplus in 1991 of R622 million notwithstanding a deficit of R840 million on agricultural trade outside the USSR (Tables 8-1 and 8-2). The volume of such trade with the rest of the world was highly skewed (a negligible 0.2 percent of exports but 22 percent of imports in 1991) and was largely confined to imports of tropical products, primarily raw sugar. Most imports from the rest of the world were procured through Moscow, hence there is very little exposure to external trade. Union trade was much higher in agricultural commodities, but in common with other interrepublican trade is likely to undergo substantial contraction and reorientation with the emerging adjustments in relative prices.

8.18   Some of the salient characteristics of agricultural trade in 1991 indicate the importance of wool as a major export item, with a net export value of R1.1 billion, and wheat as a critical import, with net imports of R187 million for 538,000 MT, equivalent to about 40 percent of domestic consumption. (In 1992 however, wheat imports were reduced to a minimum as wheat production increased substantially due to excellent rainfall and other climatic conditions.) While agricultural equipment is a net export item, tractors are a major import. Furthermore, the major agricultural equipment industry produces fodder harvesting and baling machines, and severe disruptions in imports of machine tools and new materials in 1992 are adversely affecting both exports and domestic machinery availability.

8.19   The disruption of established interrepublican trade links has caused the Government to react with a set of measures aimed at restricting key exports through quotas and licenses. For example, a portion of wool exports is restricted for barter for plant protection chemicals. Along with these, the Emergency Program proposes to promote import substitution in food production, though without a thorough assessment of comparative advantage. Such policies are likely to have adverse and unforeseen effects on production and product availability.

Table 8-1. Kyrgyzstan - Total Agricultural and Agroindustrial Trade in 1991 (mln rbl)

	Inflow	Outflow	Balance
Mineral fertilizers	123.1	0.0	(123.1)
Tractors and agri. machines	131.5	209.7	78.2
Food/fodder industrial equip.	6.6	28.7	22.0
Wool products	316.3	1,450.8	1,134.5
Other textile products	907.4	418.8	(488.6)
Leather and fur products	172.6	31.1	(141.5)
Sugar products	449.5	472.8	23.3
Tobacco products	27.5	718.8	691.3
Other food industry products	471.6	135.7	(335.9)
Wheat and barley	259.3	0.4	(258.9)
Maize	66.2	0.3	(65.9)
Vegetables and fruits	49.3	125.1	75.8
Other crops	23.5	41.9	18.4
Livestock products	24.8	17.4	(7.4)
Total	3,029.2	3,651.5	622.3

Table 8-2. Kyrgyzstan - Agricultural and Agroindustrial Trade Outside USSR in 1991 (mln rbl)[a]

	Imports	Exports	Balance
Tractors and agricultural machines	1.2	1.2	
Tea	41.8		(41.8)
Wool products	0.3	1.8	1.5
Leather and fur products	58.7	0.6	(58.1)
Raw Sugar	428.4		(428.4)
Wheat	79.0		(79.0)
Maize	64.9		(64.9)
Other grains	81.8		(81.8)
Honey		2.0	2.0
Raw Leather		1.1	1.1
Total	847.2	6.7	(840.5)

a/ These amounts are included in Table 8-1.

8.20   Credit Policies. Under the command structure in agriculture, rural finance was essentially a mechanism to distribute funds advanced by the state to the state and collective farms. Agroprombank had no deposit mobilization function, no leverage on interest rates, no influence in the assessment of credit needs (which was determined by local authorities) and, of course, there was no evaluation of credit applications for economic feasibility or risk. Within the framework of the proposed Emergency Program, the NBK has been directed to provide subsidized credit to the agricultural sector. If such subsidies are retained, they should explicitly appear on and be financed through and within the limits of the budget.

8.21   A parastatal Farmers' Bank has been established to serve mainly farmers and small agricultural trade and processing firms. However, it has extremely limited funds (R58 million) available for lending and is unlikely to have any useful impact, or even survive unless it gets massive and concessionary financial support. This is probably not justified on either economic or privatization grounds.

8.22   Water Resources and Allocation. Kyrgyzstan is endowed with abundant water resources flowing downstream through the four other states of Central Asia and the Xinjiang province of China. Of the 47.5 billion m³ average annual flow, the former Soviet Union allocated 11.5 billion m³ to Kyrgyzstan. This allocation is apparently still endorsed by the five states of Central Asia. Out of the Kyrgyzstan allocation, 5.3 billion m³ originate from the Amu Darya and Syr Darya, thus representing only 4 percent of the average annual flow of these two rivers. Any program to improve efficiency of water resources in Kyrgyzstan would therefore have limited effect on the Aral Sea. Furthermore,

Kyrgyzstan has only 400,000 ha devoted to alfalfa, one of the largest water consuming crops in the Aral Sea basin, and therefore little scope to shift to less-water consuming crops.[5]

8.23   Water Charges. Irrigation water charges are not yet applied although the Government has indicated that it plans to introduce them soon. Volumetric water charges have limited applicability. Given the present state of deterioration and the absence of water measurement devices in the minor systems, the application of volumetric water charges is feasible only at the state or collective farm level (and possibly later to water user associations when they are formed). The application of volumetric water charges in the run-of-river schemes would be more complex and would have little effect on water saving. Consequently, service fees should be calculated on a per hectare basis. Technical assistance would be necessary for a study of the technical, institutional and financial (user capacity to pay) aspects of irrigation and drainage water charges.

8.24   Rehabilitation of Irrigation Systems. Out of the reported 1.07 million irrigated ha, only 20 percent have dependable water either from storage dams or groundwater. The remaining 80 percent are supplied through diversion of mountain streams. About 135,000 ha are irrigated by sprinklers and only 12 ha by drip. The main system, particularly those downstream of large storage dams are well maintained. However, the distribution systems within the state and collective farms are generally poorly designed, built and maintained. The control structures in the distribution systems, all manually operated, are primitive and not functioning because of poor maintenance and vandalism. The pre-fabricated canaletti are of poor quality and badly installed. Seepage and leakage losses in the distribution system are considerable, resulting in a conveyance/distribution efficiency of 55 percent. Systems visited in the Fergana Valley appear, however, in better condition than in other regions of Kyrgyzstan. The steep slopes of the irrigated lands in the mountain areas and foothills of the Chu Valley combined with shallow soils should enable conversion to pressurized irrigation methods, especially where gravity pressure is feasible.

8.25   Employment. Agricultural employment has declined by about 10 percent since 1986. The reasons for this decline (unless it is a statistical artifact) are probably attributable to more factors than the reported reduction of labor-intensive tobacco production. Privatization in agriculture is likely to promote employment through more intensive use of labor, particularly family labor on private farms. However, some of the technical and administrative staff on the state and collective farms could become redundant, even though their employment as extension staff might be considered.

8.26   Agricultural Technology. The technologies currently used in crop production are outdated and a significant portion of the machinery and equipment is not functional. Major problems include a lack of improved varieties (particularly in grains, vegetables and potatoes), low quality seed, inadequate seed treatment, poor placing and timing of fertilizer applications, lack of selective and safe pesticides, highly inefficient pesticide application equipment, an inefficient irrigation system and low quality harvesting equipment. The amount of mineral fertilizers actually applied in the field has declined significantly since 1986, ranging from declines of 17 percent during 1986-90 in grain production to nearly 40 percent in fodder production. Further pronounced declines occurred this year as a result of limited availability and the more than tenfold price increase since November 1991. Forty percent of the harvesting combines need to be replaced or repaired; 20 percent of the trucks, 13 percent of tractors and

---

5.   These facts should not detract from the Government's commitment to contribute to the cooperative efforts among the riparian countries to save the Aral Sea.

30 percent of other equipment are in a similar predicament. In addition, there has been a considerable breakdown in the supply of fuel and lubricants. Through April 1992, farms had received only 62 percent of last year's supply of gasoline and fuel. Diesel fuel was in particular short supply with only 38 percent of last year's amount delivered.

8.27   Agricultural Research, Extension and Education. A thorough assessment of agricultural research and extension and agricultural education is necessary. From limited observations, it is apparent that some of the agricultural research is very advanced and the quality of the research staff is quite high. Two of the former All-Union research institutes under the Academy of Sciences, specializing in metrology and automatization of irrigation systems, are located in Bishkek and now report to the Ministry of Water Resources. These institutes have achieved advancements at the frontiers of technology in ultrasonic water measurement equipment and in telemetering and remote control equipment for canal systems, but have lost a large proportion of their staff in the past two years.

Long-Run and Transitional Policy Considerations

8.28   The long-run objective of agricultural sector reform should be aimed at creating a private and competitive free market agricultural sector that efficiently uses, and conserves, natural resources and provides equitable incomes to farm families. To achieve this objective the Government will have to complete the privatization of farms and of most support services, both upstream and downstream. It will also have to:

a)   bring relative prices close to international price relatives;

b)   integrate the sector fully into international trade for inputs and outputs;

c)   make marketing of inputs and outputs competitive; and

d)   target any remaining subsidies to the poor, for financing of public goods such as research and small farmer extension, or for correcting environmental externalities.

Items a) and b) will be achieved automatically as privatization is completed, and prices and trade are fully liberalized. Item c) will require a breaking up of input and output monopolies, and d) will require direct governmental activity on a continuing basis.

8.29   The above indicates a clear need to restructure the entire farming system. Social and communal services and activities now prevalent in the state and collective farm system should be transferred to local or national government responsibility. Input subsidies should be phased out. In the long run, government support that distorts relative prices and maintains unprofitable farms retards the adjustment process in the sector. Farms and enterprises that fail to reorganize and cease unprofitable activities or cannot be profitably restructured will have to close or will absorb growing subsidies. This adjustment process will, however, take time and may require temporary, phased intervention by the government to manage the transition.

8.30   During the transition period, the need to ensure food availability particularly for poor groups of the population may justify temporary government intervention. Certainly, one important issue during the transition is to avoid a major political crisis that could threaten the entire reform program. Food consumption problems in the city, and income problems in specific agricultural regions where people have few alternative options locally and cannot migrate in the short run, can generate massive political crises. At the same time, these interventions can lead to highly adverse support structures that are undesirable in the long run. Thus any measures taken to manage the transition period have to be chosen carefully and should avoid inconsistency with long-run policy objectives. Measures that create vested interests and which are so strong that the instruments cannot be dismantled should also be avoided. A more detailed approach to manage the transition is discussed below.

Managing the Transition

8.31   Transitional procedures should emphasize: (i) ensuring adequate food consumption of the poor (mere availability of food in the market is not sufficient); and (ii) ensuring sufficient incomes in the agricultural sector so that the objectives of agricultural reform are achievable, namely privatization of the farm sector, retention of a rural labor force consistent with comparative advantage, and sound credit policies based on nonsubsidized interest rates and repayment of credit.

8.32   Three principles should guide decisions on government efforts to facilitate the transition: (i) minimize the budget cost, and make it as transparent as possible, (ii) use instruments which provide incentives to bring about the desired structural changes (or at least not impede them), and (iii) minimize the use of and commitment to instruments that create strong vested interests. It is inappropriate to look only at narrow agricultural instruments, such as input subsidies or support prices. Any specific activity should be carefully assessed in terms of its budget implications and should only be considered if it can be clearly justified and targeted. The range of instruments for government use includes:

a)   agricultural policies such as price and export support, tariffs, credit, input subsidies, direct income support payments;

b)   general food subsidies;

c)   targeted income transfers or food and nutrition programs.

The choice of instruments depends on the nature of the short-run problem that needs to be addressed.

8.33   If there is little prospect for a specific commodity, any price support is inappropriate and domestic supply should gradually be replaced by imports from the cheapest source (FSU or international markets). The income problem of the farmers should be addressed by assisting them to move to products in which they can have a comparative advantage, and if these are few, through temporary and targeted income transfers and assistance with migration to other regions or the cities. If the prospects are good, it may be appropriate to raise output prices to bring forth the supply. If, to insure sufficient consumption of the poor, such output price increases may have to be temporarily compensated by higher targeted or untargeted consumer subsidies, this should be considered ex-ante. Sometimes it may be relatively cheaper, or create less vested interests, to temporarily subsidize an input than an output, if the subsidy can be geographically targeted to the crop.[6] Alternatively the producer can be given a temporary direct transfer tied to desired structural or systemic changes.

---

6.   An input subsidy may not add to relative price distortions if output prices, too, are below international levels, both measured at the prevailing market exchange rate.

8.34   It is clear that transition management for the food and agricultural sectors has significant operational and macroeconomic implications. The transition should not be managed by the agricultural ministries in isolation. They should be assisted and, for price and subsidy policies, guided by some interministerial body having appropriate access to the key policy makers, and with the analytical capacity and technical assistance to look at the issues intersectorally and with a view to minimize overall costs. The Government should probably allocate a maximum spending limit to such a committee, but leave it discretion on the choice of instruments to achieve the transition objectives. It has to be clear, however, that the above discussion of policy instruments refers to the transition period only and that this interministerial body is created for a limited period of time.

Summary of Recommendations

8.35   The breakdown of interrepublican trade flows has caused disruptions in agricultural production, distribution and processing, while the price decontrols have resulted in a terms of trade deterioration with potential repercussions for agricultural output. Solutions to these problems within the framework of a market economy should continue to be explored.

8.36   Incentive structure. In the medium term, agricultural production will benefit from a comprehensive analysis of comparative advantages, which is likely to call for substantial shifts in cropping patterns. In the interim, special input subsidies particularly for fuel and energy should only be considered after careful analysis of all available options, while procurement prices for perceived critical commodities should not be raised to levels that increase cropping of these commodities, if this will exacerbate current inefficiencies in cropping patterns. Prices at the retail level for bread should be raised if necessary to limit the fiscal cost of higher procurement prices of wheat.

8.37   Liberalizing agricultural commodity prices should be completed in conjunction with reductions in the Government's interventions in production decisions and input supply. The state might continue to set floor prices for certain critical commodities. State purchases should be under market conditions, using bidding procedures rather than bilateral negotiations. A state purchases program should be developed reducing commodity specific volumes (in units of basic commodity or the conversion equivalent to basic commodity units) public activity needs (schools, hospitals, military, etc.), with implementation beginning in January 1993.

8.38   Privatization. A program to completely privatize most of the current system of state and collective farms has to be developed and implemented. The mobility of resources, in particular the development of a land market for sales, rental, sharecropping arrangements as well as the use of land as collateral, is indispensable for the efficient allocation of resources in a market economy. In this respect, the Government's pilot program of land privatization in the Talas and Naryn provinces is commendable. While complete privatization over all of Kyrgyzstan may not be feasible currently feasible due to social considerations, other temporary options should be considered. One that merits serious consideration is, while maintaining state ownership of the land, to allow land lease rights which are tradeable and transferable. The Government's current program restricts transfer rights to inheritance.

8.39   After an initially rapid and enthusiastic effort to relax state control and encourage private sector activities, the program of private sector development in agriculture has slowed down and has even partly been reversed. The following critical issues will have to be addressed during the coming months to ensure a successful continuation of the privatization program:

a)   Any further suspension of the privatization program, even for a few months, should be avoided; the basic commitment of the Government to support privatization should be reinforced and publicized widely.

b)   Farmers should have the right to dispose of their output at their own discretion, preferably on the basis of advance contracts, the preferred outlets being private markets or a variety of public purchasers. Thus, any restrictions on the development of private marketing channels should be identified and eliminated.

c)   During the transition period, independent family farms should be able to compete with public farms for access to land and inputs in a fair and transparent process. The application process for land leases should be simplified and sufficient land for private farmers should be made available. The allocation of equipment, machinery, spare parts and major inputs such as fuel, lubricants, fertilizers and pesticides to private farmers should be increased temporarily and enforced, until channels of commercial input supplies are established and operate reliably.

d)   Access to competitive credit sources, and provision of adequate public infrastructure and appropriate extension services should also be ensured.

e)   The Government should make land leases (i.e., the right to use land) tradeable, through allowing the sale, rental (for cash or in kind, i.e., sharecropping), inheritance and use as collateral of all land lease rights. Privatization in agriculture, which was temporarily suspended due to the onset of the agricultural production year, should now continue, with due consideration to social conditions.

f)   Private marketing, storage, processing, exports and imports of agricultural products, inputs and spare parts should be explicitly allowed and the legislative environment for these purposes developed. The discriminatory commercial tax legislation should be reconsidered and commerce should not be taxed at a higher rate than production activities. Explicit legislation, complemented by a set of transparent by-laws and regulations that allow and facilitate the development of private sector activities is needed. This regulatory environment should also establish standards for quality and hygiene, including the critical areas of chemical residues, sanitary storage and packaging. Complementary to these activities should be an active program of privatization, including the closing of inefficient state plants, and the breakup of conglomerates into competitive firms. Private farmers and agricultural business associations should be allowed to act as professional and consultative organizations representing the interests of farmers and private business.

8.40   Research. To maintain agricultural research capacity, and the potential to export innovative technologies, technical assistance and support would be needed. In some cases the linkages of technology development and adaptive research are quite impressive as in the case of the Irrigation Research Institute. However, the overall adaptation of research to local conditions and extension structure, capacity and roles in this respect need to be studied and improved. The degree to which agricultural research, extension and education are aligning to the needs of private sector operations and market conditions undoubtedly also needs improvement. In particular, the revision of agricultural economics curricula should be a priority, aided if possible through technical assistance.

8.41   Trade. Policy decisions pertaining to trade and self-sufficiency in food production or some sub-sectors (including self-sufficiency in some inputs) need to be based on careful analysis and evaluation of the options with respect to costs, benefits and, in particular, principles of comparative advantage. In the short run, it may be advisable to work towards exploiting established comparative advantages with the CIS, providing imports can be assured. Based on a strategy of export development to be designed, the longer-term trade patterns should be based on Kyrgyzstan's comparative advantages in international markets. Policy interventions in production and processing should be fiscal in nature (e.g., compensation payments) and should not involve delivery quotas and input allocations.

8.42   Kyrgyzstan does have convertible currency export potential in agriculture though punitive surrender requirements have been a major disincentive. It should be possible to redirect wool, tobacco and fur exports to international markets. And, with proper focus on increasing quality, livestock products, particularly from small ruminants, may be exportable to neighboring countries. Production of high value irrigated crops is also a possibility that would lead to the more efficient use of valuable land and water.

8.43   Credit. The reform of the rural finance system has to be considered within the framework of the reform of the overall financial system (Chapter 4). However, it should be noted that in a competitive environment, due to higher risks and higher transactions costs, agricultural credit will have a low priority in commercial bank portfolios, even though agriculture would not have any less need for credit for working capital and longer-term investment. This issue needs to be addressed through exploring cooperative structures, mutual societies, etc., as well as trade credits for input supplies.[7]

8.44   Agro-ecological Issues. Agro-ecological problems of rangeland degradation through overgrazing, soil erosion in the arable lands, and soil and water contamination from intensive livestock production facilities and agro-processing plants need to be monitored and reversed according to an accelerated schedule. Kyrgyzstan, in the upstream Aral Sea tributary system, is dedicated to helping alleviate the Sea's environmental problems, in cooperation with the other five riparian countries. Therefore, improving water use efficiency and other natural resource conservation measures should continue to receive high priority at the technical and policy making levels. The action that reversed the ecological problems of the Issyk Kul region can serve as an example for other areas that have an impact on the ecology of the Aral Sea region.

8.45   To assess irrigation development potential, the Government should prepare an inventory of incomplete irrigation projects and those requiring rehabilitation. This inventory should include description of works, cost estimates and reassessment of economic and technical feasibility, based on world prices. There is a need to determine the priorities through a review of the economic potential of projects to rehabilitate existing systems and to construct new ones. (The proposal of the Ministry of Water Resources to increase grain production eventually by an annual production of 115,000 MT at a cost of R1.98 billion (in 1991 prices) may prove difficult to justify.) Another issue to be faced is the enhancement of farm level distribution systems as large state and collective farms are broken up into

---

7.   In other words, commercial distributors would be advanced credit which they could use for on-lending to customers against input purchases.

smaller private farms; farmers' participation in the cost of such systems, either financially or in labor contribution should be explored.

8.46   There is a need for integrated water resource development and management that takes into account the conflicting objectives of food grain production, higher-value crop production for export, energy generation and protection of the Aral Sea environment. A program should be designed for this purpose, initially with a compilation of existing projects (ongoing or arrested) found feasible after economic and environmental scrutiny, with technical assistance to support the evaluation process. This program should establish priorities for public investment as well as principles for O&M organization and funding. A system of water charges (service fees) should be introduced for the 1993 season to recover operation and maintenance and at least part of the capital costs of the irrigation and other water delivery systems. User associations should be established for each project, to collect service fees and participate in the decisions on the allocation of water and accumulated resources from water charges. In the medium term water rights should be made tradeable.

8.47   Public investment in agriculture should take budget constraints into consideration and focus on infrastructure. Investment in productive areas should increasingly be left to the private sector and legislation which would facilitate this should be submitted to the Supreme Soviet. Within budget constraints, the focus should be on infrastructural investments in the areas of irrigation, and of rural roads, market facilities, communications, etc., which improve the market environment for agriculture. By contrast the Government should withdraw from productive investments as the private sector's role in agriculture grows.

8.48   Employment in agriculture is an area that needs to be monitored carefully to prevent large-scale unemployment that induces urban migration. However, agriculture should not be forced to absorb excess labor any more than other sectors -- with due consideration to social costs -- since this would adversely affect the efficiency of production and distort the choice of technology.

Potential Areas of Foreign Assistance

8.49   To implement its economic reform program in agriculture, the Government will need to execute studies, develop strategies and legislation, and implement specific programs. In these activities, the limited human resources of Kyrgyzstan in the agricultural sector will need to be complemented by technical assistance (TA). Box 8-1 summarizes the initial TA proposals for agriculture. They are closely linked to the Government's reform program and would support the development of policies, legislation and implementation under the program.

Box 8-1. Core Areas of Technical Assistance

(a)   The historical structure of agricultural incentives (administered prices, physical control, state orders, etc.) has been pervasive, opaque and distortionary. This has resulted in an inefficient production structure which now faces a severe terms of trade shock. Potential future incentive structures have to be assessed and appropriate programs implemented to guide the agricultural sector through the transition to areas of comparative advantage. Estimated cost: US$ 500,000.

(b)   Both the farm and agroprocessing sectors have to be fundamentally restructured. The scope and speed of privatization of agricultural production and production factors with special emphasis on land reform have to be assessed and programs developed. The constraints to small-scale private sector development, farm and business management, marketing and sustainable agricultural practices (integrated pest management, small-scale machinery etc), and the development of a supporting institutional framework will have to be assessed and effective programs implemented. Estimated cost: US$ 600,000.

(c)   Restructuring of public administration in agriculture towards providing policy guidance and playing a facilitating regulatory role, divesting itself of operational involvement such as production, processing, marketing and distribution requires particular attention. Estimated cost: US$ 300,000.

(d)   New approaches are required in training and education of teachers, policy makers and managers in agricultural economics and in related areas such as agricultural policy, accounting, management, marketing, etc. Estimated cost: US$ 200,000.

(e)   Over three quarters of the cultivated lands in Kyrgyzstan are irrigated. The utilization of these irrigated areas, irrigation technologies, water use efficiency, the needs for rehabilitation and the potential for diversification and cropping pattern changes under market conditions need to be assessed. Estimated cost: US$ 300,000.

(f)   Further areas of technical and financial cooperation could include the improvement of the rural credit sector and establishment of a trade regime.

Energy

8.50   Kyrgyzstan has been a heavy consumer of energy relative to its level of industrialization and per capita income. As energy prices move to world levels, major adjustments in energy use, including substantial contraction of imported oil and gas use, are inevitable. A key unresolved issue is the extent and pace at which the authorities' desire to electrify the economy can be implemented. This, together with a rational pricing and tax structure and the ability to export electricity particularly for hard currency should be the key determinants of investment strategy, where the long-term potential for increasing hydro capacity may be favorable. Attracting foreign investment for oil and gas exploration is also a priority, for which reforms in the legal and fiscal framework, discussed earlier in this report, will be important.

Energy Balances and Outlook

8.51   Kyrgyzstan has been a major net importer of energy. Of the total primary energy demand of nearly 9 million tons of oil equivalent (toe) in 1991, about 4 million toe was produced domestically. Hydroelectricity, lignite and hard coal account for the bulk of domestic production, while consumption of oil and natural gas is almost entirely accounted for by imports. Kyrgyzstan does not posses oil refining capacity. Hence, domestically produced oil has to be exported for refining, and imports consist of relatively high priced refined grades. Among energy sources Kyrgyzstan is a net exporter only of electricity, with net exports amounting to some 31 percent of production in 1991. Table 8-3 summarizes energy consumption, production and trade in 1991, while Table 8-4 values such trade at the ruble prices prevailing in 1991.

8.52   Energy exports and imports in 1991 comprised about 3.5 percent and 10 percent of total exports and imports, respectively, producing an energy deficit of about R470 million. By comparison, valuing last year's energy trade at world prices using an average crude oil price of $18 per barrel, the energy deficit (at unchanged volumes) is estimated at $400 million.

Table 8-3. Energy Balances, 1991

	Consumption	Trade (net)	Change in Stocks	Production
Primary Energy				
Oil (tons)[a]	2,744	(2,531)	(70)	143
Coal (tons)[a]	1,570	(3)	(34)	1,533
Other solid fuels (tons)[a]	2,455	(343)	(2)	2,111
Natural gas (million m³)	2,156	(2,073)	0	83
Hydroelectricity (million kwh)	10,058			
Nuclear electricity	0	0		
Secondary Energy				
Coke and potent fuels (tons)[a]	532	(532)	0	0
Total electricity (million kwh)	9,680	4,293	0	13,972
Recovered waste heat (gcals)	14,344,269	0	0	14,344,269

a/ Quantities in tons refer to 1,000 tons.

Table 8-4. Energy Trade, 1991

	Exports		Imports	
	Quantity[a]	Value (mln rbl)	Quantity[a]	Value (mln rbl)
Oil (tons)[b]	168	27.2	2,699	471.6
Coal (tons)	0	0.0	3	0.1
Other solid fuels (tons)	1,230	14.3	1,573	70.4
Natural Gas (million m³)	55	1.7	2,129	105.5
Coke and potent fuels (tons)	0	0.0	0	0.0
Electricity (million kwh)	5,346	188.4	1,053	36.8[c]
Total		231.6		698.5[c]

a/ Quantities in tons refer to 1,000 tons
b/ Includes refined products
c/ Staff estimate

Demand

8.53 Table 8-5 shows the pattern of domestic energy consumption, of which over half was accounted for by oil and gas. At 2.3 toe per capita, Kyrgyzstan's overall energy consumption was at a similar level to Greece, Ireland or Spain, countries with substantially higher incomes, though with more moderate variations in temperature.

8.54 Nearly half of the oil consumption in 1991 was accounted for by transportation. Of this, 28 percent was for aviation uses, with most of the remainder for road transport. Of the remaining oil consumption, most is accounted for by the burning of fuel oil in the Bishkek and Osh power stations or industrial boilers. Both the Bishkek and the Osh power stations are combined heat and power (CHP) plants. Hence the fuel oil burn is concentrated in the winter months, and is very dependent on temperature. Gas demand is also concentrated in the same sectors as fuel oil, being the largest single fuel used in CHP generation. By contrast, demand for solid fuels, even lignite or sub-bituminous grades, is concentrated in the domestic and commercial sectors. This is because centralized heat distribution, though the principal source of heat in the urban areas of Bishkek and Osh, is not practical in rural areas where some 60 percent of the population reside.

Table 8-5. Primary Energy Consumption, 1991

Fuel	1,000 toe	percent share
Oil	2,744	31.3
Natural Gas	1,859	21.2
Steam coal	1,047	11.9
Lignite	810	9.2
Hydroelectricity	2,313	26.4
Nuclear	0	0
Total	8,773	100.0

Supply

8.55 Hydroelectricity is Kyrgyzstan's major energy resource. Kyrgyzstan is linked to a common grid with other Central Asian republics. Thus domestic electricity supply is linked to the need to supply water for irrigation to Uzbekistan, Turkmenistan and Kazakhstan. This, however, has resulted in the greatest supply of electricity in the summer months when energy demand is relatively low. This in turn suggests that revenues from electricity could be increased if energy prices were to exhibit greater seasonality to reflect demand variations, as is common in market economies.

8.56 Total hydroelectric capacity currently amounts to about 2.7 GW of which 2.6 GW is concentrated in major hydroelectric schemes along the Naryn river. Total electricity supply is 3.4 GW. Current hydro capacity reportedly comprises only 9 percent of the hydro power that theoretically could be developed. The previous administration had prepared plans for the development of 6.8 GW of this undeveloped potential, with average cost per MW reported at $1,100 - $1,500 per kw, comparing favorably with the best international levels. Work had begun at two sites, the largest being Kambaratin (2.26 GW). Most of this capacity was not envisaged as being installed until after the year 2000. The authorities regard the expansion of hydro capacity as particularly important in that it would permit more electricity to be supplied in winter to regional markets; load patterns could thus be revolutionized and fossil fuels replaced in both urban and rural areas.

8.57 Kyrgyzstan is also well endowed with solid fuel reserves. Hard coal and lignite deposits are spread across the country. But mines tend to be relatively small and mountain roads prevent any significant trade, though exports of lignite into power stations in southern Kazakhstan occur along the northern border. Higher priced Kazakh hard coals are imported for domestic, commercial and industrial uses. Acute difficulties are currently being experienced by the mining sector in obtaining raw materials and supplies, resulting in a 25 percent fall in coal output in the first quarter of 1992. Substantial investment would apparently be required to raise output in order to meet local demand. Moreover, as incomes rise, domestic coal demand tends to fall as households substitute less labor intensive fuels. Though this trend may be delayed in Kyrgyzstan, the potential offered by electricity is likely to be more attractive economically and hence coal investment would appear unattractive in the longer term.

8.58   The reserve base in oil and gas is uncertain. Exploration had been neglected for the past 15-20 years reflecting the Union's priorities. Oil and gas production has thus fallen continuously for the past decade. Thus, in 1991, oil production was under 3,000 b/d (143,000 tons) and gas production was only 83 million m³. Recent deep, large discoveries in the Fergana depression in Uzbekistan are thought to extend into Kyrgyzstan. Source rocks extend from this basin across the country into China where oil fields have been discovered and developed. The existence of both hydrocarbon source rocks and deeply buried coal deposits is considered by local geologists as indicative of probable gas reserves, for example, around Lake Issyk-Kul. With adequate investment, the long-term decline in oil and gas production could, almost certainly, be reversed. The key to future supply is the price, tax and licensing arrangements to be adopted.

8.59   Most prices for fossil fuels had risen by a factor of 20 or more in early 1992,[8] whereas the rise in electricity prices was somewhat less, from 2 to 28 kopek/kwh. Accompanying these overall trends, however, was a widening of price differentials charged to the productive versus household sectors -- with prices being raised faster for the former, except for instances of specialized subsidy as in the case of certain farm categories.

8.60   The declines in domestic production of energy sources varied considerably in the first quarter, with electricity output falling by less than 2 percent, oil production down by about 9 percent, compared to declines of 21 and 25 percent for gas and coal, respectively. The extent of decline of imported energy sources is not available but may have been even larger, given the estimated falls in road and air transport in the first quarter of 33 and 45 percent, respectively.

Outlook

8.61   The evolution of energy demand over the medium term is likely to be dominated by the trends of overall output and relative price changes. On both counts it would appear that a major downward shift in demand is likely since output levels may not recover to pre-reform levels for much of this decade, and the trend of increased relative prices of energy may continue for a number of years as imported energy prices move to international levels. The latter adjustment should lead to a shift from higher to less intensive energy use in industry and could result in the closure of energy intensive plants where restructuring of existing technology is not feasible. While energy intensive mining activity may rise, it is apparent that overall consumption of oil and gas will fall precipitously in the 1990s relative to the pre-reform era.

8.62   The trend of electricity consumption will of course depend in part on pricing policy (discussed below) and the extent to which it is economically feasible to substitute existing use of fossil

---

8.   For example, the Turkmenistan gas price of R43/1,000 m³ at end 1991 stood at R960 by March; gasoline prices had risen from 299 to 7,100 rubles per ton; diesel from 192 to 3,500 R/t; fuel oil from 120 to 4,000 R/t; coal prices from 15 to over 300 R/t.

fuels for industrial and household uses into electricity use. Since this will have an important bearing on investment strategy, a study of the pace of such conversion possibilities is of high priority. In the short term, it would appear that the income effect will dominate so that electricity consumption will also decline, but this trend can be expected to reverse in due course.

Policy Issues

Price and Tax Policy

8.63   To guide current and future investment decisions in a non-distortive manner, it is essential to move as rapidly as possible to a relative price structure for energy that is reflective of international levels. Thus, increases in imported oil, gas and coal prices should be passed on fully. Subsidies on domestic coal production should be eliminated and energy prices for households should be raised as rapidly as feasible to remove fiscal subsidies.

8.64   Electricity pricing should be based on long-run marginal cost (LRMC). Until such a price structure is devised, domestic electricity prices should be adjusted on a cost-plus basis to at least ensure that the relevant enterprises involved in the generating and distribution processes remain profitable. An alternative means of electricity pricing in the short run would be to maintain approximate parity with adjustments in imported oil prices; such a rule would appear particularly appropriate in pricing exports within the ruble zone. Kyrgyzstan should also study the practices of other major electricity producers, for example, Norway to align its price structure to variations in demand as a means of increasing revenue.

8.65   Energy tax policies should be coordinated as far as possible within a common ruble zone framework. Excise taxes on gasoline and other fuels may be an effective way of raising revenue. In designing such taxes, Kyrgyzstan should strive to shift demand away from high priced gasoline towards less expensive (in terms of import cost) and more efficient diesel. Thus, it may be desirable to increase the tax on gasoline from the proposed rate of 20-25 percent.

8.66   Since Kyrgyzstan is considering licensing oil and gas acreage under the new mining code, early advice is essential on the structure of royalty and other charges to be levied on any oil or gas produced. Though production sharing contracts (PSCs) are attractive, as they can be implemented speedily, the creation of a licensing and fiscal regime under a separate hydrocarbon law has many long-term advantages. One, of particular relevance, is the ability to raise significant sums in revenue for very low cost. Another is that such terms are normal in the developed world and provide a more effective means of modifying, on a continuing basis, the shares of hydrocarbon income between the government and the companies.

Investment Strategy

8.67   The key to the future investment strategy in Kyrgyzstan is electricity. If, as reported by the authorities, the hydro sites are world class and the technology of dam construction is very advanced, then new hydro capacity should be capable of delivering energy into the economy at resource costs lower than other fuels. Moreover, replacement of fossil fuels in power and heat generation would be an environmentally superior strategy. Given the relatively high altitude of Kyrgyzstan's proposed hydro sites, resettlement costs will also be relatively low. Finally, the safety of existing dams is considered highly acceptable. Thus the long-term strategy proposed by the authorities -- an increase in the degree of electrification of the economy -- appears sound.

8.68   Two potential difficulties complicate the short-term investment strategy, however: the uncertain outlook for electricity demand at prices that permit profitable operations; and fiscal constraints on further investment. Hence in 1992-93 it would be advisable to give priority to those projects that are due for completion in the next 1-2 years. Other projects already initiated should continue to be provided resources, provided they are still considered viable, but some cutbacks may be inevitable in 1992-93. Major new investments should not be initiated until a study of electricity demand in the new environment is available. The exception to this conclusion would be if significant contracts can be concluded for export outside the CIS where payments would be in hard currency. If such contracts are concluded, the authorities should seriously explore the opportunities for private sector involvement through "build-operate-transfer" (BOT) type schemes, incorporating the advice of international institutions such as the World Bank with prior expertise in this area.

8.69   During the next 5 to 10 years, moves can be made preparatory to shifting the economy towards a new energy structure. Small hydro dams, which are associated with irrigation schemes and which at present have mainly idle turbines could be reconstructed cheaply and effectively. Measures could be taken, possibly via joint ventures with foreign companies, to consider what level of manufacturing capability should be created to supply the new heating markets or provide the necessary maintenance resource for Kyrgyzstan or the wider region. Peak and seasonal load variations will need to be considered in depth before investment to serve new markets is undertaken. Meters can be installed to establish the precise efficiency of the systems in use, to assist in pricing the fuels delivered and assessing the returns to investment.

8.70   Of the fossil fuels, coal resources are likely to have limited long-term interest to investors. While the hydrocarbon sector will never play the same role as electricity, every effort should be made to develop these resources, if necessary by direct foreign investment. This depends critically upon the legal and fiscal framework, but the potential for discoveries of significant value to a small economy should not be ignored.

Mining and Metallurgical Sector

8.71   The broader issues of structural reform in the industrial sector were discussed in Chapter 5. This section contains a separate assessment of the mining and metallurgical sector since this sub-sector of industry constitutes an important area for potential growth in the medium term.

Current Minerals Production

8.72   Data and statistics on mineral production, extraction and processing, grade and tonnage, and basic geology are considered classified. The unavailability of complete and verifiable data makes it difficult to come to more than general conclusions about the sector. The information below should hence be regarded as preliminary.

8.73   In 1991, the estimated value of minerals (excluding rare earth metals) produced in Kyrgyzstan was about $60 million at world market prices. The non-ferrous metals sector contributed about 4.5 percent of total production in 1991. Official statistics indicate that the non-ferrous mining and metallurgical sector employs approximately 10,000 persons, representing three percent of the industrial workforce. This figure is probably understated because it may not include the 8,000 work force at the uranium processing facility or the 6,000 employees of the State Committee on Geology. In terms of ability to generate hard currency export revenue the sector is a more significant contributor. Assuming that half the uranium production and all of gold production were sold on world markets, it is estimated that $30 million could be earned from uranium oxide and gold, which is higher than Kyrgyzstan's estimated convertible currency export earnings in 1991. Table 8-6 contains very preliminary estimates regarding current minerals production valued at recent world prices.

Table 8-6. Estimates of Mineral Production, 1991

Commodity	Amount	Price(US$)	Value (US$M)
Uranium Oxide U308, (tons)	1,000	20.00/kg	20.0
Antimony Metal (tons)	5,000	1.80/kg	9.0
Mercury, tons	725	3,190.00/ton	2.3
Gold, kgs	1,000	10,850.00/kg	10.8
Molybdenum, export (tons)	500	7.39/kg	3.7
Rare Earths	N.A.	-	-
Total Value at world market prices			45.8

8.74   By international standards Kyrgyzstan has a small, highly specialized mining and metallurgical industry. With the exception of gold, world markets for Kyrgyzstan's currently produced minerals -- uranium oxide, antimony, mercury, molybdenum, and rare earths -- are very modest in size. For instance, total world trade in mercury and antimony, two commodities for which Kyrgyzstan can claim a significant portion of world production, was only about $120 million in 1991. The world market for uranium oxide remains weak because electric utilities are still working off stocks built up by virtue of long-term contracts signed in the 1970s and because of safety concerns about nuclear power.

8.75   Nonetheless, Kyrgyzstan possesses good minerals potential. The mercury and antimony operations may be small but could be highly profitable. The in-situ leach methods presently used to mine uranium are generally a cost effective extraction method and the 2.4 percent U grades reported are respectable by international standards. Gold, especially, may present good possibilities for expansion given the large number of deposits already identified by the State Committee on Geology. The belt of rocks within which the Morantau gold deposit is located in Uzbekistan, one of the largest such deposits in the world, extends into Kyrgyzstan. The Malmak gold deposit, currently Kyrgyzstan's only producing mine, may be similar geologically to Morantau. The international gold market is more robust and much larger in size than the markets for Kyrgyzstan's other mineral commodities. Gold is also a fungible commodity and is easily transported and sold on international exchanges.

8.76   Very little of Kyrgyzstan's mineral production is used by local industries. In fact, a common source of complaint is that prior policies relegated the republic to the position of raw materials supplier to industries located elsewhere in the USSR, depriving the economy of the value added to be gained from processing. It should be noted, however, that the types of commodities Kyrgyzstan produces are not necessarily amenable to downstream processing. Unlike major metals such as copper or iron ore which can be fashioned into final products, the mercury produced in Kyrgyzstan, for instance, is used as a catalyst in industrial production processes. Antimony is, in fact, processed in Kyrgyzstan to final metal stage, using not only locally produced but also ores brought in from other republics. Kyrgyzstan's uranium oxide is processed into nuclear fuel in other republics as well as outside the CIS. In principle, this commodity could be processed further in Kyrgyzstan but the viability of such activity would be difficult to justify under present market conditions.

8.77   The authorities also complain that under the previous system Kyrgyzstan was regarded as a strategic minerals reserve. This has meant that identified deposits were left undeveloped in favor of other areas in the former USSR. More importantly, the basic exploration philosophy of the command economy was simply to prove the physical presence of minerals in accordance with targets and plans received from the central ministry. This is significantly different from exploration driven by commercial principles, which relates the physical presence of minerals to cut-off grades and dilution factors based on world market prices to determine the economic viability of extracting and processing the ore. The result is that the ore grades and reserve tonnages as presently stated by the State Committee on Geology may over or under estimate the true economic value of a deposit. Considerable scope therefore exists to apply market oriented principles to exploration with good potential for discovering new deposits.

Institutional and Government Structure

8.78   Given the speed with which events have evolved in the past several months it is understandable that clear lines of authority, responsibility, and jurisdiction for government management of the sector have yet to be established. As presently configured, the various organizations in Kyrgyzstan that intervene in the mining sector comprise:

a)   the State Committee on Geology, responsible for exploration of minerals and hydrocarbons;

b)   the Ministry of Industry, responsible for oversight of the sector and allocation of budget and other resources to producing entities;

c)   various production entities, "combinates", responsible for the extraction, beneficiation, processing, and smelting of mineral products;

d)   the Committee on Foreign Economic Relations, the State Committee on Environmental Protection, the Academy of Sciences, and other organs also intervene in the sector.

Such a structure is not ideally suited for effective management of minerals and metallurgical development.

8.79   Other countries have found that the sector is best managed by clearly distinguishing roles for:

a)   conducting basic research into the earth sciences;

b)   formulating overall government policy and development strategy in respect of the sector;

c)   regulating and registering the issuance of exploration licenses and mining titles;

d)   monitoring various producing enterprises;

e)   attracting and retaining new investment; and

f)   enforcing environmental, health and safety standards.

The present configuration of ministries in Kyrgyzstan does not adequately serve these functions.

8.80   The task of promoting exploration would be better served if the State Committee on Geology were to concentrate on basic geological research, play the catalytic role in the development of technical programs, and serve as the national repository for geological and technical data. Detailed exploration and delineation of ore bodies generally should be left to the producing enterprise or to new investors willing and able to assume the exploration risk. In particular, attracting foreign and local investment will critically depend on providing complete access to all technical, scientific, financial, and production information regarding deposits and basic geology. The role of collecting and disseminating basic information on the earth sciences to all interested parties is critical. Ideally, this information should be retrievable using information processing systems.

8.81   No official entity currently exists with the clear mandate to implement mining related legislation, issue exploration and exploitation licenses, maintain a central registry of mining titles, evaluate proposed work programs and expenditure minimums, and to supervise procedures for mineral asset disposals. These functions are typically handled in other countries by a government department of mines that is responsible for the implementation and enforcement of mining legislation, and a similar arrangement may be appropriate in Kyrgyzstan.

8.82   The Ministry of Industry is directly responsible for minerals production, operational budgeting, and capital investment decisions for producing mines and metallurgical plants. The government's intention to grant greater autonomy to producing enterprises makes this structure and role inappropriate. In order to maximize efficiency and enhance competitive advantage, individual production units should be free to make production and marketing decisions, develop operational and capital budgets, and finance operations and expansion from internally generated funds. The Ministry of Industry should concentrate on setting overall industrial policy, monitoring performance of the sector in line with such policies, and ensuring coordination among other ministries as well as other CIS governments on industrial matters.

8.83   The State Committee on Ecology should play an increasingly important role in devising and enforcing appropriate environmental standards for the metallurgical industry. In particular, the Committee and producing enterprises should make the proper disposal of industrial and uranium wastes a priority. The Committee on Foreign Economic Relations, advisory bodies within the President's office, and other entities are reportedly to be involved in negotiations with foreign investors for the acquisition of State mineral properties as well as exploration acreage. The role of these entities to facilitate the gathering of information by the investor, streamline investment administrative procedures, ensure coordination among the relevant ministries, and provide a conduit to senior government officials of information concerning the progress of the project would be more useful if the responsibilities of each are clearly spelled out in a legal text or government policy decision.

8.84   The Government is contemplating setting-up a state-owned entity which will have exclusive monopoly rights to explore, develop, and exploit Kyrgyzstan's gold resources. While it is recognized that gold may be a substance of considerable economic importance for the Government, the manner in which the contemplated entity is to be structured as well as the monopoly control over gold resources by the new entity is a matter of deep concern. Such a development would appear to run counter to the Government's announced intention to promote investment in the sector and require enterprises to become responsive to the requirements of the market economy.

Legal and Fiscal Environment

8.85   The Government is in the formative stages of developing legislation in respect of mining activities. A mines and minerals code has been prepared, but has not yet been passed by Parliament. Review of a draft copy of this legislation, however, indicates that it is seriously deficient when compared to international standards. Specifically, the draft code does not provide for sufficient security of tenure and contains excessive government discretionary authority. Taxes and royalties are not defined and expectations on the part of some government officials about the amount of taxation a mineral deposit is able to support are too high. A Mining Code should serve as the fundamental legal instrument through which the state, as owner of sub-soil resources, grants to physical and juridical persons rights to explore and exploit such resources. Several principles are common to such codes. They:

a)   apply without discrimination to all investors, public and private, domestic and foreign;

b)   define jurisdiction over the resources: national, oblast, or regional;

c)   provide for clear, transparent, and rapid mining title issuance procedures;

d)   guarantee security of tenure to permit holders (i.e., the progression from exploration to exploitation);

e)   ensure that land under permit is worked effectively through a system of minimum work obligations and escalating surface rents;

f)   limit government discretionary powers and precisely state under which circumstances licenses may be refused; and

g)   provide an appeal procedure through an independent judicial system and/or international arbitration.

8.86   In the absence of such a code, the Foreign Investment Law, summarized in Chapter 5, and Law on Concessions and Foreign Concessional Enterprises (March 1992) are presently the two pieces of legislation that are most pertinent to the sector, though other recently adopted legislation could apply as well. The recently passed Law on Concessions is particularly important for the mining sector since it provides for the leasing of state assets, including mineral deposits, to physical and juridical persons. While acceptable in principle, certain ambiguities in the text of this law should be clarified in the enabling regulations and/or the concession contract. For instance, a competitive bidding process is to be used to select concessionaires for designated assets, but the criteria for evaluating the bids as well as the procedures to be followed are not specified in the law. A concession agreement is to be negotiated to detail the investors' obligations, tax treatment, period of contract, accounting and record keeping, methods of payment, supervision by state bodies and other financial arrangements of the venture. It is unclear if this agreement is in addition to or in lieu of the agreement to be negotiated under the terms of the Law on Foreign Investment. These negotiations will likely prove tedious and time consuming in the absence of fixed conditions and enabling regulations. In addition, expectations regarding the degree of investor interest as well as the prices to be paid for the properties may be overly optimistic. For example, government valuations of deposits based on the gross market value of in-situ minerals are wholly unrealistic since no allowance is made for dilution of reserves in mining and processing, the cost of production, or technical and market risk. Standard practice in the international mining industry would be to reduce the value of in-situ reserves by appropriate technical coefficients and to further adjust the value by discounting the cash flows of anticipated production.

8.87   Mining and metallurgical industries can be substantial contributors to government tax revenues. The challenge for government is to devise the right mix of policies and taxes that permit financial rewards to those assuming the investment risk while at the same time maximizing revenues to the state from exploitation of a depletable resources. Most countries have found that a combination of taxes based on earnings (taxes on profits, corporate income, and dividends) together with a modest (if any) royalty on production fulfills these criteria.

8.88   Our understanding of the current mix of taxes in Kyrgyzstan is that they are principally based on levies on output and secondarily on profit. The combined effect of this mix of taxes is far in excess of international norms. Enterprises report that they must surrender 40-50 percent of foreign exchange proceeds either by virtue of an explicit export tax or punitive rates used to convert foreign exchange into rubles. Ruble profits are taxed at 35 percent. A value added tax of 28 percent is assessed on critical inputs and it is unclear if a proportionate amount of this tax is refunded for exported products. The Foreign Investment Law does provide for certain fiscal advantages such as a five year tax holiday for qualified investments. While this may be attractive to some, most foreign investors would prefer a fair, straightforward, and reasonable level of taxation without special favors. Given these high taxes it is unlikely that foreign or local investors would find financial returns in the sector sufficiently attractive to justify new investment. Experience in other countries has demonstrated that tax revenues are better maintained by a uniform level of tax on profits for all industrial sectors with, perhaps, the provision for accelerated depreciation of the heavy capital investments involved with mining and metallurgical plants.

Comparative Advantage

8.89   A major short-term challenge will be to objectively assess the international comparative advantage and competitiveness of Kyrgyzstan's mineral production enterprises. In an open market economy international mineral commodity prices will condition the performance of the sector, even though the main orientation of these enterprises may remain to supply other industrial enterprises in the CIS with mineral products.

8.90   Given Kyrgyzstan's heavy dependence on the CIS for markets as well as essential equipment it is understandable that the authorities seek investment in downstream processing. However, this should be resisted if based solely on a desire to express national autonomy. Firstly, minerals presently produced may not be amenable to downstream processing. Secondly, investment in facilities to make finished or semi-finished goods, even if the mineral in question is amenable to such processing, should be judged on a case-by-case basis and according to strict market criteria using international prices for all inputs. The incremental cost of such facilities will often not be justified in terms of additional value added.

8.91   Plant managers as well as government officials express the view that injection of new Western technology will allow mines and metallurgical facilities to better compete on international markets. It is certainly true that equipment and technology generally in use in the mining sector is twenty to forty years out of date by modern standards. Some gains in efficiency could be achieved through investment in new production and processing technologies, but these investments should also be studied on a case-by-case basis and judged on strict economic criteria.

8.92   Moreover, considerable efficiency could be achieved in existing plants by improving management and organization, scheduling preventive maintenance, rationalizing staffing levels, and applying modern concepts of cost and financial accounting. For instance, enterprises generally carry a heavy burden of non-productive expenditures for worker lodging, health care, vacation and recreation facilities, commissary privileges, etc. Considerable scope therefore exists to improve efficiency in existing plants without expensive retro-fitting of new technology.

8.93   A significant impediment to effectively competing on international markets is the system of state orders. In the past, enterprises simply received orders from the appropriate ministry to produce a given volume of mineral product at a given price. The price paid to the enterprise was arrived at by averaging the production costs of several similar enterprises and adding a small margin. Enterprises are now theoretically free to market mineral products at negotiated prices. In practice, the state order still takes between 70 and 100 percent of total production, much of which is destined for the export market. Phasing out the state order will enable enterprises themselves to establish direct contacts with customers and realize the full international market value for the commodities sold. In fact, this is currently being done by Uhzpolymetal, which has entered into a trading relationship with a Washington D.C. based firm for the sale of uranium oxide in the United States.

Environmental Aspects

8.94   Even though the overall environmental situation is better in Kyrgyzstan than in neighboring republics, individual mining and metallurgical plants are heavy polluters. Some, such as the uranium tailings disposal dump at the Uhzpolymetal facility in Kara Balta, pose clear and immediate dangers to the health of workers and residents in proximity to the plant.[9] Industrial wastes transported from other republics and processed at this facility may also create serious health risks. The processing of mercury ores in the southern part of the country could pose serious health hazards in and around the facilities. In planning environmental policy the Government should prioritize those abuses that present the severest health and safety hazards to the population.

8.95   Health and safety standards observed at several facilities are far below acceptable international standards. Foundry workers at the Frunze tractor factory lack hard hats, safety glasses, aprons, masks, safety shoes, or other protective garments. The mandatory retirement age in the uranium processing mill in Kara Balta is 50 years for men and 45 years for women, below the age at other mills in the same complex, and perhaps indicative of the health and safety standards in the plant. Ironically, the Kara Balta facility produces the only radioactive dust masks made in the CIS and used in the clean-up after the Chernobyl disaster.

8.96   Clearly the improper disposal of industrial and mine wastes should be given the closest attention. Air quality is also a problem but does not present as severe a hazard as the industrial waste issue.

---

9.   At Kara Balta, no attempt was observed to cover or bury these tailings so as to prevent leaching into the ground water table of heavy metals and harmful radioactive elements. Radioactive dust lifted from the tailings pile by winds would also be a hazard. Disposal of tailings at the mercury and antimony processing centers was also not observed. The processing and use of mercury is especially hazardous to plant personnel as well as inhabitants in proximity to the works. Air pollution and emissions of fly ash, SO_2, NOx, arsenic, phosphorus, and other noxious elements are prevalent in proximity to plants and mills and hence of concern to those living in proximity.

CHAPTER 9

The Infrastructure for Production

Telecommunications

9.01   Kyrgyzstan's telecommunication infrastructure is insufficient to support the desired outward orientation of the economy, posing a major constraint to the expansion of economic ties outside the CIS. While local and interregional communications within the CIS are available to all subscribers, international communications are extremely restricted with all traffic routed through a network in Moscow. Total capital expenditure in the sector over the last five years amounted to less than one percent of gross domestic investment, indicating the historically low priority accorded to telecommunications development. The average age of the network is approximately 15 years and parts of it badly need replacement. Investment in the short term should focus on higher revenue generating international services and the needs of emerging business subscribers. The tariff structure will need to be revised to permit such investments on a commercial basis. Regulatory and institutional reforms are also needed to establish autonomous entities that can be commercialized to improve the quality of service and financial viability.

Structure and Recent Performance

Structure

9.02   The Ministry of Communications (MOC) is the monopoly provider of telecommunications services in Kyrgyzstan. The MOC is responsible for strategic planning, regulation, policy, and day-to-day implementation and operations activities for telecommunications. It has accountability for local, national, and international telephone, telex, telegraph, and data communication activities. In addition, MOC has responsibility for postal services, express mail, subscription and delivery of press publications, radio and television broadcasting, construction of buildings for affiliated enterprises, and money transfers. Planning and day-to-day operations are done at a regional level. Plans are submitted to the Ministry for comment and approval. Six regions and 54 districts operate as separate profit and loss centers though results from all activities (i.e. post, telecommunications, press, etc.) are combined in the regional and consolidated financial statements. It is not clear how major capital investment decisions are currently made.

9.03   Existing Facilities. As of end 1991 telephones were available to 325,300 subscribers or about 7 percent of the population. This density is comparable to other Central Asian states but is slightly higher than countries with comparable per capita income. Capacity utilization is approximately 87 percent which leaves little room for expansion. Specialized networks are provided to customers such as the railways, security services, etc. They represent approximately 2 - 3 percent of capacity to the country's network but would be difficult to convert for use on the public network.

9.04   Historically the development plans were established in Moscow. As in other former Soviet republics, the networks therefore use analogue transmission techniques and electromechanical switches at all levels of interconnection. Over time, this equipment has become obsolete and the manufacture of it and spare parts are rapidly being discontinued worldwide. Coaxial cable has been used on a limited basis for medium distance transmission. Digital techniques were recently introduced. All exchanges are automatic in urban and rural areas with automatic dialing for domestic services. With the exception of 1000 digital channels manufactured by Nokia (Finland), all equipment in the network is from the former Soviet Union and Eastern Europe. Much of the equipment was installed in the 1980s and is functional, but the microwave, overhead transmission, and exchanges from the early 1970s need to be replaced.

9.05   The network interconnects with other CIS republics via 600 channels and with the rest of the world via 60 channels in Moscow. The latter provides 1 channel per 5000 subscribers which is extremely low. The channels in the Russian network are semi-automatic service and require operator assistance.

9.06   The staff ratio (number of telecommunications staff per 1000 connected lines) is about 14. Considering the rural character and low population density of Kyrgyzstan this compares normally with ratios of to 10 in industrialized countries and favorably with ratios of 30 to 150 in Asia and Africa. About 38 percent of the subscribers are in Bishkek, 34 percent in other urban areas, and 28 percent in rural areas. 20 percent of subscribers are business customers.

Performance

9.07   Technical. The network appears to operate poorly. The fault rate (average yearly number of faulty lines per 100 subscribers) of 2 is very high and the traffic congestion on the lines at peak hours is quite high. Yearly growth in connected capacity averaged 7% during the last five years and the exchange fill (percent of connected lines to installed capacity) is 7%. This leaves only a small margin of about 40,000 lines available for new subscribers. The registered waiting list of unfilled applications is 107,000 though it is unclear to what extent this demand will remain if tariffs are increased and the economy continues to deteriorate.

9.08   Financial. Telecommunications historically has been a small but reasonably profitable sector, despite low tariffs. It has been self-sufficient (independent of the government budget) since 1986. The overall rate of return on net fixed assets for all communication activities was 12 percent in 1991, but this number is potentially misleading since asset values were arbitrary and have not been revalued.

9.09   Telecommunication revenues equalled R81.8 million in 1991 or 45 percent of total communications revenue. Assuming that telecommunications generated an equivalent level of expenses and taxes,[1] the telecom operating profit would have been R17.4 million (21 percent of revenue) and net income 10.1 million. This is equivalent to R252 of revenue and R31 of net income per connected subscriber line. By comparison in Western countries the average revenue per connected subscriber is 600.

---

1.   Under their current accounting practices, expense and tax amounts are combined for all communication activities. It is therefore virtually impossible to identify the expenses or taxes generated by each activity.

Policy Issues and Recommendations

9.10   During 1991, MOC began revising its strategic plan in light of the ongoing political changes within the former Soviet Union. It has recently submitted a proposal to separate telecommunication activities from postal and press functions but the proposal has yet to be approved by the Supreme Soviet. In the interim period, the focus has been on maintaining the existing level and quality of service despite high inflation, a contracting economy, and resulting cash flow shortages.

Sector Restructuring

9.11   To introduce a market orientation will require developing a new sector strategy that includes clear objectives, priorities among objectives, and a short and medium-term implementation plan. A first step in this process would be to commercialize and modernize operations. Important initial steps to consider in commercializing will be to:

a)   establish telecommunications and postal activities as separate, independent, and autonomous operating entities with separate financial statements;

b)   after establishing separate entities, privatize ancillary, independent activities such as the subscription and delivery of press publications, sound and television broadcasting, construction activities, and money transfers; and

c)   provide improved telecommunication services to subscribers who will promote overall economic development and who have an ability to pay. Important issues will be to i) improve service, ii) identify priority sectors and identify how to meet their requirements given limited resources, iii) introduce payment for international communications in foreign currency for entities with access to foreign exchange (i.e. hotels, embassies, international trade, etc.), and iv) reinvest a significant portion of foreign exchange income into the sector.

Regulatory Framework

9.12   A sound regulatory framework is essential to successful commercialization. Regulatory and policy activities should be separated from operational activities with the former under the direct responsibility of the MOC. A regulatory body would ideally promote an investor friendly environment, i.e. with appropriate laws on property ownership, competition, repatriation of profits, tariff setting policies, licensing, frequency allocation, etc. A legally separate, commercial firm, with the Ministry as the sole or primary shareholder could carry out operating activities. This would enable the Ministry to retain indirect control of the firm through regulations and through its role as a stockholder while enabling the firm to establish commercial operations, improve efficiency, and possibly attract private investment.

9.13   Without a sound regulatory framework and a legally separate operating firm, it is unlikely that foreign entities will invest in telecommunications. Furthermore such a framework will enable the Ministry to begin to possibly privatize the operating firm and introduce competition in value added services (mobile communications, data transmission, access to data banks and information facilities, electronic mail, etc.).

Institutional Restructuring

9.14   MOC or a new operating firm should review existing business practices and organization structure. This would include financial and accounting policies and procedures, operations practices, and human resource requirements; particularly training. Internationally accepted financial and accounting procedures and control tools should be introduced.[2] Restructuring should include establishing marketing, sales, and customer service groups; revamping existing departments; and revising the relationship between the headquarters and regional operating entities. The planning and coordination activities should be done in close cooperation between headquarters and the regional operating firms while the day-to-day activities are done by the regional staff. These regional entities should continue to operate as separate profit and loss centers though the cost allocation methods (allocation of revenue and expenses) should be reviewed.

9.15   An estimated 4-5,000 employees work specifically with telecommunications. These staff are well educated but have little or no education in international business concepts or the latest telecommunication technology used internationally. A major staff retraining program is therefore required for telecom staff. The quality of the retraining effort will be a major determinant of the success of the commercialization effort. Creative training techniques and strategies should therefore be explored. A training program could be implemented in phases with a few staff being trained as trainers who would then train other staff.

9.16   Establishing sound wage and incentive programs to properly motivate staff will be required to improve productivity. Over the longer term, other human resource activities such as career development, benefits, etc. will need to be reviewed and incorporated into a comprehensive human resource development program.

Development Program

9.17   For historical reasons, the Ministry lacks adequate development planning, procurement, and implementation capabilities. Currently, no comprehensive development plan exists. The main emphasis in planning thus far has been to devise a method to develop international communication capabilities that are independent of Moscow. There is wide recognition however of the need to rehabilitate and expand the existing local and regional networks. Regional communications will need to be strategically and technically planned in cooperation with the regional cooperative venture, Intertelecom. Outside assistance will be required to advise on and strengthen the Ministry's and operating entities' development planning, procurement, and implementation capabilities.

Tariff Policy

9.18   Tariffs need to be revised on an ongoing basis to adjust for inflation and devaluation. This was not the case in 1991 leading to an increase in operating expense as a percentage of revenue to 90 percent from 4 percent in 1990. Tariffs were raised an average of 500 percent on January 1, 1992, but given the pace of recent price increases, will have to be adjusted on a monthly or quarterly basis to maintain their level in real terms. Moreover, tariffs will have to rise in real terms to provide the funds for future investments. Hence, a thorough tariff and demand analysis to determine optimal levels, timing of tariff adjustments, and the appropriate market segments to target is necessary.

---

2.   Accounting procedures should be adopted in common with other sectors (Chapter 3).

Investment Strategy

9.19   Given the expected contraction of the economy, in the next 1 - 2 years the Ministry should concentrate on expanding higher revenue generating international services,[3] providing service to emerging business subscribers, and maintaining and improving the existing quality of national, interrepublic, and local services to business and residential subscribers. In 1993 and possibly 1994, it is likely that telephone lines currently used by government agencies will become available as the size of government activities shrinks. These telephone lines can be made available to emerging business subscribers. Investment of $1 - 2 million will probably be required for cables and other equipment to connect these subscribers. As the business community grows, it will be necessary to develop additional telephone capacity, to provide additional services to business as well as residential subscribers in urban and rural areas, and to replace obsolete equipment.

9.20   Import requirements of about $3.5 million in 1992-93 comprising of cables and outside plant equipment for local networks; spare parts and extension units for multiplex transmission, local and trunk switching, traffic control installations, and maintenance improvement; teleprinters and facsimile terminal equipment; and tools, measuring instruments, machinery, and specialized vehicles for construction and maintenance of local cable and overhead line networks would be needed to fulfill such an agenda. In addition, installation of an international satellite communications system is of high priority.

9.21   The priority for such investments would of course be linked to an assessment of the development capacity of private enterprise, as well as competing demands from other sectors. However, the very high correlation (close to one) between the growth of international trade and telecommunications services, and the current inadequacies within Kyrgyzstan point to the need for early investments in these directions. Because Kyrgyzstan is a mountainous and land-locked country, high quality and readily accessible telecommunications services are particularly important to its development.

Transportation

9.22   Kyrgyzstan's transport sector is relatively developed and potentially able to serve the needs of the economy adequately. The infrastructure appears to be of sound quality and equipment is available in sufficient quantity. A major challenge of the coming years will be to ensure that these assets are properly maintained and efficiently operated. This will require a judicious allocation of resources for funding, adjustments in the price and tax system to eliminate user subsidies, and creation of a competitive transport market. Reform of the existing organization of the sector is also a priority, as is acceleration of privatization of transport and construction companies.

The Transport System

9.23   Kyrgyzstan has a relatively developed transport network, well adapted to its unique geographical characteristics, in particular the concentration of the population in only two clusters in the north, around Bishkek, and the southwest, around Osh, and the vast mountainous and scarcely populated areas in between. The road network is the backbone of the transport system. With about 21,000 km of inter- and intra-urban roads, road density is about 0.1 km/sq km and there are 220 persons/km, which

---

3.   International communications accounted for only one percent of total telephone revenue in recent years.

compares well with similar countries. The network serves the entire country and is particularly dense around Bishkek and Osh. The proportion of paved roads is relatively high (50 percent) and the network is generally in good condition. It is an asset of great value and unusual quality, given Kyrgyzstan's level of development. It probably does not need to be developed for the time being but will require a high level of funding to be adequately maintained. Air transport is also unusually developed in Kyrgyzstan with two international airports (Bishkek and Osh) and a large number of local runways that are served by the national company recently formed out of the break up of Aeroflot. The railway consists of a small line (340 km) in the north of the country, which links to Russia through Kazakhstan.

9.24   Three main government departments are responsible for the transport sector. First, the Ministry of Transport provides the road infrastructure, most passenger transport services by road, and about a third of all road freight transport services. It is also beginning to become involved in the development of sector regulations. Second, the State Civil Aviation Agency manages airports, all domestic air transport services and about half of international air services. Third, the Bishkek Railway Department is responsible for rail transport. There is currently no systematic coordination among these agencies.

Transport Demand

9.25   Kyrgyzstan's economy is highly transport intensive. There are approximately 1.3 tons per km of freight transport for each US $ of 1991 GNP, less than in the former USSR (4.7), but much more than in countries like Bulgaria (0.8) and those of Western Europe (about 0.25). Road transport is predominant with 72 percent of total freight tons per km and 95 percent of total passenger per km movements. Given the well developed road infrastructure, though, road traffic is on the whole moderate ranging from about 15,000 vehicles/day on a few high traffic corridors to less then 1000 vehicles/day on many secondary roads.

9.26   As the economy restructures and energy prices continue to rise, it is likely that transport demand will decline. Transport demand during the first half of 1992 was generally quoted as being 30 percent below the demand of previous years. Demand will also certainly diversify. Kyrgyzstan now makes, for example, only marginal use of container transport, which may change rapidly. The transport share of larger and heavier trucks is also likely to increase substantially. Air transport may decline as prices become better linked to costs. In general, except for urban buses, there is ample capacity in the transport system to meet demand.

9.27   Given the integration of Kyrgyzstan's economy within that of the former Soviet Union and the remote origin and destination of many imports/exports, international transport demand is very large. The railway's total freight transport within Kyrgyzstan, only a fraction of the total international transport of the country, is already about 2.4 billion tons per km. Kyrgyzstan's economy is thus highly dependent on the performance of the rail systems of other countries. It will therefore be of strategic importance for Kyrgyzstan, in the long term, to ensure that it has access to several alternative international routes. In the medium term, however, the benefits of such security of access must be weighed against the probably very high cost of infrastructure development.

Issues and Recommendations

9.28   Although the transport sector appears to serve current demand relatively well, there are many inefficiencies that effect its economic cost and undermine its ability to adapt to future demand.

9.29   Expenditures. There is an acute need to increase the funding of road maintenance. The 1992 maintenance budget (R170 million) allows maintenance of about 80 km of roads, or only about 15-20 percent of the need. In the medium term, the consequences of such underfunding could be dramatic. Without timely reseal, the paved roads of Kyrgyzstan, which have often not been well constructed and thus do not have a strong structure, could deteriorate very quickly. As a result, vehicle operating costs would increase drastically and reconstruction expenditures several times the cost of maintenance would later be needed. Many gravel roads could also become impassable. An adequate level of funding must thus be reinstated as soon as possible. If, however, increased funding is not available, plans should be formulated to concentrate existing resources on a smaller network of priority roads while substantially lowering the standards of low volume roads.

9.30   Given the likelihood of declining transport demand and the relative overcapacity of the transport system, there is probably very little need for investment in transport in the coming years, except for replacement of some key equipment. Maintenance should, in any case, be given priority. The few investment projects that could be entertained should therefore be submitted to a rigorous analysis, including economic and financial analysis. Equipment replacement, in particular, should be considered only if transport demand cannot be satisfied at a reasonable cost by improving operations and/or increasing productivity of the existing assets.

9.31   Pricing and Regulations. The prices of almost all transport services are fixed by the Government. In general, price levels do not take account of depreciation based on actual replacement value. Some prices are also well below costs, especially for urban bus services. There is evidence that this pricing system prevents the best use of existing assets. It is also likely to discourage innovation and investment. In addition, as the economy adjusts and transport input prices (especially energy prices) continue to increase in absolute and relative terms, such a system will become exceedingly difficult to manage. Particularly in road transport there are substantial variations in the type of service provided, which should be (but currently are not) reflected in prices.

9.32   The system of road user taxation in Kyrgyzstan is inadequate. The efficient use of the road infrastructure requires that the users be charged for the marginal costs that they impose on society (deterioration of the road, congestion, and environmental costs). The main instruments for this purpose are, in most countries, an annual vehicle registration tax and, most importantly, a diesel and gasoline tax which is directly related to the quantity of road use. However, there is currently no fuel tax in Kyrgyzstan and the revenues from the vehicle registration tax are very small. There is also a small tax on transport expenditures which is only indirectly related to road use. As a result, even if the price of petroleum products reflected opportunity cost (which it currently does not), road users would be subsidized by the general public. This needs to be changed; in particular, a fuel tax needs to be established. An efficient road user taxation system would also help Government mobilize the additional funds critically needed for road maintenance.

9.33   A new licensing system for road transport companies is being prepared by the Ministry of Transport. This system would establish very rigid rules as to where and when any road transport company can provide service. The experience of other countries, for example, Mexico, with such a type of licensing has resulted in many distortions and high total costs to the economy. Road transport works much better in a deregulated and competitive environment. Companies should only be submitted to the laws and regulations regarding, in general, commerce and labor practices, and, specifically, drivers' licensing, vehicle weight and dimensions limits, and technical safety and environmental standards. A simple and non-restrictive registration system and rules on consumer information may also prove useful. The Government should strive to put such a regulatory environment in place. In addition, to ensure competition, it is important that a large number of independent private transport companies be established as soon as possible.

9.34   <u>Institutional Aspects</u>. Privatization in the transport sector is progressing very slowly. There do not seem to be any precise plans currently for this purpose. Yet, the potential for privatization in the sector is very high, especially regarding road transport and the construction industry. Indeed, to achieve efficiency in these activities requires adaptation to many different market demands and special circumstances, rapid reaction to changes, and high flexibility in organization and personnel, characteristics that, in most cases, only active private entrepreneurs have. The current organization of road transport and construction in Kyrgyzstan also renders the creation of a competitive market relatively more straightforward than in other sectors.

9.35   In the current structure of the Ministry of Transport, there are a large number of medium size transport and construction companies that already function in a quasi-autonomous way and, in most cases, could be privatized almost as they are, provided that the current boundaries of their territories are eliminated so as to create a competitive environment. There are limited economies of scale in general in road transport and construction at Kyrgyzstan's stage of development and the existing companies could function at a high level of efficiency. It would therefore be of great benefit to accelerate substantially the pace of privatization in road transport and construction, including, to the largest extent possible, such companies of other ministries. In construction, however, the Government should also ensure that appropriate contractual arrangements and supervision procedures are developed in parallel. Privatization of Kyrgyzstan's airline could be a longer-term objective. However, prior to this, competition and efficiency in the air transport subsector should be encouraged by opening it to private participation.

9.36   Although there already appear to be good capabilities and useful systems and procedures within governmental institutions, some key improvements are needed. These relate especially the roads subsector:

a)   First, better supervision of civil works, including systematic quality control, is needed. Despite generally sound designs, the quality of road pavements and especially their service life appears to be poor, reflecting a low quality of construction materials and practices. Detailed procedures to control and enforce quality at every stage of construction would therefore help to considerably reduce the costs of maintaining and using roads in the longer term;

b)   Second, competition should be promoted among construction companies and fair and efficient relationships need to be established between the Government and construction companies. For this purpose, a system of adequate procedures needs to be in place for selecting contractors, as well as standard tendering and contract documents for civil works, and contract administration procedures;

c)   Third, the current system of periodic analysis of pavement conditions   should be complemented by some objective measurements (for example, of the percentage of cracking and potholes). Decisions on what type of periodic treatment is most appropriate on a road (for example, single or double seal, asphalt concrete) could also be helped greatly by the use of computer models, now widely available, which can assess the costs and benefits of various alternatives; and

d)   Fourth, a road research unit should be created to gather available information on road technologies to help improve or introduce more efficient technologies in Kyrgyzstan.

All the former Soviet republics may be confronted with similar problems as Kyrgyzstan in the above areas. It would hence be of benefit if comparable systems and procedures could be established, since the costs of preparation and the lessons of experience could then be shared.

9.37   Although action is most needed in the short term in the roads subsector, key institutional improvements are also possible with the railways and the airline. As is now the practice in many countries, the Government should establish "performance plans" or "contract plans" between itself and these companies. Such plans would set out clear operational and financial objectives for the companies, including performance targets, and provide a framework for revising tariffs; they would enable companies to function autonomously on a commercial basis while ensuring sufficient government supervision.

9.38   There is also a need to better define government responsibilities in the transport sector and, possibly, centralize these or, at least, create coordination mechanisms. For example, there is apparently no unit clearly in charge of setting the standards for the weight, dimensions, and other technical characteristics of vehicles. There is no authority responsible for centralizing all transport relevant information, analyzing trends and emerging problems in surface transport, and monitoring implementation of transport policies. Responsibility for road safety is also split among several institutions and possibly not fully covered. In addition, there appears to be little coordination between road and rail transport, especially regarding investments, and no knowledge nor promotion of multimodel transport. These deficiencies need to be remedied.

9.39   Although the experience of other countries indicates no ideal way to allocate government responsibilities in the transport sector, the disaggregation found in Kyrgyzstan is unusual. The expansion of the Ministry of Transport to cover the areas mentioned above and, possibly, the supervision of the railways should be considered. A reorganization of the State Civil Aviation Agency would also be useful. Its main objective should be to clearly separate the function of regulation and policy formulation from the management of infrastructure and provision of air transport services. In particular, the airline and the airports should be fully autonomous agencies with a well-defined supervisory role by the Agency.

Box 9-1. Technical Assistance Requirements in the Transport Sector

Technical assistance will be needed in the short term to:

- Help Government prepare regulations for the competitive tendering of civil works and train contractors, consultants, and government staff in basic techniques of the construction business.

- Help the highway department set up methods and procedures for supervision and quality control of civil works.

- Improve the formulation of road rehabilitation and maintenance programs and the selection of technologies.

The total estimated cost is US$ 500,000.

The Environment

9.40   Kyrgyzstan has made great strides since 1988 in establishing the basic tools for environmental protection. The State Committee for Environmental Protection (**Goskompriroda**) is well-structured and staffed to deal with the environmental problems likely to be faced: localized air pollution around the main cities; more extensive water pollution, with agricultural complexes and industries the main contributors; and the need to safeguard the soils, forests and wildlife of the country. In contrast to some other states of the former USSR, the situation is not of crisis proportions but could deteriorate if sound policies and programs are not pursued.

Environmental Status

9.41   In comparison with some other East European and former Soviet countries, environmental problems are only moderate in severity and do not appear to pose immediate threats to human health or sustainable development. Nevertheless, air quality in the major cities is unsatisfactory, with particulate levels (from power production, industry and motor vehicles) up to five times standards and benzopyrenes (from motor vehicles) up to 15 times standards.[4] Though lead is not systematically monitored it is also likely to be a problem. Intensive livestock complexes and agro-processing factories for meat and milk are among the major sources of water pollution. Tailings from mining operations probably pose significant health hazards, especially the uranium mine at Kara Balta (Chapter 8). There is no disposal facility for industrial hazardous wastes and municipal waste disposal is inadequate. Little attention is paid to occupational health and safety. Though no data are available on food safety, this is another area of potential concern.

9.42   Forests cover 3.7% of the territory of Kyrgyzstan and past overcutting appears to have been arrested. Overgrazing of the mountain pastures is being brought under control. Protected areas

---

4.   As discussed below, Kyrghyzstan's standards are often unnecessarily strict. Even so, exceedances of these magnitudes indicate real problems.

cover 0.4% of the territory, with plans to expand this to 2%; this might well be increased further, given the large amount of very scenic, biologically diverse and thinly populated land that Kyrgyzstan possesses.

Laws and Institutions

9.43   Kyrgyzstan has a relatively well developed institutional framework for environmental regulation, with **Goskompriroda** having a staff of 340 and branches in each of the **oblasts**; Bishkek city government has an environment department with 14 staff. Shortages of technical staff do not appear to be a problem. **Goskompriroda** has a good understanding of the problems faced and is developing the necessary tools: a new Environmental Law; draft laws for air, water, soils, nature etc; environmental assessment and auditing procedures; market based instruments, such as pollution permits, fees and fines; and plans to expand the system of protected areas. Even so, the full implications of economic restructuring and the new relationship between the Government and polluters and users of natural resources have yet to be fully realized. As in many countries, **Goskompriroda**'s links with the economic policy-makers are undeveloped.

Standards and Enforcement

9.44   Kyrgyzstan still uses the standards of the former USSR which, in many cases (especially in ambient air standards), are stricter than necessary to ensure human health. It is recommended that, in revising legislation, standards consistent with European Community (or other international) practice be introduced, perhaps in stages, together with strict enforcement to give credibility to the process. As in most other former centrally planned countries, strict laws were ineffective in the past, as it was difficult for one branch of government to regulate another, exceptions were readily granted, and, in the absence of market prices, pollution fees and fines could be passed on to the customer. To overcome these problems, Kyrgyzstan needs to establish a system of pollution permits for existing industrial and municipal sources, starting with the major sources of air and water pollution. Permitted discharges would be calculated -- and then negotiated on a case by case basis with the enterprise -- based on best available technology and on the contribution of the source to ambient air or water degradation. In most cases, some reasonable period (2 to 5 years) would be allowed to reach compliance. For discharges within the permitted limit, fees would be paid; higher discharges would lead to fines or, if persistent, more drastic penalties. It will be important that the introduction of this system be closely linked to the economic restructuring process, especially with respect to privatization.

9.45   Fees and fines should be progressively raised until they begin to offer an incentive to the polluter to lower his emissions by investment in pollution control. In the meantime, the fees and fines offer a useful source of revenue for the **oblast** environment funds. Criteria for the use of these funds may need to be further developed.

9.46   Use of **environmental assessments** to analyze the environmental impact of proposed new projects has begun; its use should be extended to all projects with significant impacts in the public and private sectors, with opportunity for public participation.

Links with Economic Restructuring

9.47   The restructuring of the economy provides short-term opportunities that should not be missed for addressing environmental objectives. Rising energy prices will lead consumers to take conservation measures, which, together with cutbacks in industrial production and the shift to less energy intensive industrial technology, will lead to reduced demand for energy and consequently less polluting emissions, to the extent that such energy demand is met from more highly polluting fuels. Environmental costs should be included in assessing the costs of alternative fuels.

9.48   The privatization program also provides opportunities for achieving environmental goals, especially in agriculture. It would not be difficult to attach provisions to privatization plans requiring the new owners to reduce pollution to acceptable levels within an agreed time period. This should particularly be the case for intensive livestock units, which are among the major contributors to water pollution, and where the technology is well-established and the stabilized wastes can have considerable value in the farm operation. For industries producing hazardous wastes, the question of liability for past environmental neglect will need to be clarified; in most cases, the State, as previous owner, should accept liability. Foreign investors, in particular, will require reassurance on this point.

Issues and Recommendations

9.49   Over the <u>medium term</u>, Goskompriroda should give priority to the following tasks:

a)   establishment of technically sound permits ("ecological passports") for all polluting enterprises, close monitoring of actual levels and vigorous enforcement of sanctions;

b)   raising pollution fees and fines first to offset the effects of inflation and then, over time, to begin to influence enterprises to install pollution control devices;

c)   development of a system for setting priorities for allocating funds from the Environment Funds at oblast level;[5]

d)   continued training of its own staff and the staff of other government agencies and enterprises, both locally and abroad, especially in adapting previous regulatory practices to a market economy;

e)   stepping up its efforts to ensure that environmental impact assessments are provided for all new projects in the public and private sector and to undertake industrial environmental audits in existing facilities, with an emphasis on no-cost and low-cost measures;

f)   beginning analytical studies of important pollution "hot spots", such as Bishkek, Osh or Kara Balta, to assess the relative risks from various pollution sources and cost-effective mitigation strategies;

g)   expanding the size of protected areas for nature conservation, by balancing the needs of conservation (protection of threatened species and ecosystems), recreation (local and foreign tourism) and economic activities (grazing, mining etc);

---

5.   The pros and cons of such earmarking have been extensively debated. As long as such funds are included in the overall budgetary framework, there are often advantages of transparency in earmarking environmental charges to special funds, particularly when this occurs at the local level, where there are few alternative revenue sources. All the countries of Central and Eastern Europe are following this approach.

h)   continuing its participation in efforts to address global environmental problems, such as the Global Climate Change Convention.

9.50   In the longer term, the environmental community should be very active in shaping Kyrgyzstan's energy policy, especially in supporting efforts to emphasize cleaner sources, such as hydro-electric power and natural gas, in both industry and domestic heating. Reduction of emissions from motor vehicles will require a coordinated approach with neighboring states, particularly with respect to tax policy, in lowering the levels of lead and other pollutants in fuels and in regulating long-distance truck traffic. Meanwhile, much could be done within Kyrgyzstan to require improved maintenance, especially of diesel engines.

9.51   Kyrgyzstan has expressed a willingness to step up its efforts, in cooperation with other Central Asian Republics, to promote sustainable land and water development in the Aral Sea Basin (see Annex). This will be a long-term program, requiring considerable international assistance; mobilization of such assistance is now beginning. The plans of the Ministry of Land Reclamation and Irrigation to promote more efficient irrigation technology and to introduce water charges will provide important policy support to such efforts.

9.52   Goskompriroda has indicated that it would welcome international assistance in: researching low waste technology; disposal of hazardous wastes; environmental assessment; development of laws and standards; access to international data banks; provision of modern monitoring equipment; and, training of its specialists. The City of Bishkek would welcome financial assistance in expanding its wastewater treatment plant, building a separation plant for its solid waste, and developing a disposal system for industrial hazardous wastes. These priorities are fully consistent with the above recommendations.

ANNEX: ARAL SEA ISSUES

Background[1]

The Aral Sea lies between Kazakhstan and Uzbekistan in a vast geological depression in the Kyzylkum and Karakum deserts. In 1960, the Aral Sea was the fourth largest inland lake in the world. Since then, however, it has shrunk significantly because of nearly total cutoff of river inflow from the Amu Dar'ya (river) and Syr Dar'ya as a result of heavy withdrawals for irrigation. By 1989 the sea level had fallen by 14.3 meters and the surface area had shrunk from 68,000 km^2 to 37,000 km^2. The salinity of the sea had increased to 2.8 times its 1960 level.

The Aral Sea basin extends over 690,000 km^2, including the republics of Kazakhstan, Kyrgyzstan, Tadjikistan, Turkmenistan and Uzbekistan. A small portion of its headwaters is located in Afghanistan, Iran and China. The basin is formed by two of the largest rivers of Central Asia - Amu Dar'ya and Syr Dar'ya - both fed by the snow melts and glaciers from the mountains. The Amu Dar'ya sources are mostly located in Tadjikistan, with a few watercourses originating in northeastern Afghanistan. The Syr Dar'ya originates mainly in Kyrgyzstan. It runs across small portions of Tadjikistan and Uzbekistan and through the Kazakh provinces of Chimkent and Kzyl-Orda.

The total population of the Aral basin is estimated at 35 million based on the 1989 census. Uzbekistan, with 19.9 million, is the most populated among the countries in the region, Kazakhstan has a population of 16.5 million of which 2.48 million live in the Aral Basin. The rate of natural population increase in the region averaged 2.54% over the period 1979-89 compared to a national (FSU) rate of 0.87%.

The Aral Basin has three distinctive ecological zones: the mountains, the deserts, and the Aral with its deltas. The Tian Shan and Pamir mountains in the south and southwest are characterized by high altitudes (with peaks over 7000 m) and by high moisture coefficients, with average annual precipitation ranging from 800 to 1600 mm. The mountains host large forest reserves and some national parks. In their foothills and valleys, soil and temperature conditions are favorable for agriculture. The lowland deserts of Karakum and Kyzylkum cover most of the basin area, and are characterized by low precipitation (under 100 mm/year) and high evaporation rates. Both the rivers' banks and deltas and the Aral Sea islands are characterized by a variety of vegetation and wildlife resources. For example, the Barsakelmes Island, in the main part of the Aral Sea, is a natural reserve for endangered species such as the Kulan (Asiatic wild burro) and Siagak, an ancient variety of antelope. The sea itself was the habitat for more than 24 species of fish, and a number of other aquatic organisms.

Issues

The main issues relating to the Aral Sea basin area are the following: the reduction of the sea, the destruction of its aquatic ecosystem, the lowering of soil quality in the Aral Sea Basin, pollution of surface and groundwater of the delta draining into the Aral Sea, depressed economy and

---

1. For reference, the issues surrounding the Aral Sea Basin have been studied by a number of individuals and organizations. In particular, UNEP has produced "The Diagnostic Study for the Development of an Action Plan for the Aral Sea," which was issued in July 1992. This report presents a comprehensive analysis of the causes of the Aral Sea crisis and provides a basis for elaboration and analysis of the strategies for future activities for mitigating the ecological disaster.

adverse health impact on the population due to lack of potable water and inadequate sanitation.

The causes as well as the regional effects of the Aral Sea shrinkage can be enumerated. Inefficient irrigation practices coupled with heavy chemical applications, cultivation of cotton and rice, and inappropriate development policies are among the important causes. For the last three decades, Soviet policy in the region focussed on massive irrigation projects along the Amu Dar'ya and Syr Dar'ya with the primary goal of creating a Central Asian cotton belt. Urban and industrial water use, though still a small fraction of total water use, has also risen. The irrigation techniques have lead to high rates of leakage and evaporation as well as waterlogging and salinity build-up. As a result, the two river flows that feed the Aral Sea are nearly completely expended before they ever reach the Sea.

Numerous reports and articles have been written by experts, both national and foreign, during the past decade on this crisis, attracting world-wide attention. Environmental experts, scientists, engineers and economists from all over the world have joined their counterparts from the FSU. Their findings have been presented in several publications during the past decade and discussed in many international seminars. Recently, in June 1992, the Stockholm Environment Institute, Boston Center, published the results of a microcomputer model for simulating current water balances and evaluating water management strategies in the Aral Sea region. The study presented a picture of an unfolding and deepening crisis situation and concluded that, in the absence of an action plan to save the Aral Sea, its surface areas would decrease from its 1987 level of 41 square kilometers to 9 square kilometers by 2015, and that the sea would turn into several small residual brine lakes.

The United Nations Environment Program (UNEP) considers that, in terms of its ecological, economic, and social consequences, the Aral Sea is one of the most staggering ecological disasters of the twentieth century. Recognizing the crucial need to save the disappearing Aral Sea and the need to provide an overall perspective of the Aral Region, the UNEP issued a diagnostic study of the state of its environment, its population and its economics in July 1992. The report presents a comprehensive analysis of the causes of the Aral Sea crisis, but it does not recommend a specific action plan. It provides, however, a basis for elaboration and analysis of the strategies for future activities for mitigating the ecological disaster.

The Bank's Assessment of the Aral Sea Crisis[2]

Despite a decade of studies by national and international experts a viable plan for addressing the Aral Sea problems has not been formulated. Ideas and suggestions abound, but their technical, economic, financial and political feasibility has not been examined. The studies indicate that the solutions may be extremely costly, difficult to finance, and would take decades to implement. Thirty major action programs suggested in these reports broadly cover the following categories of action:

(a)   Actions proposed to increase the inflows to the Aral Sea (4 major projects and programs);

(b)   Actions proposed to save a part of the water currently used for irrigation and other purposes and use the saved water to increase the inflows to the

---

2.   This assessment is based on numerous reports written by experts and on the findings of the Bank's Aral Sea Reconnaissance mission, which visited the Aral Sea basin in September 1992.

Aral Sea (14 major projects and programs);

(c)   Measures to improve the health and environment of the population in the Aral Sea Region (8 major projects and programs);

(d)   Rationalization of water rights in the Aral Sea Basin across Central Asia and Kazakhstan (4 major projects and programs);

The technical, economic, financial, and political feasibility of these programs have not been determined. They seem to constitute a master program costing, around $30 billion to $50 billion that would require a period of 40 to 50 years to implement. The authors of these programs have not considered how essential are these projects; who will finance them; and whether the Republics are willing to share such large costs.

The proposed projects and programs underline one overriding objective: to increase the inflows to the Aral Sea and restore it to its pre-disaster conditions, or to some level that would save the sea. The rationale of this objective is not clear.

The feasibility of some grand schemes such as diverting the rivers flowing north to the Arctic Sea, or transferring water from the Caspian Sea, for increasing the inflows to the Aral Sea is questionable. Aside from their huge costs, these schemes could involve serious political and environmental issues.

The feasibility and sustainability of some proposals for increasing the inflows to the Aral Sea by reducing the existing uses is also questionable. They include, for example, limiting water deliveries from the Amu and Syr rivers for irrigation and other purposes; and reducing the area of cotton and rice crops. It may be necessary to take these actions for other economic reasons, but it seems unrealistic to expect that the water saved from these actions would be available for increasing the inflows to the Aral Sea on a sustainable long-term basis.

The Bank's assessment of the Aral Sea crisis is classified under three categories: (a) Aral Sea and Aral Sea related issues; (b) regional issues; and, (c) development issues that should receive high priority although not directly related to the Aral Sea problems.

Aral Sea and Aral Sea Related Issues

(i)   There are differences in views and uncertainty regarding the extent of the existing and future adverse effects of the Aral Sea. The problems appear more manageable than indicated in a number of previous reports.

(ii)   The proposals to divert water from outside the basin (from the Arctic rivers and Caspian Sea) to fill the Aral Sea do not appear viable.

(iii) Conserving the water resources of the basin by reducing waste, improving water management, diversifying crops, and other measures are important and should receive priority. However, the political feasibility and economic justification of diverting the saved water to fill the Aral Sea is questionable.

(iv)   The available information indicates that it is not possible to restore the Sea to its pre-disaster conditions. However, it may be necessary to stabilize the Sea at a sustainable level based on available flows.

(v)   The living conditions of the people in the zone around the Aral Sea that has been seriously affected by the changes in the Aral Sea are deplorable. Lack of potable water, water borne diseases, inadequate health facilities, depressed economy, lack of employment opportunities, adverse effects of sand and salt storms and the deteriorating ecosystem are some of the major problems. This disaster zone covers parts of Kazakhstan, Uzbekistan and Turkmenistan. Improving the living conditions and environment of the people in this area should receive high priority. The suggestions made in some reports to shift the most severely affected population appear unrealistic. The people need development assistance, not migration assistance.

Regional Issues

(i)   The Agreement signed on February 15, 1992 between the Aral Sea Basin Republics, and the Protocol and Resolutions established during April-August, 1992 for cooperation on management, utilization and protection of water resources, and for joint measures for solution of the Aral Sea problems are commendable. Preliminary review, however, indicates that they are not adequate to constitute binding legal treaties. Some subdued complaints about the fairness of allocations are already simmering and other riparians (China, Afghanistan, and Iran) have not been consulted yet. It is advisable to improve these agreements to internationally accepted standards to avoid possible conflicts in the future.

(ii)   The Republics have established an Inter-ministerial Committee and two River Basin Commissions (BVOs) for allocating water, monitoring water use and quality and for data collection, analysis, management and forecasting. These arrangements are working satisfactorily and are commendable. However, the capacity and effectiveness of these institutions should be enhanced by increasing their decision making and regulatory powers and providing them with advanced equipment, facilities and technologies to play their role most effectively.

(iii)   The need for comprehensive planning and management of water resources, both quantity and quality, and for the short and long term, was stressed at some meetings. Given the scarcity of water resources, increasing demands, and the fact that the river flows have been almost fully diverted for irrigation and other purposes at present, the need and importance of developing strategies for comprehensive management of the water resources should be underscored.

(iv)   The high caliber of researchers and scientists of research institutes and academies of sciences dealing with water resources, ecology and pollution control is impressive. However, there a continuing depletion of talent due to the lack of funds, advanced equipment and facilities, and career development opportunities. These problems require urgent attention.

(v)   The Central Asian Research Institute of the region has now become an institute of the

Republic in which it was located. The need for a regional institution to address regional and Aral Sea research needs and to provide research support to the BVOs should be considered as a high priority.

Development Issues

The Republics' concerns with their country-specific development issues and the high priority they attach to water supply and sanitation, health, ecology, population, salinity and waterlogging, drainage, pollution control and food self-sufficiency programs in their respective countries is overwhelming. These programs should receive high priority for external assistance.

Statistical Appendix

Statistical Appendix - Contents

Table 1.1: Kyrgyzstan - Population and Employment - Summary Table 1/

	1980	1985	1986	1987	1988	1989	1990	1991
				(in thousands)				
Total Population	3593.2	3975.7	4051.6	4133.6	4213.0	4290.5	4367.2	4422.2
Males	1744.5	1933.2	1971.1	2013.1	2054.2	2094.3	2134.6	2165.3
Females	1848.7	2042.5	2080.5	2120.5	2158.8	2196.2	2232.6	2256.9
Urban	1379.9	1509.7	1537.7	1567.9	1601.7	1640.9	1663.8	1684.3
Rural	2213.3	2466.0	2513.9	2565.7	2611.3	2649.6	2703.4	2737.9
Total Employment of which:	1424.6	1614.3	1651.1	1702.7	1716.1	1738.9	1747.9	1750.0
on private plots and at home	88.7	107.2	122.2	176.8	185.3	190.6	186.9	189.6
				(in percent)				
Total Population	100.0	100.0	100.0	100.0	100.0	100.0	100.0	100.0
Males	48.6	48.6	48.6	48.7	48.8	48.8	48.9	49.0
Females	51.4	51.4	51.4	51.3	51.2	51.2	51.1	51.0
Urban	38.4	38.0	38.0	37.9	38.0	38.2	38.1	38.1
Rural	61.6	62.0	62.0	62.1	62.0	61.8	61.9	61.9
Below Active Age	39.6	39.0	39.1	39.3	39.4	39.5	39.6	39.6
Active Age	50.8	51.1	51.0	50.7	50.5	50.4	50.4	50.4
Over Active Age	9.6	9.9	9.9	10.0	10.1	10.0	10.0	10.0
Total Employment	100.0	100.0	100.0	100.0	100.0	100.0	100.0	100.0
State sector	78.6	78.7	78.4	76.0	75.1	74.4	74.1	71.7
Cooperatives	15.1	14.7	14.2	13.6	14.1	14.6	15.1	15.2
Collective farms	12.1	11.9	11.4	10.7	10.7	10.1	10.2	11.0
Consumer cooperatives	3.0	2.8	2.8	2.8	2.8	2.9	3.0	3.0
Goods and services coops	-	-	-	0.1	0.6	1.6	1.9	1.2
Sphere of individual labor	6.3	6.6	7.4	10.4	10.8	11.0	10.8	13.1
Total in national economy	100.0	100.0	100.0	100.0	100.0	100.0	100.0	100.0
Industry and construction	27.9	27.3	27.3	26.8	26.9	28.0	27.8	26.5
Agriculture and forestry	32.0	32.8	32.7	33.9	33.6	33.2	32.8	35.5
Transport and communication	7.6	7.5	7.4	6.9	6.5	5.5	5.4	5.3
Trade, catering, procurment	7.2	6.9	6.8	6.7	6.8	6.5	6.6	6.3
Health, physical education, social security, education, culture and arts, science and science services	18.1	18.3	18.5	18.3	18.9	19.6	20.3	19.8
Administration, credit and insurance	3.0	3.1	3.1	3.1	3.0	2.8	2.8	2.5
Other sectors	4.2	4.1	4.2	4.3	4.3	4.4	4.3	4.1

1/ 1989 Population data is from the January 12 Census; for the other years it is the data from the beginning of the year.

Source: Statistical Yearbook for Kyrgyzstan, 1990 and State Statistical Commitee.

Table 1.2: Kyrgyzstan - Labor Force

	1980	1985	1986	1987	1988	1989	1990	1991
				(in thousands)				
State Sector Employment	1163.0	1315.0	1341.0	1342.0	1338.0	1345.0	1350.0	1309.8
Percent of Women	46.6	46.6	47.0	47.0	46.8	46.8	47.6	47.7
Cooperatives	..	..	..	..	10.0	27.6	33.0	21.0
Percent of Women	..	..	..	..	25.0	24.3	22.1	25.2
Collective Farms	172.0	192.0	188.0	181.0	183.0	175.0	178.0	193.8
Percent of Women	45.0	..	..	..	..	40.1	40.4	47.1
Private Agriculture 1/	88.3	106.9	122.0	175.2	182.4	188.2	183.8	223.9
Percent of Women	35.1	..	..	..	..	43.3	42.4	..
Private Non-agriculture	0.4	0.3	0.2	1.6	2.9	2.4	3.1	5.1
Percent of Women	75.0	66.7	50.0	62.5	62.1	66.7	80.6	73.3
Total Employment	1423.7	1614.2	1651.2	1702.2	1716.3	1738.2	1747.9	1754.1
Percent of Women	45.7	..	..	..	..	45.4	45.6	..
Unemployed	154.6	134.8	141.2	107.9	119.9	129.3	134.5	165.2
of which:								
"Discouraged Workers"	75.9	61.7	67.8	54.8	68.4	73.2	73.5	72.7
Searching for a Job	14.5	12.0	11.8	11.0	10.0	10.0	11.0	11.5
Seasonally Unemployed	64.0	60.2	60.3	41.0	40.0	40.0	43.5	46.0
Unemployed Graduates	0.2	0.9	1.3	1.1	1.5	6.1	6.5	35.0
Percent of Women	64.1	64.1	64.3	64.0	64.5	64.6	64.5	64.7
Total Labor Force	1578.3	1749.0	1792.4	1810.1	1836.2	1867.5	1882.4	1919.3
Percent of Women	47.5	..	..	..	..	46.8	47.2	..
Memorandum Items:								
Share of State Employment								
(including Collective Farms)	93.8	93.4	92.6	89.5	88.6	87.4	87.4	85.7
Unemployment Rate	9.8	7.7	7.9	6.0	6.5	6.9	7.1	8.3
Working Age Population	1847.0	2037.0	2068.0	2097.0	2127.0	2165.0	2198.0	2216.0
Participation Rate 2/	85.5	85.9	86.7	86.3	86.3	86.3	85.6	86.1
Participation Rate - Women	82.7	..	..	..	..	82.9	82.9	..
Participation Rate - Men	88.1	..	..	..	..	89.4	88.3	..

1/ Includes persons officially classified as "employed in auxiliary activities".
2/ Participation rate is defined as the percent of labor force in the working age population (age 16-54 for women and 16-59 for men).

Source: State Statistical Committee.

Table 1.3: Kyrgyzstan - Employment by Sector

	1980	1985	1986	1987	1988	1989	1990	1991
	(in thousands, yearly average)							
Total employment 1/	1424.6	1614.3	1651.1	1702.7	1716.1	1738.9	1747.9	1750.0
Material sphere	1045.7	1180.3	1203.5	1247.8	1251.9	1264.4	1261.0	1264.0
Industry	295.1	321.7	327.1	331.4	333.1	333.0	332.1	332.8
Agriculture 2/	364.5	419.0	414.2	398.8	391.6	386.2	385.5	384.9
Forestry	3.2	3.3	3.4	3.3	3.4	3.0	2.9	2.9
Transport and communication 3/	65.1	73.5	73.8	71.3	67.3	57.1	56.6	56.4
Construction	102.5	119.4	123.0	123.8	126.5	151.5	152.8	151.7
Trade	102.7	111.0	112.0	114.0	116.1	113.6	115.1	115.0
Other types of activity of material production sphere (residual)	112.6	132.4	150.0	205.2	213.9	220.0	216.0	220.3
Non-material sphere 1/	378.9	434.0	447.6	454.9	464.2	474.5	486.9	486.0
Health, athletics and social security	73.9	85.2	89.1	91.1	95.4	101.3	104.6	104.3
Education, culture and art	150.2	174.0	180.2	185.6	194.8	204.6	215.5	215.3
Science and science services	34.4	35.9	36.2	35.1	34.1	34.2	34.6	35.0
Other	120.4	138.9	142.1	143.1	139.9	134.4	132.2	131.4
	(in percent of total)							
Total employment 1/	100.0	100.0	100.0	100.0	100.0	100.0	100.0	100.0
Material sphere	73.4	73.1	72.9	73.3	73.0	72.7	72.1	72.2
Industry	20.7	19.9	19.8	19.5	19.4	19.2	19.0	19.0
Agriculture 2/	25.6	26.0	25.1	23.4	22.8	22.2	22.1	22.0
Forestry	0.2	0.2	0.2	0.2	0.2	0.2	0.2	0.2
Transport and communication 3/	4.6	4.6	4.5	4.2	3.9	3.3	3.2	3.2
Construction	7.2	7.4	7.4	7.3	7.4	8.7	8.7	8.7
Trade	7.2	6.9	6.8	6.7	6.8	6.5	6.6	6.6
Other types of activity of material production sphere	7.9	8.2	9.1	12.1	12.5	12.7	12.4	12.6
Non-material sphere 1/	26.6	26.9	27.1	26.7	27.0	27.3	27.9	27.8
Memorandum items:								
Women employed (% of state sector)	48.4	48.3	48.7	48.3	48.6	48.7	49.5	49.0
State employees (excluding blue collar)	328.1	372.9	380.2	371.3	378.8	384.3	389.0	388.1
Working on private plots and at home	88.7	107.2	122.2	176.8	185.3	190.6	186.9	189.6

1/ Including working on private plots and at home.
2/ Excluding working on private plots.
3/ Servicing material production sphere.

Source: State Statistical Committee.

Table 2.1: Kyrgyzstan - Gross Domestic Product at Current Prices

	1985	1986	1987	1988	1989	1990	1991 a)
			(in millions of rubles)				
Total Gross Domestic Product	6,109	6,098	6,278	6,940	7,620	8,320	15,839
Net Value Added	5,152	5,079	5,263	5,742	6,367	6,995	12,936
Depreciation	957	1,019	1,015	1,198	1,253	1,325	2,903
Gross Material Product	5,151	5,127	5,260	5,840	6,464	7,007	13,273
By source:							
Agriculture	1,826	1,905	2,002	2,160	2,510	2,805	4,505
Net Value Added	1,649	1,717	1,806	1,960	2,315	2,599	4,058
Depreciation	177	188	196	200	195	206	447
Industry	1,898	1,755	1,875	2,081	2,250	2,348	5,985
Net Value Added	1,612	1,449	1,569	1,708	1,849	1,919	5,054
Depreciation	287	306	306	373	401	429	931
Construction	639	643	648	760	785	840	1,100
Net Value Added	568	567	587	647	671	720	864
Depreciation	71	76	61	113	114	120	236
Transport	284	306	314	351	357	397	672
Net Value Added	155	169	169	188	200	231	307
Depreciation	129	137	145	163	157	166	365
Other	503	518	421	489	562	617	1,011
Net Value Added	454	466	379	444	520	557	869
Depreciation	49	52	42	45	42	60	142
Gross Non-Material Product	958	971	1,018	1,100	1,157	1,313	2,566
Net Value Added	714	711	753	796	813	969	1,784
Depreciation	244	260	265	304	344	344	782
By end use:	7,098	7,111	7,444	8,088	9,301	9,727	15,926
Consumption	4,935	4,911	5,142	5,595	6,286	6,942	10,481
Personal	3,991	3,967	4,112	4,465	5,036	5,572	7,971
Public	944	944	1,030	1,130	1,250	1,370	2,510
Gross Capital Formation	2,163	2,200	2,301	2,493	3,015	2,785	5,445
Fixed Capital	1,707	1,797	1,882	1,943	2,390	2,337	4,353
Changes in Stocks	456	403	419	550	625	448	1,092
Trade Balance	-989	-1,013	-1,166	-1,147	-1,681	-1,407	-4
Exports	..	..	2,324	2,595	2,600	2,499	6,371
Imports	..	..	3,490	3,745	4,296	3,926	6,385
Foreign Trade Operations	63	58	0	2	15	20	10

a) *Preliminary; the Text Tables in Volume I of the Report reflect a revision as of October 1992 for which full details were not available.*

Note: *See Methodology Notes at end of Section 2.*

Source: *State Statistical Committee and World Bank mission estimates.*

Table 2.1a: Kyrgyzstan - Gross Domestic Product at Current Prices

	1985	1986	1987	1988	1989	1990	1991 a)
(in percent of Gross Domestic Product)							
Total Gross Domestic Product	100.0	100.0	100.0	100.0	100.0	100.0	100.0
Net Value Added	84.3	83.3	83.8	82.7	83.6	84.1	81.7
Depreciation	15.7	16.7	16.2	17.3	16.4	15.9	18.3
Gross Material Product	84.3	84.1	83.8	84.2	84.8	84.2	83.8
By source:							
Agriculture	29.9	31.2	31.9	31.1	32.9	33.7	28.4
Net Value Added	27.0	28.2	28.8	28.2	30.4	31.2	25.6
Depreciation	2.9	3.1	3.1	2.9	2.6	2.5	2.8
Industry	31.1	28.8	29.9	30.0	29.5	28.2	37.8
Net Value Added	26.4	23.8	25.0	24.6	24.3	23.1	31.9
Depreciation	4.7	5.0	4.9	5.4	5.3	5.2	5.9
Construction	10.5	10.5	10.3	11.0	10.3	10.1	6.9
Net Value Added	9.3	9.3	9.3	9.3	8.8	8.7	5.5
Depreciation	1.2	1.2	1.0	1.6	1.5	1.4	1.5
Transport	4.6	5.0	5.0	5.1	4.7	4.8	4.2
Net Value Added	2.5	2.8	2.7	2.7	2.6	2.8	1.9
Depreciation	2.1	2.2	2.3	2.3	2.1	2.0	2.3
Other	8.2	8.5	6.7	7.0	7.4	7.4	6.4
Net Value Added	7.4	7.6	6.0	6.4	6.8	6.7	5.5
Depreciation	0.8	0.9	0.7	0.6	0.6	0.7	0.9
Gross Non-Material Product	15.7	15.9	16.2	15.8	15.2	15.8	16.2
Net Value Added	11.7	11.7	12.0	11.5	10.7	11.6	11.3
Depreciation	4.0	4.3	4.2	4.4	4.5	4.1	4.9
By end use:	116.2	116.6	118.6	116.5	122.1	116.9	100.5
Consumption	80.8	80.5	81.9	80.6	82.5	83.4	66.2
Personal	65.3	65.1	65.5	64.3	66.1	67.0	50.3
Public	15.5	15.5	16.4	16.3	16.4	16.5	15.8
Gross Capital Formation	35.4	36.1	36.7	35.9	39.6	33.5	34.4
Fixed Capital	27.9	29.5	30.0	28.0	31.4	28.1	27.5
Changes in Stocks	7.5	6.6	6.7	7.9	8.2	5.4	6.9
Trade Balance	-16.2	-16.6	-18.6	-16.5	-22.1	-16.9	0.0
Exports	..	..	37.0	37.4	34.1	30.0	40.2
Imports	..	..	55.6	54.0	56.4	47.2	40.3
Foreign Trade Operations	1.0	1.0	0.0	0.0	0.2	0.2	0.1

Source: Table 2.1.

Table 2.2: Kyrgyzstan - Gross National Disposable Income, Savings and Sector Balances

	1985	1986	1987	1988	1989	1990	1991 a)
			(in millions of rubles)				
All Sectors:							
Gross Domestic Product	6,109	6,098	6,278	6,940	7,620	8,320	15,839
Net Foreign Transfers	400	400	390	620	540	910	1,930
Gross National Disposable Income	6,509	6,498	6,668	7,560	8,160	9,230	17,769
Consumption	4,935	4,911	5,142	5,595	6,286	6,942	10,481
Gross National Savings	1,575	1,587	1,526	1,966	1,874	2,288	7,288
Capital Formation	2,163	2,200	2,301	2,493	3,015	2,785	5,445
Domestic Balance							
(= Current Account Balance)	-589	-614	-776	-527	-1,141	-497	1,843
Government Sector:							
Tax Revenues			1,760	1,830	2,130	2,180	2,660
Non-tax Revenues			230	150	220	120	840
Net Transfers from the Union			390	620	540	910	1,930
Total Receipts			2,380	2,600	2,890	3,210	5,430
Subsidies			370	400	380	570	750
Other Domestic Transfers			520	590	710	760	1,280
Total Transfers			890	990	1,090	1,330	2,030
Disposable Income			1,490	1,610	1,800	1,880	3,400
Consumption			1,030	1,120	1,250	1,370	2,510
Saving			460	490	550	510	890
Capital Formation			310	390	390	480	190
Sector Balance			150	100	160	30	700
Memorandum Item:							
Government Outlays on Consumption and Capital Formation			1,340	1,510	1,640	1,850	2,700
Enterprise and Household Sector:							
Gross Disposable Income			5,178	5,950	6,360	7,350	14,369
Consumption			4,112	4,475	5,036	5,572	7,971
Saving			1,066	1,476	1,324	1,778	6,398
Capital Formation			1,991	2,103	2,625	2,305	5,255
Sector Balance			-926	-627	-1,301	-527	1,143

a) *Preliminary; the Text Tables in Volume I of the Report reflect a revision as of October 1992, for which full details are not available.*

Note: *See Methodology Notes at end of Section 2.*

Source: *State Statistical Committee and World Bank mission estimates.*

Table 2.2a : Kyrgyzstan - Composition of Disposable Income, Savings and Sector Balances

	1985	1986	1987	1988	1989	1990	1991 a)
(in percent of Gross Domestic Product)							
All Sectors:							
Gross Domestic Product	100.0	100.0	100.0	100.0	100.0	100.0	100.0
Net Foreign Transfers	6.5	6.6	6.2	8.9	7.1	10.9	12.2
Gross National Disposable Income	106.5	106.6	106.2	108.9	107.1	110.9	112.2
Consumption	80.8	80.5	81.9	80.6	82.5	83.4	66.2
Gross National Savings	25.8	26.0	24.3	28.3	24.6	27.5	46.0
Capital Formation	35.4	36.1	36.7	35.9	39.6	33.5	34.4
Domestic Balance							
(= Current Account Balance)	-9.6	-10.1	-12.4	-7.6	-15.0	-6.0	11.6
Government Sector:							
Tax Revenues			28.0	26.4	28.0	26.2	16.8
Non-tax Revenues			3.7	2.2	2.9	1.4	5.3
Net Transfers from the Union			6.2	8.9	7.1	10.9	12.2
Total Receipts			37.9	37.5	37.9	38.6	34.3
Interest							
Payments to CIS							
Subsidies			5.9	5.8	5.0	6.9	4.7
Other Domestic Transfers			8.3	8.5	9.3	9.1	8.1
Total Transfers			14.2	14.3	14.3	16.0	12.8
Disposable Income			23.7	23.2	23.6	22.6	21.5
Consumption			16.4	16.1	16.4	16.5	15.8
Saving			7.3	7.1	7.2	6.1	5.6
Capital Formation			4.9	5.6	5.1	5.8	1.2
Sector Balance			2.4	1.4	2.1	0.4	4.4
Memorandum Item:							
Government Outlays on Consumption							
and Capital Formation			21.3	21.8	21.5	22.2	17.0
Enterprise and Household Sector:							
Gross Disposable Income			82.5	85.7	83.5	88.3	90.7
Consumption			65.5	64.5	66.1	67.0	50.3
Saving			17.0	21.3	17.4	21.4	40.4
Capital Formation			31.7	30.3	34.4	27.7	33.2
Sector Balance			-14.7	-9.0	-17.1	-6.3	7.2

Source: Table 2.2.

Table 2.3: Kyrgyzstan - Gross Domestic Product at Constant Prices

	1985	1986	1987	1988	1989	1990	1991 a)
			(in millions of 1983 rubles)				
Total Gross Domestic Product	5,846	6,045	6,076	6,869	7,133	7,361	7,094
Net Value Added	5,005	5,063	5,148	5,770	6,012	6,242	5,950
Depreciation	841	982	928	1,100	1,121	1,118	1,144
Gross Material Product	4,945	5,089	5,103	5,800	6,063	6,212	5,982
By source:							
Agriculture	1,644	1,749	1,788	1,966	2,047	2,160	1,988
Net Value Added	1,489	1,568	1,609	1,782	1,873	1,986	1,812
Depreciation	155	181	179	184	174	174	176
Industry	1,924	1,897	1,933	2,292	2,404	2,381	2,388
Net Value Added	1,672	1,602	1,653	1,950	2,045	2,019	2,021
Depreciation	252	295	280	342	359	362	367
Construction	625	644	652	740	750	761	714
Net Value Added	562	571	596	637	648	660	621
Depreciation	63	73	56	104	102	101	93
Transport	268	301	302	338	324	348	354
Net Value Added	155	169	169	188	184	208	210
Depreciation	113	132	133	150	140	140	144
Other	484	497	428	464	537	561	537
Net Value Added	441	447	390	423	499	511	481
Depreciation	43	50	38	41	38	51	56
Gross Non-Material Product	901	956	973	1,070	1,070	1,149	1,112
Net Value Added	686	706	731	790	762	859	804
Depreciation	215	251	242	279	308	290	308
By end use:	6,897	7,069	7,140	7,834	8,853	8,129	7,124
Consumption	4,967	4,956	5,083	5,509	6,078	5,947	4,989
Personal	4,023	4,010	4,049	4,408	4,846	4,637	3,722
Public	944	946	1,034	1,101	1,232	1,310	1,268
Gross Capital Formation	1,930	2,113	2,056	2,325	2,775	2,182	2,134
Fixed Capital	1,500	1,732	1,720	1,783	2,138	1,973	1,717
Changes in Stocks	431	381	336	542	637	209	417
Trade Balance	-1,051	-1,024	-1,064	-965	-1,720	-768	-30

a) Preliminary; the Text Tables in Volume I of the Report reflect a revision as of October 1992
   for which full details were not available.

Note: See Methodology Notes at end of Section 2.

Source: State Statistical Committee and World Bank mission estimates.

Table 2.3a: Kyrgyzstan - Gross Domestic Product at Constant Prices

	1985	1986	1987	1988	1989	1990	1991 a)
		(percentage change)					
Total Gross Domestic Product		3.4	0.5	13.1	3.8	3.2	-3.6
Net Value Added		1.2	1.7	12.1	4.2	3.8	-4.7
Depreciation		16.8	-5.6	18.5	2.0	-0.2	2.3
Gross Material Product		2.9	0.3	13.7	4.5	2.5	-3.7
By source:							
Agriculture		6.4	2.2	9.9	4.2	5.5	-8.0
Net Value Added		5.3	2.6	10.8	5.1	6.0	-8.8
Depreciation		16.9	-1.1	2.5	-5.0	-0.3	1.2
Industry		-1.4	1.9	18.6	4.9	-0.9	0.3
Net Value Added		-4.2	3.2	17.9	4.9	-1.3	0.1
Depreciation		17.1	-5.2	22.4	4.8	0.9	1.3
Construction		3.2	1.2	13.5	1.4	1.5	-6.2
Net Value Added		1.7	4.4	6.7	1.9	1.8	-5.9
Depreciation		16.3	-23.9	86.0	-1.7	-0.7	-8.2
Transport		12.2	0.2	11.9	-3.9	7.4	1.7
Net Value Added		8.8	0.0	11.2	-2.1	13.2	1.1
Depreciation		16.9	0.4	12.9	-6.1	-0.2	2.8
Other		2.6	-13.9	8.4	15.7	4.6	-4.3
Net Value Added		1.3	-12.9	8.5	18.1	2.3	-5.8
Depreciation		16.6	-23.4	7.6	-9.0	34.8	10.6
Gross Non-Material Product		6.1	1.7	9.9	0.0	7.4	-3.2
Net Value Added		2.9	3.5	8.2	-3.6	12.6	-6.3
Depreciation		16.6	-3.4	15.2	10.3	-5.7	6.1
By end use:		2.5	1.0	9.7	13.0	-8.2	-12.4
Consumption		-0.2	2.6	8.4	10.3	-2.2	-16.1
Personal		-0.3	1.0	8.9	9.9	-4.3	-19.7
Public		0.2	9.3	6.5	11.8	6.4	-3.2
Gross Capital Formation		9.5	-2.7	13.1	19.4	-21.4	-2.2
Fixed Capital		15.5	-0.7	3.7	19.9	-7.7	-13.0
Changes in Stocks		-11.6	-11.7	61.1	17.5	-67.2	99.7
Trade Balance		..	..	-9.3	78.2	-55.4	-96.1

Source: Table 2.3.

Table 2.4: Kyrgyzstan - Gross Domestic Product, Implicit Deflators

	1985	1986	1987	1988	1989	1990	1991 a)
(1983=100)							
Total Gross Domestic Product	104.6	100.9	103.3	101.0	106.8	113.0	223.3
Net Value Added	102.9	100.3	102.2	99.5	105.9	112.1	217.4
Depreciation	113.8	103.7	109.4	109.0	111.8	118.5	253.8
Gross Material Product	104.2	100.8	103.1	100.7	106.6	112.8	221.9
By source:							
Agriculture	111.1	108.9	111.9	109.9	122.6	129.9	226.6
Net Value Added	110.7	109.5	112.2	110.0	123.6	130.9	224.0
Depreciation	113.8	103.7	109.4	109.0	111.8	118.5	254.0
Industry	98.8	92.5	97.0	90.8	93.6	98.6	250.6
Net Value Added	96.4	90.4	94.9	87.6	90.4	95.1	250.1
Depreciation	113.8	103.7	109.4	109.0	111.8	118.5	253.7
Construction	102.5	99.8	99.3	102.7	104.7	110.3	154.0
Net Value Added	101.1	99.3	98.4	101.6	103.5	109.1	139.1
Depreciation	113.8	103.7	109.4	109.0	111.8	118.5	253.8
Transport	106.1	101.6	104.1	104.0	110.1	114.0	189.7
Net Value Added	100.0	100.0	100.0	100.0	108.8	111.1	146.0
Depreciation	113.8	103.7	109.4	109.0	111.8	118.5	253.5
Other	103.9	104.2	98.5	105.3	104.6	109.9	188.2
Net Value Added	102.9	104.3	97.4	104.9	104.1	109.0	180.6
Depreciation	113.8	103.7	109.4	109.0	111.8	118.5	253.6
Gross Non-Material Product	106.9	101.5	104.7	102.9	108.1	114.2	230.8
Net Value Added	104.2	100.7	103.1	100.7	106.6	112.8	221.9
Depreciation	113.8	103.7	109.4	109.0	111.8	118.5	253.9
By end use:	103.0	100.6	104.3	103.2	105.1	119.7	223.6
Consumption	99.3	99.1	101.2	101.6	103.4	116.7	210.1
Personal	99.1	98.9	101.6	102.0	103.9	120.2	214.2
Public	100.0	99.8	99.6	99.9	101.5	104.6	198.0
Gross Capital Formation	112.1	104.1	111.9	107.2	108.7	127.7	255.2
Fixed Capital	113.8	103.7	109.4	109.0	111.8	118.5	253.5
Changes in Stocks	105.9	105.9	124.7	101.5	98.2	214.6	261.9
Trade Balance	94.1	98.9	109.5	118.9	97.7	183.3	293.3

a) Preliminary; the Text Tables in Volume I of the Report reflect a revision as of October 1992
for which full details were not available.

Note: See Methodology Notes at end of Section 2.

Source: State Statistical Committee and World Bank mission estimates.

Table 2.5: Kyrgyzstan - Conversion from MPS to SNA 1/ - Final Use of National Income and Gross Domestic Product

	1980	1985	1986	1987	1988	1989	1990
	(in millions of rubles)						
A1. Personal consumption (domestic) of goods and material services (or individual consumption, or consumption of the population)	2894.7	3678.0	3671.4	3824.3	4199.5	4855.0	5316.4
plus: Value of non-material services (including housing services) purchased by households	787.5	949.1	984.2	1080.1	1124.2	1201.2	1410.6
minus: Material cost of housing services allocated to households (including owner occupied dwellings), and depreciation of dwellings	..	..	..	..	..	..	..
minus: Expenditure for material goods and services during business travel	44.8	63.3	67.6	65.4	75.6	65.8	70.3
minus: Material expenditure by enterprises on cultural, sport and similar facilities for their employees	83.6	85.3	144.5	180.7	183.1	234.5	287.4
minus: Material expenditure by government on health, education, culture and other services provided free to individuals	634.0	772.7	812.7	872.3	931.7	943.4	1100.4
plus: Direct consumer expenditure abroad and transferes abroad by enterprises	..	..	..	..	..	..	..
minus: Direct consumer expenditure on domestic market by non-republican enterprises and transfers from abroad	..	..	..	..	..	..	..
minus: Material services of non-material sphere used in material sphere	100.0	120.0	118.0	131.9	120.9	150.0	163.0
equals: **B1. Final consumption expenditures by resident households**	2819.8	3585.8	3512.8	3654.1	4012.4	4662.5	5105.9
A2. Other final consumption (social) (material consumption of units in non-material sphere serving the community)	404.2	542.0	529.1	564.8	599.3	618.4	657.0
plus: Material expenditure by government on health, education, culture and other services provided free to individuals	634.0	772.7	812.7	872.3	931.7	943.4	1100.4
plus: Government expenditures on fixed assets that have military uses	..	..	..	..	..	..	..
plus: Difference between the material and non-material services produced by government, their material cost and depreciation	..	..	..	..	..	..	..
plus: Difference between the material and non-material cost, depreciation and compensation of employees of extrateritorial bodies representing Kyrgyzstan abroad and analogous expenditures of bodies representing other countries and international organizations in Kyrgyzstan	..	..	..	..	..	..	..
minus: Material services of non-material sphere used in matrial sphere	..	..	..	..	..	..	..
equals: **B2. Government final consumption expenditure**	1038.2	1314.7	1341.8	1437.1	1531.0	1561.8	1757.4

(continued)

Table 2.5 : Kyrgyzstan - Conversion from MPS to SNA 1/ - Final Use of National Income and Gross Domestic Product

	1980	1985	1986	1987	1988	1989	1990
			(in millions of rubles)				
A3. Increase in fixed capital (net fixed investment)	540.8	708.0	651.0	897.0	769.0	966.0	708.0
minus: Government expenditure on fixed assets that have military use	..	..	..	..	..	..	..
plus: Depreciation of fixed capital	734.0	957.0	1019.0	1015.0	1198.0	1253.0	1325.0
plus: Increase of unfinished construction (including roads, dams, ports, etc.)	-33.7	42.1	127	-30	-24.2	171.1	304.3
plus: Losses from natural disasters	8.3	34.3	56.9	51.0	51.2	62.1	78.5
equals:							
B3. Gross fixed capital formation	1249.4	1741.4	1853.9	1933.0	1994.0	2452.2	2415.8
A4. Capital formation in stocks (incl. unfinished construction)	347.6	423.0	454.9	303.7	438.8	711.3	637.8
minus: Unfinished construction	-33.7	42.1	127.0	-30.0	-24.2	171.1	304.3
equals:							
B4. Increase in Stocks	381.3	380.9	327.9	333.7	463.0	540.2	333.5
A5. Exports of goods and material services	..	..	..	..	..	..	..
plus: Difference between the export value of non-material services and material cost and depreciation included in these services	..	..	..	..	..	..	..
plus: Consumption expenditure and outlays in fixed capital formation by extraterritorial bodies of foreign government and international organizations located in Kyrgyzstan	..	..	..	..	..	..	..
plus: Direct purchases on the domestic market by non-resident households and gifts sent abroad by households	..	..	..	..	..	..	..
minus: Sale abroad by an external trade organization of goods that have not crossed the border of Kyrgyzstan as well as of goods that crossed the border but that are re-exported without being processed	..	..	..	..	..	..	..
minus: The difference between exported monetary gold and the value of sales of newly produced gold ingots and bars	..	..	..	..	..	..	..
equals:							
B5. Exports of goods and non-factor services	..	..	..	..	..	..	..

(continued)

Table 2.5 : Kyrgyzstan - Conversion from MPS to SNA 1/ - Final Use of National Income and Gross Domestic Product

	1980	1985	1986	1987	1988	1989	1990
(in millions of rubles)							
A6. Imports of goods and material services	..	..	..	..	..	..	..
plus: Difference between the import value of non-material services and material cost and depreciation included in these services	..	..	..	..	..	..	..
plus: Consumption expenditure and outlays in fixed capital formation by extrateritorial bodies that represent Kyrgyzstan abroad	..	..	..	..	..	..	..
plus: Direct purchases abroad by residents and gifts received from abroad by households	..	..	..	..	..	..	..
minus: Purchase abroad by an external trade organization of goods that have not crossed the border of Kyrgyzstan as well as of goods that crossed the border but that are re-exported without being processed	..	..	..	..	..	..	..
minus: The value of imported monetary gold	..	..	..	..	..	..	..
equals: Imports of goods and non-factor services	..	..	..	..	..	..	..
B6. Trade Balance	-511.0	-988.5	-1013.5	-1165.8	-1147.2	-1681.2	-1407.2
A7. Losses in Fixed Capital and Stocks	46.0	75.0	75.0	85.6	86.9	84.9	114.5
A. Net Material Product (A1+A2+A3+A4+B6+A7)	3722.3	4437.5	4367.9	4509.6	4946.3	5554.4	6026.5
B. Gross Domestic Product (B1+B2+B3+B4+B6+A7)	5023.7	6109.3	6097.9	6277.7	6940.1	7620.4	8319.9

1/ A = aggregates of MPS (Material Product System)
   B = aggregates of SNA (System of National Accounts)

Note: See Methodology Notes at end of Section 2.

Source: State Statistical Committee.

Table 2.5a: Kyrgyzstan - Transition from Net Material Product to Gross Domestic Product
Summary Table

	1980	1985	1986	1987	1988	1989	1990
	(in millions of rubles)						
Net Material Product	3722.3	4437.5	4367.9	4509.6	4946.3	5554.4	6026.5
plus: Amortization of fixed capital in material and non-material sphere, incl. roads, bridges	734.0	957.0	1019.0	1015.0	1198.0	1253.0	1325.0
plus: Losses of material circulation means (Money)	8.3	34.3	56.9	51.0	51.2	62.1	78.5
plus: Transfer expenses for purchase and sale of existing maintenance capital	..	..	..	..	..	..	..
plus: Value added in the sphere of non-material services	787.5	949.1	984.2	1080.1	1124.2	1201.2	1410.6
minus: Non-material services of non-material sphere used in material sphere 1/	100.0	120.0	118.0	131.9	120.9	150.0	163.0
minus: Material expenditure of enterprises for cultural, sports and other services for their workers	83.6	85.3	144.5	180.7	183.1	234.5	287.4
minus: Expenditure for goods and material services during business trips in material and non-material spheres	44.8	63.3	67.6	65.4	75.6	65.8	70.3
equals: **Gross Domestic Product**	5023.7	6109.3	6097.9	6277.7	6940.1	7620.4	8319.9
Memorandum Item:							
GDP/NMP	1.35	1.38	1.40	1.39	1.40	1.37	1.38

1/ Figures for 1987 and 1988 are final; for the other years they are estimates based on the 1987-88 averages.

Source: State Statistical Committee.

Table 2.5b: Kyrgyzstan - Transition from the System of Material Product to the System of National Accounts (Production Methodology)

	1980	1985	1986	1987	1988	1989	1990
			(in millions of rubles)				
A1. Gross Social Product	8406.5	11041.2	11282.1	11486.6	12118.3	12953.7	13415.7
Gross output of non-material services (+)	1014.8	1244.4	1290.2	1388.3	1480.5	1599.7	1811.1
Purchases by enterprises of cultural and recreational services (-)	..	..	..	..	..	..	..
B1. Gross Output	9421.3	12285.6	12572.3	12874.9	13598.8	14553.4	15226.8
A2. Intermediate material consumption (including amortization)	4684.2	6603.7	6914.2	6977.0	7172.0	7399.3	7389.2
Material consumption of economic units in non-mat. sphere (incl. amort.)(+)	..	..	..	..	..	..	..
Material expenditures of enterprises for culture, sport and other serv.(+)	83.6	85.3	144.5	180.7	183.1	234.5	287.4
Material (excl. amort.) and non-mat. expenditures of households (+)	100.0	120.0	118.0	131.9	120.9	150.0	163.0
Expenditures for goods and material services on business trips (+)	44.8	63.3	67.6	65.4	75.6	65.8	70.3
Losses of reserves due to natural causes (-)	8.3	34.3	56.9	51	51.2	62.1	78.5
Consumption of fixed capital in material sphere (-)	506.7	661.7	713.0	706.8	841.7	854.5	924.5
B2. Intermediate Consumption	4397.6	6176.3	6474.4	6597.2	6658.7	6933.0	6906.9
Net Material Product (A1-A2)	3722.3	4437.5	4367.9	4509.6	4946.3	5554.4	6026.5
Gross Domestic Product (B1-B2)	5023.7	6109.3	6097.9	6277.7	6940.1	7620.4	8319.9

A = aggregates of SMP (System of Material Product)
B = aggregates of SNA (System of National Accounts)

Source: State Statistical Committee.

Table 2.6: Kyrgyzstan - Components of Net Material Product and Gross Domestic Product on the Basis of Value Added

	1980	1985	1986	1987	1988	1989	1990
	(in millions of rubles)						
A. Net Material Product (A1 + A2)	3722.3	4437.5	4367.9	4509.6	4946.3	5554.4	6026.5
A1. Primary Income of the Population	2059.2	2755.4	2874.6	2937.6	3194.3	3502.2	3874.8
+a. Wages and Salaries of Employees in the Non-material Sphere (+)	699.9	873.2	899.7	992.7	1038.9	1086.6	1253.8
+b. Social/Cultural Expenditures of Material Sphere for Employees (+)	-	-	-	-	-	-	-
-c. Income from Personal and Subsidiary Plots of the Population (-)	442.8	676.2	729.1	808.5	899.4	1019.0	1143.8
+d. Employers Contributions to Social Security in Material and Non-mat. Spheres (+)	154.4	247.7	247.7	241.7	265.6	282.4	322.1
-e. Business Travel Expenses in Material and Non-material Spheres (-)	44.8	63.3	67.6	65.4	75.6	65.8	70.3
B1. Compensation of Employees (A1+a+b-c+d-e)	2425.9	3136.8	3225.3	3298.1	3523.8	3786.4	4236.6
A2. Primary Income of Enterprises (Net Product in Material Sphere minus Wages)	1663.1	1682.1	1493.3	1572.0	1752.0	2052.2	2151.7
+a. Income from Personal and Subsidiary Plots of the Population (+)	442.8	676.2	729.1	808.5	899.4	1019.0	1143.8
+b. Profit in Non-mat. Sphere (excluding Revenues from Private Enterprises (+)	34.8	21.4	28.4	29.6	24.9	53.2	88.2
-c. Employers Contributions to Social Security in the Material Sphere (-)	101.6	193.2	191.6	183.9	205.2	221.0	253.5
-d. Purchase of Non-material Services in the Material Sphere (-)	-	-	-	-	-	-	-
-e. Expenditure in Connection with the Provision of Cultural, etc. Facilities of Industries in the Material Sphere (-)	83.6	85.3	144.5	180.7	183.1	234.5	287.4
+f. Losses in Reserves in the Material Sphere (+)	8.3	34.3	56.9	51.0	51.2	62.1	78.5
-g. Non-material Services of Non-material Sphere used in Material Sphere (-)	100.0	120.0	118.0	131.9	120.9	150.0	163.0
B2. Profit (including Net Indirect Taxes) (A2+a+b-c-d-e+f-g)	1863.8	2015.5	1853.6	1964.6	2218.3	2581.0	2758.3
B3. Consumption of Fixed Capital in Material and Non-material Sphere	734.0	957.0	1019.0	1015.0	1198.0	1253.0	1325.0
B. Gross Domestic Product (B1+B2+B3)	5023.7	6109.3	6097.9	6277.7	6940.1	7620.4	8319.9

A = aggregates of MPS (Material Production System)
B = aggregates of SNA (System of National Accounts)

Source: State Statistical Committee.

Table 2.7: Kyrgyzstan - Net Material Product at Current Prices

	1980	1985	1986	1987	1988	1989	1990	1991 a)
				(in millions of rubles)				
Total Net Material Product	3722.3	4437.5	4367.9	4509.6	4946.3	5554.4	6026.5	11152.0
By source:								
Agriculture	1127.0	1648.9	1716.8	1805.8	1960.1	2314.8	2599.2	4058.0
Industry	1425.3	1611.7	1449.0	1568.8	1707.5	1849.1	1919.2	5054.0
Construction	365.5	567.7	567.0	586.6	647.0	671.3	720.0	864.0
Transport and Communication	116.5	155.3	168.7	169.0	187.9	200.1	231.1	307.0
Foreign Trade Operations	357.3	62.9	58.0	0.1	2.2	14.6	20.1	10.0
Other	330.7	391.0	408.4	379.3	441.6	504.5	536.9	859.0
By end use:	4233.3	5426.0	5381.4	5675.5	6093.5	7235.6	7433.7	11156.0
Consumption	3298.9	4220.0	4200.5	4389.2	4798.8	5473.4	5973.4	8614.0
Private	2894.7	3678.0	3671.4	3824.4	4199.5	4855.0	5316.4	7314.0
Government	404.2	542.0	529.1	564.8	599.3	618.4	657.0	1300.0
Net Capital Formation	934.4	1206.0	1180.9	1286.3	1294.7	1762.2	1460.3	2542.0
Fixed Capital	507.1	750.1	778.0	867.0	744.8	1137.1	1012.3	1450.0
Changes in Stocks	427.3	455.9	402.9	419.3	549.9	625.1	448.0	1092.0
Trade balance	-511.0	-988.5	-1013.5	-1165.9	-1147.2	-1681.2	-1407.2	-4.0
Exports	..	..	..	2323.8	2595.4	2600.2	2498.8	6371.0
Imports	..	..	..	3489.8	3744.8	4296.0	3926.1	6385.1
Foreign Trade Operations	357.3	62.9	58	0.1	2.2	14.6	20.1	10.1
				(in percent of Net Material Product)				
Total Net Material Product	100.0	100.0	100.0	100.0	100.0	100.0	100.0	100.0
By source:								
Agriculture	30.3	37.2	39.3	40.0	39.6	41.7	43.1	36.4
Industry	38.3	36.3	33.2	34.8	34.5	33.3	31.8	45.3
Construction	9.8	12.8	13.0	13.0	13.1	12.1	11.9	7.7
Transport and Communication	3.1	3.5	3.9	3.7	3.8	3.6	3.8	2.8
Foreign Trade Operations	9.6	1.4	1.3	0.0	0.0	0.3	0.3	0.1
Other	8.9	8.8	9.4	8.4	8.9	9.1	8.9	7.7
By end use:	113.7	122.3	123.2	125.9	123.2	130.3	123.4	100.0
Consumption	88.6	95.1	96.2	97.3	97.0	98.5	99.1	77.2
Private	77.8	82.9	84.1	84.8	84.9	87.4	88.2	65.6
Government	10.9	12.2	12.1	12.5	12.1	11.1	10.9	11.7
Net Capital Formation	25.1	27.2	27.0	28.5	26.2	31.7	24.2	22.8
Fixed Capital	13.6	16.9	17.8	19.2	15.1	20.5	16.8	13.0
Changes in Stocks	11.5	10.3	9.2	9.3	11.1	11.3	7.4	9.8
Trade balance	-13.7	-22.3	-23.2	-25.9	-23.2	-30.3	-23.4	0.0
Exports	..	..	..	51.5	52.5	46.8	41.5	57.1
Imports	..	..	..	77.4	75.7	77.3	65.1	57.3

a) Preliminary; the Text Tables in Volume I of the Report reflect a revision as of October 1992 for which full details were not available.

Note: See Methodology Notes at end of Section 2..

Source: State Statistical Committee.

Table 2.8: Kyrgyzstan - Net Material Product at Constant Prices

	1980	1985	1986	1987	1988	1989	1990	1991 a)
			(in millions of constant 1983 rubles)					
Total Net Material Product	3567.0	4319.1	4357.0	4417.0	4979.1	5249.5	5383.9	5145.7
By source:								
Agriculture	768.5	1489.0	1568.0	1609.0	1782.3	1873.0	1986.0	1812.0
Industry	1685.0	1672.0	1602.0	1653.2	1949.7	2045.0	2019.0	2021.0
Construction	380.0	561.5	571.0	596.3	636.5	648.4	660.0	621.3
Transport and Communication	129.4	155.3	169.0	169.0	187.9	183.9	208.1	210.3
Foreign Trade Operations	313.1	62.1	57.0	0.1	2.2	13.7	23.6	15.0
Other	291.0	379.2	390.0	389.4	420.5	485.5	487.2	466.1
By end use:	3994.5	5370.0	5381.0	5481.4	5944.1	6969.5	6151.5	5147.7
Consumption	3193.7	4280.5	4250.5	4352.7	4718.8	5315.6	5088.2	4158.8
Private	2794.1	3738.5	3720.5	3785.6	4118.8	4706.3	4459.9	3502.2
Government	399.6	542.0	530.0	567.1	600.0	609.3	628.3	656.6
Net Capital Formation	800.8	1089.5	1130.5	1128.7	1225.3	1653.9	1063.3	988.9
Fixed Capital	537.9	659.0	750.3	792.5	683.6	1017.4	854.5	572.0
Changes in Stocks	262.9	430.5	380.2	336.2	541.7	636.5	208.8	416.9
Trade Balance	-427.5	-1050.9	-1024.0	-1064.4	-965.0	-1720.0	-767.6	-2.0

	1980-85 b)		*(percentage change)*					
Total Net Material Product	4.0	0.9	1.4	12.7	5.4	2.6	-4.4	
By source:								
Agriculture	14.1	5.3	2.6	10.8	5.1	6.0	-8.8	
Industry	-0.2	-4.2	3.2	17.9	4.9	-1.3	0.1	
Construction	8.1	1.7	4.4	6.7	1.9	1.8	-5.9	
Transport and Communication	3.7	8.8	0.0	11.2	-2.1	13.2	1.1	
Foreign Trade Operations	-27.6	-8.2	-99.8	2100.0	522.7	72.3	-36.4	
Other	5.4	2.8	-0.2	8.0	15.5	0.4	-4.3	
By end use:	6.1	0.2	1.9	8.4	17.3	-11.7	-16.3	
Consumption	6.0	-0.7	2.4	8.4	12.6	-4.3	-18.3	
Private	6.0	-0.5	1.7	8.8	14.3	-5.2	-21.5	
Government	6.3	-2.2	7.0	5.8	1.5	3.1	4.5	
Net Capital Formation	6.4	3.8	-0.2	8.6	35.0	-35.7	-7.0	
Fixed Capital	4.1	13.9	5.6	-13.7	48.8	-16.0	-33.1	
Changes in Stocks	10.4	-11.7	-11.6	61.1	17.5	-67.2	99.7	
Trade Balance	-19.7	2.6	-3.9	9.3	-78.2	55.4	99.7	

a) *Preliminary; the Text Tables in Volume I of the Report reflect a revision as of October 1992 for which full details were not available.*

b) *This column represents the annual average change for the period 1980-1985.*

Note: *See Methodology Notes at end of Section 2.*

Source: *State Statistical Committee and World Bank mission estimates.*

Table 2.9: Kyrgyzstan - Net Material Product Implicit Price Deflators

	1980	1985	1986	1987	1988	1989	1990	1991 a)
				(1983 = 100)				
Total Net Material Product	104.4	102.7	100.3	102.1	99.3	105.8	111.9	216.7
By source:								
Agriculture	146.6	110.7	109.5	112.2	110.0	123.6	130.9	224.0
Industry	84.6	96.4	90.4	94.9	87.6	90.4	95.1	250.1
Construction	96.2	101.1	99.3	98.4	101.6	103.5	109.1	139.1
Transport and Communication	90.0	100.0	99.8	100.0	100.0	108.8	111.1	146.0
Foreign Trade Operations	114.1	101.3	101.8	100.0	100.0	106.6	85.2	66.7
Other	113.6	103.1	104.7	97.4	105.0	103.9	110.2	184.3
By end use:	106.0	101.0	100.0	103.5	102.5	103.8	120.8	216.7
Consumption	103.3	98.6	98.8	100.8	101.7	103.0	117.4	207.1
Private	103.6	98.4	98.7	101.0	102.0	103.2	119.2	208.8
Government	101.2	100.0	99.8	99.6	99.9	101.5	104.6	198.0
Net Capital Formation	116.7	110.7	104.5	114.0	105.7	106.5	137.3	257.1
Fixed Capital	94.3	113.8	103.7	109.4	109.0	111.8	118.5	253.5
Changes in Stocks	162.5	105.9	106.0	124.7	101.5	98.2	214.6	261.9
Trade balance	119.5	94.1	99.0	109.5	118.9	97.7	183.3	200.0

a) *Preliminary; the Text Tables in Volume I of the Report reflect a version as of October 1992
for which full details were not available.*

Note: *See Methodology Notes at end of Section 2..*

Source: *State Statistical Committee and World Bank mission estimates.*

Table 2.10: Kyrgyzstan - Gross Output, Input and Net Material Product by Sector 1/

	1985	1988	1989	1990
	(in millions of current rubles)			
Industry				
Gross Output	6,156	6,633	7,035	6,946
Material Input	4,544	4,926	5,186	5,027
Net Product	1,612	1,708	1,849	1,919
Agriculture				
Gross Output	2,749	3,136	3,459	3,845
Material Input	1,100	1,176	1,144	1,246
Net Product	1,649	1,960	2,315	2,599
Construction				
Gross Output	1,213	1,363	1,360	1,457
Material Input	645	716	689	737
Net Product	568	647	671	720
Transport and Communication				
Gross Output	339	393	407	434
Material Input	183	205	206	203
Net Product	155	188	200	231
Other Sectors				
Gross Output	571	631	749	739
Material Input	117	187	230	182
Net Product	454	444	519	557
Total Economy				
Gross Output	11,027	12,155	13,009	13,421
Material Input	6,589	7,209	7,455	7,394
Net Product	4,438	4,946	5,554	6,027

1/ Material Input includes Capital Depreciation.

Source: Statistical Yearbook for Kyrgyzstan, 1990 and State Statistical Committee.

Methodology Notes to Tables 2.1 - 2.10

The basic source for Kyrgyzstan National Accounts in Section 2 is a set of tables compiled by the State Statistical Committee (SSC) early in 1992 for the IMF. These tables included, among many other subjects, Net Material Product (NMP) for 1985-90 in current and constant prices, with detail by origin of product and by its final uses. These figures appear in Appendix Tables 2.7 and 2.8.[1] SSC tables also included adjustments, shown in Tables 2.5 and 2.6, to convert NMP figures on <u>uses</u> of products into uses of gross domestic production (GDP) for those years. For 1991 the tables carried very preliminary estimates for NMP by origin in current and constant prices, and they included 1991 final uses of NMP only in current prices. None of the adjustments for NMP to GDP were included for 1991.

For Appendix Tables 2.1 and 2.3, sources of GDP are approximated for each industry group as the sum of the group's NMP and its depreciation charges as made available separately by the SSC to the Bank mission. This sum is incomplete as a NMP-to-GDP adjustment on an industry basis, but it makes the major adjustment. Tables 2.1 and 2.3 on GDP include a residual industrial source, Gross Non-Material Product, that covers all sources of GDP not covered by material-industry NMP plus Depreciation. In final uses of GDP, the Depreciation total is added Fixed Capital outlays, and the rest of the adjustment falls into Personal Consumption.

GDP final uses in Table 2.1 differ in two respects from SSC adjustments in Table 2.5: i) Government Consumption is taken from budget data as reported in Appendix Table 4.2, rather than from Table 2.5; and ii) Fixed Capital outlays exclude the item for natural disasters, which is not in Table 9.1 and ambiguous in Table 2.5a. Both of these differences are offset in Personal Consumption.

The 1991 GDP account reflects several Bank estimates and adjustments. Two changes were made in constant price output without modifying the SSC's current price figures for 1991: agricultural output was fitted more closely with separate SSC data on agricultural output (in Table 6.4), and industry constant price output was fitted more closely to the figures on industrial production that appear in Table 7.2. These changes affected total NMP in constant prices and, with current price NMP unchanged for 191, the implicit 1991 deflators of NMP. Current price <u>uses</u> of NMP in Table 2.7 for 1991 are from the SSC tables except the Trade Balance, which reflects more recent data on imports and exports. The adjustment to trade is offset in Personal Consumption.

Constant price final uses of NMP in 191 were calculated from Indices of Prices and Wages. Capital goods prices reflect a weighted change from 1990 to 1991 in Wholesale Prices of machinery (40% weight) and construction materials (30%0, and of wages in construction (30%). Prices of stocks reflect a broader range of prices, and Government Consumption includes a heavier weight for wages of government workers. The deflator for Personal Consumption is an implicit residual.

1/ "Change in construction work in progress" in the SSC tables is included in outlays for Fixed Capital in this Appendix. Similarly, the SSC item for "Losses" is included in Changes in Stocks.

Adjustments from NMP to GDP for 1991 consisted of staff estimates for Depreciation by industry and for a single figure to cover all other differences between NMP and GDP. Depreciation was based on the detailed listings of 1990 Capital Stocks and adjustments that appear in Table 9.1; for each industry 1990 depreciation was extended to 1991 and inflated to 1991 prices with the same price index that was used to deflate 1991 Fixed Capital outlays to constant prices. "All other" differences from NMP were taken as the stable 16% of NMP that appears for recent years.

Table 3.1: Kyrgyzstan - Imports of Goods, Including Interrepublican Trade

	1987	1988	1989	1990	1991
(in millions of rubles)					
Total Imports	3490.0	3744.8	4296.0	4242.7	6782.8
Industry	3391.0	3610.2	4021.8	3893.5	6311.1
Electric energy	36.0	29.9	28.6	33.8	37.1
Oil and gas industry	291.0	314.3	324.6	268.6	578.0
Coal industry	42.0	31.4	32.2	38.1	84.6
Ferrous metallurgy	176.0	194.9	172.8	170.5	302.8
Non-ferrous metallurgy	75.0	88.6	99.2	97.5	283.2
Chemical and petrochemical	329.0	358.3	409.2	373.5	609.9
Machine building	773.0	991.0	1089.4	985.3	1271.6
Lumber and paper	133.0	122.3	136.3	129.6	200.5
Industrial construction materials	62.0	68.1	71.5	80.4	84.5
Light industry	790.0	742.3	894.7	966.2	1513.6
Food industry	633.0	611.8	692.0	663.0	1080.0
Other industries a)	51.0	57.3	71.3	87.0	265.3
Agriculture	92.0	127.4	183.4	247.0	422.1
Other, including goods N.E.S.	7.0	7.2	90.8	102.2	49.6
(in percent of total)					
Total Imports	100.0	100.0	100.0	100.0	100.0
Industry	97.2	96.4	93.6	91.8	93.0
Electric energy	1.0	0.8	0.7	0.8	0.5
Oil and gas industry	8.3	8.4	7.6	6.3	8.5
Coal industry	1.2	0.8	0.7	0.9	1.2
Ferrous metallurgy	5.0	5.2	4.0	4.0	4.5
Non-ferrous metallurgy	2.1	2.4	2.3	2.3	4.2
Chemical and petrochemical	9.4	9.6	9.5	8.8	9.0
Machine building	22.1	26.5	25.4	23.2	18.7
Lumber and paper	3.8	3.3	3.2	3.1	3.0
Industrial construction materials	1.8	1.8	1.7	1.9	1.2
Light industry	22.6	19.8	20.8	22.8	22.3
Food industry	18.1	16.3	16.1	15.6	15.9
Other industries a)	1.5	1.5	1.7	2.1	3.9
Agriculture	2.6	3.4	4.3	5.8	6.2
Other, including goods N.E.S.	0.2	0.2	2.1	2.4	0.7

a) For 1991 includes: pharmaceuticals, medical equipment and tools, and other industrial products.

Source: State Statistical Committee and World Bank mission estimates.

Table 3.2: Kyrgyzstan - Exports of Goods, Including Interrepublican Trade

	1987	1988	1989	1990	1991
	(in millions of rubles)				
Total Exports	2324.0	2595.4	2600.2	2498.8	6546.0
Industry	2182.0	2471.4	2478.2	2387.9	6337.9
Electric energy	42.0	78.1	80.2	67.1	188.4
Oil and gas industry	11.0	11.4	11.0	9.8	29.4
Coal industry	20.0	21.6	22.4	21.9	14.3
Ferrous metallurgy	6.0	8.2	10.5	7.7	11.8
Non-ferrous metallurgy	132.0	145.6	141.9	163.9	499.3
Chemical and petrochemical	23.0	24.7	24.3	23.6	217.7
Machine building	674.0	949.7	951.0	892.6	2017.5
Lumber and paper	5.0	4.5	4.5	3.5	24.5
Industrial construction materials	19.0	12.7	17.1	13.1	67.2
Light industry	657.0	664.6	660.1	648.3	1901.1
Food industry	579.0	526.9	528.9	515.7	1317.0
Other industries	14.0	23.4	26.3	20.7	49.7
Agriculture	137.0	118.8	101.6	92.3	185.1
Other, including goods N.E.S.	5.0	5.2	20.4	18.6	23.0
	(in percent of total)				
Total Exports	100.0	100.0	100.0	100.0	100.0
Industry	93.9	95.2	95.3	95.6	96.8
Electric energy	1.8	3.0	3.1	2.7	2.9
Oil and gas industry	0.5	0.4	0.4	0.4	0.4
Coal industry	0.9	0.8	0.9	0.9	0.2
Ferrous metallurgy	0.3	0.3	0.4	0.3	0.2
Non-ferrous metallurgy	5.7	5.6	5.5	6.6	7.6
Chemical and petrochemical	1.0	1.0	0.9	0.9	3.3
Machine building	29.0	36.6	36.6	35.7	30.8
Lumber and paper	0.2	0.2	0.2	0.1	0.4
Industrial construction materials	0.8	0.5	0.7	0.5	1.0
Light industry	28.3	25.6	25.4	25.9	29.0
Food industry	24.9	20.3	20.3	20.6	20.1
Other industries	0.6	0.9	1.0	0.8	0.8
Agriculture	5.9	4.6	3.9	3.7	2.8
Other, including goods N.E.S.	0.2	0.2	0.8	0.7	0.4

Source: State Statistical Committee and World Bank mission estimates.

Table 3.3: Kyrgyzstan - Imports of Goods 1/

	1982	1987	1988	1989	1990
(in millions of rubles)					
Total Imports	547.5	722.8	773.0	934.4	1063.3
Industry	534.6	698.9	710.1	838.5	982.8
Electric energy	..	..	..	..	..
Oil and gas industry	..	..	..	..	..
Coal industry	..	..	..	..	..
Other fuel industry	..	..	..	..	..
Ferrous metallurgy	8.3	9.0	7.6	5.0	3.3
Non-ferrous metallurgy	2.4	1.7	1.2	8.0	1.4
Chemical and petrochemical	27.6	30.0	19.7	60.0	50.5
Machine building	20.6	30.4	42.2	69.9	106.1
Lumber and paper	12.2	15.1	15.2	7.6	15.3
Industrial construction materials	4.8	3.4	3.5	4.5	11.1
Light industry	238.1	262.5	271.4	334.9	364.3
Food industry	218.7	345.7	348.3	347.8	415.1
Other industries	1.9	1.1	1.0	0.8	15.7
Agriculture	12.9	23.9	62.9	95.3	79.9
Other types of material production	..	..	..	0.6	0.6
(in percent of total)					
Total Imports	100.0	100.0	100.0	100.0	100.0
Industry	97.6	96.7	91.9	89.7	92.4
Electric energy	..	..	..	..	..
Oil and gas industry	..	..	..	..	..
Coal industry	..	..	..	..	..
Other fuel industry	..	..	..	..	..
Ferrous metallurgy	1.5	1.2	1.0	0.5	0.3
Non-ferrous metallurgy	0.4	0.2	0.2	0.9	0.1
Chemical and petrochemical	5.0	4.2	2.5	6.4	4.7
Machine building	3.8	4.2	5.5	7.5	10.0
Lumber and paper	2.2	2.1	2.0	0.8	1.4
Industrial construction materials	0.9	0.5	0.5	0.5	1.0
Light industry	43.5	36.3	35.1	35.8	34.3
Food industry	39.9	47.8	45.1	37.2	39.0
Other industries	0.3	0.2	0.1	0.1	1.5
Agriculture	2.4	3.3	8.1	10.2	7.5
Other types of material production	..	..	..	0.1	0.1

1/ Imports from outside of ruble zone.

Source: State Statistical Committee and World Bank mission estimates.

Table 3.3a: Kyrgyzstan - Imports of Goods in 1991 1/

	(in thousands of rubles)	(in percent of total)
Total Imports	1373968.9	100.0
Industry of which:	1132396.6	82.4
Machines, equipment and vehicles including:	86229.6	6.3
Eqipment for food and light industry	41605.4	3.0
Ferrous metals including:	10570.9	0.8
Rolled ferrous metals	7025.1	0.5
Steel pipes	1035.8	0.1
Other ferrous metals	2478.0	0.2
Non-ferrous metals including:	5857.0	0.4
Copper	1683.0	0.1
Rolled copper	4078.0	0.3
Chemicals, fertilizers, synthetic rubber including:	20891.9	1.5
Chemicals	6157.8	0.4
Paints, laquers and tanning materials	5246.7	0.4
Fertilizers and pesticides	3519.5	0.3
Synthetic rubber, rubber and rubber-asbestos products	3240.5	0.2
Synthetic soaps	2655.0	0.2
Construction matrials and components including:	1956.2	0.1
Construction materials	1927.9	0.1
Products of glass, and china-pottery industry	1972.0	0.1
Wood products and celluloze-paper products including:	1716.0	0.1
Paper and cardboard	690.5	0.1
Furniture	22988.6	1.7
Wool	86826.6	6.3
Raw leather and leather	12088.7	0.9
Cotton yarn	2439.0	0.2
Fabrics	22439.6	1.6
Knitts	39991.0	2.9
Shoes, including rubber shoes	51571.8	3.8
Sewn products	53149.0	3.9
Other light industry products	6850.5	0.5
Raw sugar	428378.4	31.2
Natural coffee	4296.0	0.3
Instant coffee	5646.0	0.4
Tea	52378.0	3.8
Infant and diet foods	918.0	0.1
Pasta	935.0	0.1
Milk and milk products	13479.0	1.0
Vegetable oil	1800.0	0.1
Cigarettes and other tobacco products	23746.0	1.7
Confectionery	1705.3	0.1
Flour and cereal products	34222.0	2.5
Cosmetics	14397.0	1.0
Other food industry products	28450.9	2.1
Fodder	13915.5	1.0
Medication	22858.8	1.7
Medical equipment	1455.9	0.1
Protein-vitamin additives	7467.0	0.5
Agriculture of which:	241572.3	17.6
Wheat	93363.7	6.8
Barley	27864.4	2.0
Other grains	48634.3	3.5
Maize	69294.3	5.0
Potatoes	756.6	0.1
Other crops	1659.0	0.1
Other	48809.4	3.6

1/ Imports from outside of ruble zone.

Source: State Statistical Committee.

Table 3.4: Kyrgyzstan - Exports of Goods 1/

	1982	1987	1988	1989	1990
	(in millions of rubles)				
Total Exports	39.1	55.3	58.6	51.2	52.9
Industry	27.4	32.2	47.5	45.2	47.9
Electric energy	..	..	..	..	..
Oil and gas industry	..	..	..	..	..
Coal industry	..	..	..	..	..
Other fuel industry	..	..	..	..	..
Ferrous metallurgy	..	..	..	2.0	0.6
Non-ferrous metallurgy	8.9	10.2	17.0	17.8	19.2
Chemical and petrochemical	..	..	..	..	0.6
Machine building	4.3	10.6	10.9	5.1	10.9
Lumber and paper	..	..	..	..	..
Industrial construction materials	0.4	..	..	0.4	..
Light industry	11.7	3.3	13.8	10.0	8.6
Food industry	2.1	8.1	5.8	9.9	7.9
Other industries	..	..	..	..	0.1
Agriculture	11.6	23.1	11.1	5.9	4.9
Other types of material production	0.1	..	..	0.1	0.1
	(in percent of total)				
Total Exports	100.0	100.0	100.0	100.0	100.0
Industry	70.1	58.2	81.1	88.3	90.5
Electric energy	..	..	..	..	..
Oil and gas industry	..	..	..	..	..
Coal industry	..	..	..	..	..
Other fuel industry	..	..	..	..	..
Ferrous metallurgy	..	..	..	3.9	1.1
Non-ferrous metallurgy	22.8	18.4	29.0	34.8	36.3
Chemical and petrochemical	..	..	..	..	1.1
Machine building	11.0	19.2	18.6	10.0	20.6
Lumber and paper	..	..	..	..	..
Industrial construction materials	1.0	..	..	0.8	..
Light industry	29.9	6.0	23.5	19.5	16.3
Food industry	5.4	14.6	9.9	19.3	14.9
Other industries	..	..	..	..	0.2
Agriculture	29.7	41.8	18.9	11.5	9.3
Other types of material production	0.3	..	..	0.2	0.2

1/ Exports to outside of ruble zone

Source: State Statistical Committee and World Bank mission estimates.

Table 3.4a: Kyrgyzstan - Exports of Goods in 1991 1/

	(in thousands of rubles)	(in percent of total)
Total Exports	40644.4	100.0
Industry	26769.0	65.9
of which:		
Non-ferrous metals	7758.9	19.1
Plastics and glass fibre products	12.9	0.0
Paints and laquers	10.9	0.0
Rubber shoes	12.5	0.0
Power engineering	4.4	0.0
Cranes	430.7	1.1
Electric engeneering	4193.8	10.3
Cables	589.0	1.4
Metal working and wood processing, and pressing machines	89.2	0.2
Tools, instruments, appliances	478.1	1.2
Vehicles equipmet	345.5	0.9
Spare parts for tractors	1111.5	2.7
Agricultural machines	132.4	0.3
Equipment for stores and restaurants	312.0	0.8
Household appliences	49.6	0.1
Audio-visual equipment	79.2	0.2
Metal products	227.9	0.6
Raw wood products	7064.0	17.4
Finished wood	22.7	0.1
Furniture	219.0	0.5
Construction materials from natural stone	310.4	0.8
Cotton fiber	29.0	0.1
Cotton/paper products	30.4	0.1
Wool products	1837.0	4.5
Clothing and other sewn products	375.0	0.9
Leather and fur products	605.0	1.5
Raw leather	388.4	1.0
Meat and meat products	41.7	0.1
Other industrial goods	7.9	0.0
Agriculture	2762.9	6.8
of which:		
Honey	1991.7	4.9
Leather as raw material	672.3	1.7
Other agricultural products	98.9	0.2
Other	11110.0	27.3

1/ *Exports to outside of ruble zone.*

Source: State Statistical Committee and World Bank mission estimates.

Table 3.5: Kyrgyzstan - Trade in Domestic and World Prices in 1990

(in millions of rubles)

	Interrepublican Trade				Extrarepublican Trade				Total Trade			
	Domestic Prices		World Prices		Domestic Prices		World Prices		Domestic Prices		World Prices	
	Export.	Import	Export	Import	Export	Import	Export	Import	Export	Import	Export	Import
INDUSTRY	2340	2911	1903	2703	48	983	51	706	2388	3894	1954	3408
POWER	67	34	101	51	0	0	0	0	67	34	101	51
OIL AND GAS	10	269	34	605	0	0	0	0	10	269	34	605
Oil Products	9	0	31	0	0	0	0	0	9	0	31	0
Refineries	0	237	0	528	0	0	0	0	0	237	0	528
Gas Products	1	31	3	77	0	0	0	0	1	31	3	77
COAL	22	38	21	36	0	0	0	0	22	38	21	36
OTHER FUELS	0	0	0	0	0	0	0	0	0	0	0	0
Combustible Shales	0	0	0	0	0	0	0	0	0	0	0	0
Peat	0	0	0	0	0	0	0	0	0	0	0	0
FERROUS	7	167	9	189	1	3	0	4	8	171	9	194
Ferrous Ores	0	0	0	0	0	0	0	0	0	0	0	0
Ferrous Metals	7	126	9	156	0	3	0	4	7	129	9	160
Coking Products	0	4	0	6	0	0	0	0	0	4	0	6
Fire Resistant	0	2	0	3	0	0	0	0	0	2	0	4
Metal Products	0	35	0	25	1	0	0	0	1	36	0	25
NON-FERROUS	145	96	235	156	19	1	32	1	164	98	267	157
Non-ferrous Ores	60	38	94	59	0	0	0	0	60	38	94	59
Non-ferrous Metals	84	58	141	98	19	1	32	1	104	60	173	99
CHEMICALS	23	323	19	269	1	51	1	37	24	374	20	307
Mineral Chemistry	0	1	1	1	0	0	0	0	0	1	0	1
Basic Chemicals	1	89	1	64	1	3	0	2	1	92	1	66
Chemical Fibers	0	25	0	18	0	3	0	2	0	29	0	20
Synthetic Resins	0	9	0	7	0	1	0	0	0	10	0	8
Plastic Products	11	20	9	16	0	1	0	1	11	21	9	16
Paints and Laquers	2	24	1	18	0	4	0	4	2	28	1	22
Synthetic Paints	0	4	0	3	0	2	0	2	0	6	0	5
Synthetic Rubber	0	3	0	2	0	0	0	0	0	3	0	2
Organic Chemicals	0	7	0	6	0	1	0	1	0	8	0	7
Tires	0	52	0	51	0	0	0	0	0	52	0	51
Rubber and Asbestos	0	30	0	26	0	7	0	4	0	37	0	30
Other Products	0	38	0	38	0	5	0	2	0	43	0	40
Pharmaceuticals	9	22	8	20	0	23	0	20	9	44	8	39
MACHINERY	882	879	1099	906	11	106	13	79	893	985	1112	985
Energy and power	0	4	0	4	0	0	0	0	0	4	0	4
Technology	0	0	0	0	0	0	0	0	0	0	0	0
Mining	0	5	0	7	0	0	0	0	0	5	0	8
Transportation	6	11	8	15	0	1	1	1	6	12	9	16
Railway Equipment	0	5	0	4	0	2	0	2	0	7	0	6
Electro-technical	206	96	189	88	1	1	1	1	207	96	190	88
Cables	28	16	28	16	0	0	0	0	28	16	28	16

(continued)

Table 3.5: Kyrgyzstan - Trade in Domestic and World Prices in 1990

(in millions of rubles)

	Interrepublican Trade				Extrarepublican Trade				Total Trade			
	Domestic Prices		World Prices		Domestic Prices		World Prices		Domestic Prices		World Prices	
	Export	Import	Export	Import	Export	Import	Export	Import	Export	Import	Export	Import
Pumps	23	26	26	30	0	3	0	3	23	30	26	33
Machine Tools	25	15	29	17	0	3	0	2	25	18	29	20
Forging/Pressing	4	6	3	5	0	0	0	0	4	6	3	5
Casting Equipment	0	2	0	2	0	0	0	0	0	2	0	2
Precision Instr.	34	13	21	8	3	0	2	0	37	13	22	8
Synthetic Diamonds	0	5	0	5	0	0	0	0	0	5	0	5
Tools and Dies	48	76	44	62	0	18	0	17	48	94	44	79
Autos & Parts	120	173	202	148	1	8	3	8	121	181	205	156
Bearings	0	9	0	7	0	0	0	0	0	9	0	7
Tractors & Agri.Eq.	87	76	118	103	4	5	5	5	91	81	123	108
Construction M&E	1	21	1	30	0	1	0	1	1	22	1	30
Communal M&E	0	5	0	7	0	1	0	1	0	6	0	8
Light Ind. M&E	0	15	0	17	0	7	0	6	0	22	0	22
Food M&E	3	6	3	8	0	21	0	16	3	27	3	24
Trade M&E	22	5	33	8	0	0	0	0	22	5	33	8
Printing M&E	0	1	0	1	0	2	0	2	0	3	0	2
Appliances	18	37	10	17	0	11	0	4	18	48	10	21
Sanitary Eng.	0	11	0	6	0	0	0	0	0	11	0	6
Shipbuilding	0	0	0	1	0	0	0	0	0	1	0	1
Radio Electronics	91	101	90	66	1	5	1	3	92	106	91	69
Other Ind. M&E	145	100	275	191	1	1	0	1	145	101	275	192
Metal Construction	1	4	1	5	0	0	0	0	1	4	1	5
Metal Products	21	30	17	24	0	9	0	2	21	39	17	26
M&E Repair	0	2	0	3	0	0	0	0	0	2	0	3
Medical Equipment	1	3	1	3	0	7	0	6	1	10	1	9
WOOD AND PAPER	4	114	2	80	0	15	0	9	4	130	2	89
Logging	0	19	0	12	0	0	0	0	0	19	0	12
Sawmill	0	43	0	32	0	0	0	1	0	43	0	33
Plywood	0	5	0	4	0	0	0	0	0	5	0	4
Furniture	1	18	1	8	0	0	0	7	1	30	1	15
Paper and Pulp	2	29	2	24	0	12	0	2	2	31	2	25
Chemistry Prod.	0	1	0	0	0	2	0	0	0	1	0	0
CONSTR. MATERIALS	13	69	13	64	0	11	0	3	13	80	13	67
Cement	3	1	2	1	0	0	0	0	3	1	2	1
Asbestos Products	1	7	2	10	0	0	0	0	1	7	2	10
Roofing	0	10	0	10	0	0	0	0	0	10	0	10
Precast Concrete	3	1	3	1	0	0	0	0	3	1	3	1
Wall Materials	0	1	0	0	0	0	0	0	0	1	0	0
Ceramics	0	2	0	2	0	0	0	0	0	3	0	2
Construction Products	0	2	0	2	0	0	0	0	0	3	0	2
Other	1	12	1	15	0	0	0	0	1	12	6	15
Glass and Porcelain	6	31	6	21	0	10	0	3	6	42	6	24
Medical Products	0	2	0	2	0	0	0	0	0	2	0	2

(continued)

Table 3.5: Kyrgyzstan - Trade in Domestic and World Prices in 1990

(in millions of rubles)

	Interrepublican Trade				Extrarepublican Trade				Total Trade			
	Domestic Prices		World Prices		Domestic Prices		World Prices		Domestic prices		World Prices	
	Export	Import	Export	Import	Export	Import	Export	Import	Export	Import	Export	Import
LIGHT INDUSTRY	640	602	174	200	9	364	2	90	648	966	176	290
Cotton Products	121	132	41	53	1	29	0	9	122	161	41	63
Flax Products	0	13	0	5	0	2	0	2	0	15	0	7
Wool Products	383	119	94	31	7	21	1	6	390	140	95	37
Silk Products	66	72	12	12	1	14	0	4	67	85	12	16
Hosiery/Knitwear	8	47	3	16	0	79	0	14	8	126	3	30
Other Textiles	14	29	8	16	0	9	0	2	14	38	8	17
Sewn Goods	19	117	6	38	1	117	0	27	20	235	7	66
Leather	27	74	10	28	0	93	0	26	27	168	10	54
FOOD PRODUCTS	508	248	182	103	8	415	3	477	516	663	184	580
Sugar	199	18	78	7	0	322	0	441	199	340	78	449
Bread Products	0	4	0	2	0	1	0	0	0	5	0	3
Confections	0	14	0	7	0	1	0	0	0	15	0	7
Vegetable Oils	2	43	1	16	1	12	0	7	3	55	1	24
Perfume Oils	0	32	0	22	0	28	0	10	0	59	0	32
Distilleries	0	0	0	0	0	0	0	0	0	0	0	0
Wines	28	1	4	0	0	2	0	0	28	2	4	1
Fruit/Vegetables	8	2	3	1	0	3	0	2	8	5	3	3
Tobacco	247	12	85	4	2	8	1	3	249	20	86	7
Other Food	9	48	5	13	2	28	1	7	11	76	5	20
Meat Products	2	5	1	2	2	0	1	0	5	5	2	2
Dairy Products	0	7	0	4	0	7	0	2	0	14	0	6
Fish Products	0	33	0	14	0	4	0	2	0	37	0	16
Flour and Cereals	13	30	5	12	0	1	0	0	13	31	5	12
OTHER INDUSTRY	21	71	16	43	0	16	0	5	21	87	16	48
Microbiology	0	9	0	7	0	0	0	0	0	9	0	7
Animal Feed	4	6	4	5	0	0	0	0	4	6	4	5
Other Products	16	57	13	31	0	16	0	5	17	72	13	35
AGRICULTURE	87	167	31	93	5	80	1	53	92	247	31	146
Crops	62	159	23	91	0	59	0	46	62	218	23	137
Animal Husbandry	25	8	8	2	5	21	1	8	30	29	9	10
OTHER PROD.	19	102	20	114	0	1	0	1	19	102	20	115
Information Services	0	0	0	0	0	0	0	0	0	0	0	0
Other Services	5	9	5	9	0	0	0	0	5	10	5	9
Transport Expenses	14	93	15	106	0	1	0	1	14	93	15	106
TOTAL	2446	3179	1954	2910	53	1063	52	759	2499	4243	2006	3669

Source: FSU Data Base, IECSE.

Table 4.1: Kyrgyzstan - State Government Revenue and Grants, 1987-92

	1987	1988	1989	1990	1991	1992 Budget a)
(in billions of rubles)						
Tax revenue	**1.76**	**1.83**	**2.13**	**2.18**	**2.66**	**11.41**
Turnover tax 1/	0.86	0.92	1.15	1.17	1.17	--
Value-added tax 2/	--	--	--	--	0.30	5.13
Excise taxes 3/	--	--	--	--	--	3.26
Enterprise profits taxes	0.32	0.29	0.27	0.36	0.65	2.72
Profits tax on co-ops	0.04	0.03	0.05	0.06	0.10	0.06
Personal income taxes 4/	0.26	0.28	0.32	0.20	0.38	0.22
Social security contributions 5/	0.26	0.29	0.31	0.36	--	--
Other taxes 6/	0.02	0.02	0.02	0.03	0.05	0.03
Nontax revenue	**0.23**	**0.15**	**0.22**	**0.12**	**0.84**	**0.55**
Road user fees	--	--	--	--	0.13	0.21
Windfall on stock re-evaluation	--	--	--	--	0.21	0.10
Other fees and charges	0.23	0.15	0.22	0.12	0.50	0.24
Total revenue except grants	**1.99**	**1.98**	**2.35**	**2.30**	**3.50**	**11.97**
Union payments (net)	0.39	0.62	0.54	0.91	1.93	--
Grants	0.28	0.56	0.51	0.56	2.55	--
Other payments (net) 7/	0.11	0.06	0.03	0.35	-0.62	--
Total revenue and grants	**2.38**	**2.60**	**2.89**	**3.21**	**5.43**	**11.97**
Memorandum Item:					b)	c)
GDP at current prices	6.28	6.94	7.62	8.32	16.92	64.00
(shares of GDP)						
Tax revenue	28.0	26.4	27.9	26.2	15.7	17.8
Taxes on goods and services 8/	13.7	13.3	15.1	14.1	8.7	13.1
Profits tax	5.1	4.2	3.5	4.3	3.8	4.3
Other taxes	9.2	8.9	9.2	7.8	3.1	0.5
Nontax revenue	3.7	2.2	2.9	1.4	5.0	0.9
Union grants (net)	6.2	8.9	7.1	10.9	11.4	0.0

a) *Revised as of January 1992.*

b) *Revised as of October 1992.*

c) *Estimate of GDP for 1992 underlying the revised budget prepared in January 1992.*

1/ *The turnover tax was abolished in 1992.*

2/ *The-value added tax was introduced January 1, 1992. A sales tax was instituted in 1991 rescinded as of January 1, 1992.*

3/ *Excise taxes were introduced with the 1992 budget effective January 1, 1992.*

4/ *The revenue from the personal income tax was split between the Republic and the Union in 1990. In other years, the entire funds went to the republic.*

5/ *The social security tax prior to 1990 was collected by the Republic and transfered to the trade unions that ran the pension funds. As of 1991, a separate pension fund was established that collects the contributions directly.*

6/ *Local taxes, cinema tax, and others.*

7/ *Includes a rub 200 million payment to the Union in 1991 that was classified in the budget as expenditure.*

8/ *Includes turnover tax, sales tax (1991 only), value-added tax, and excises.*

Source: Ministry of Finance, Office of the President, IMF and World Bank mission estimates.

Table 4.2: Kyrgyzstan - State Government Expenditure and Financing, 1987-92

	1987	1988	1989	1990	1991	1992 Budget a)	
(In billions of rubles)							
Current expenditure	**1.92**	**2.11**	**2.34**	**2.71**	**4.53**	**14.10**	
Wages and salaries	0.43	0.46	0.48	0.53	1.11	3.18	
Other goods and services	0.41	0.45	0.53	0.58	0.97	3.13	
Operation and maintenance	0.19	0.21	0.24	0.26	0.43	1.40	
Subtotal: Consumption	1.03	1.12	1.25	1.37	2.51	7.71	
Interest on debt							
Foreign	--	--	--	--	--	--	b)
Domestic	--	--	--	--	--	--	b)
Transfers	0.52	0.59	0.71	0.76	1.28	4.13	
Subsidies	0.37	0.40	0.38	0.57	0.75	1.49	
CIS payments	--	--	--	--	--	0.77	
Capital expenditure	**0.31**	**0.39**	**0.39**	**0.48**	**0.19**	**0.75**	
Social	0.07	0.09	0.11	0.11	0.05	n.a.	
Material economy	0.24	0.30	0.28	0.36	0.15	n.a.	
Total expenditure	**2.23**	**2.50**	**2.73**	**3.18**	**4.73**	**14.85**	b)
Total revenue and grants	**2.38**	**2.60**	**2.89**	**3.21**	**5.43**	**11.97**	
Surplus/Deficit (-)	**0.15**	**0.10**	**0.16**	**0.03**	**0.70**	**-2.89**	b)
Financing of expenditure							
Domestic borrowing	0.02	0.02	0.02	0.02	0.01	n.a.	
Borrowing from the Union	--	--	--	--	0.23	n.a.	
Other borrowing	--	--	--	--	--	n.a.	
Implied use of cash balances	-0.17	-0.12	-0.18	-0.05	-0.94	n.a.	
Memorandum Item:						c)	d)
GDP at current prices	**6.28**	**6.94**	**7.62**	**8.32**	**16.92**	**64.00**	
(share of GDP)							
Current expenditure	30.6	30.4	30.7	32.6	26.8	22.0	
Wages	6.8	6.6	6.3	6.4	6.6	5.0	
Other consumption	9.6	9.5	10.1	10.1	8.3	7.1	
Transfers	8.3	8.5	9.3	9.1	7.6	6.5	
Subsidies	5.9	5.8	5.0	6.9	4.4	2.3	
CIS payments	--	--	--	--	--	1.2	
Capital expenditure	4.9	5.6	5.1	5.8	1.1	1.2	

a) Revised as of January 1992.
b) The State budget includes no allowance for interest payments. See Text Table 2.4. for estimates
   of interest due in 1992.
c) Revised as of October 1992.
d) Approximation of GDP for 1992 implied in revised budget,.

Source: Ministry of Finance, Office of the President, IMF and World Bank mission estimates.

Table 4.3: Kyrgyzstan - State Government Expenditures by Function

	1990	1991	1992 a)
(in millions of rubles)			
Total Expenditures	**3,184**	**4,727**	**17,053** b)
National economy	1,553	1,573	3,276
Social/cultural expenditure	1,416	2,782	9,539
Education	604	1,096	4,231
Health	318	565	2,283
Culture and mass media	79	96	328
Social security	416	1,008	2,697
Science	33	19	138
Law enforcement	--	68	616
Other	182	285	515
CIS contributions	--	--	773
Memo Item:			
GDP at current prices	**8,320**	**16,924** c)	**64,000**
(shares of GDP)			
Total Expenditures	**38.3**	**27.9**	**26.6**
National economy	18.7	9.3	5.1
Social/cultural expenditure	17.0	16.4	14.9
Education	7.3	6.5	6.6
Health	3.8	3.3	3.6
Culture and mass media	0.9	0.6	0.5
Social security	5.0	6.0	4.2
Science	0.4	0.1	0.2
Law enforcement	--	0.4	1.0
Other	2.2	1.7	0.8
CIS contributions	--	--	1.2

a) *Revised Budget as of January 1992.*
b) *Excludes interest payments.*
c) *Revised as of October 1992.*

Source: Ministry of Finance, Office of the President, and World Bank mission estimates.

Table 5.1: Kyrgyzstan - Illustrative Monetary Survey

	Year -end 1991	June 1992
(in billions of rubles)		
Net Foreign Assets		
Foreign Exchange	0.0	-0.7
Net Domestic Assets	10.0	16.5
Credit to Government	-0.5	-1.2
Credit to the Economy	8.3	19.7
Other Items, Net	2.2	-2.0
Money Stock	10.0	15.8
Currency Outside Banks	2.8	5.6
Deposits	7.2	10.2
(in percent of GDP)		
Net Foreign Assets		
Foreign Exchange	0.0	0.5
Net Domestic Assets	49.0	12.4
Credit to Government	-2.5	-0.9
Credit to the Economy	40.8	14.8
Other Items, Net	10.8	-1.5
Money Stock	49.0	11.9
Currency Outside Banks	13.9	4.2
Deposits	35.1	7.7
Monetary Velocities		
Money Stock	2.0	8.4
Currency Outside Banks	7.3	23.7
Deposits	2.8	13.0
GDP at Annual Rate	20.4	133.0

Source: National Bank of Kyrgyzstan and World Bank mission estimates.

Table 6.1: Kyrgyzstan - Total Land Area and its Allocation by Different Uses as of November 1, 1991

	Total land area	Total land under cultivation	Plowed land	of which: Tree crops	Hay	Pasture
(in thousands of hectares)						
Total land (territory)	20265.0	10854.0	1383.7	67.4	204.2	9186.6
Agricultural enterprises and farms	15969.8	10048.5	1365.4	64.5	196.7	8410.0
Collective farms	6999.7	4498.7	586.7	14.7	54.7	3836.8
Land for general use	6957.4	4464.5	559.6	8.6	53.7	3836.8
Land for employees' individual use	42.3	34.2	27.1	6.1	1.0	-
State farms	8359.0	5136.3	702.9	31.1	135.6	4260.9
Inter-farm agricultural enterprises and organizations	2.6	2.4	0.2	1.9	-	0.3
Individual use	76.4	68.6	49.5	16.3	2.8	-
City residents with farms	81.8	68.4	11.9	0.5	1.1	54.9
Land reserve and forest organizations	3184.6	668.0	13.9	1.4	6.3	646.3
Other land uses	1110.8	137.4	4.4	1.6	1.1	130.3
Agriculture cooperatives and organizations	450.6	272.3	12.5	-	2.4	257.1

Source: State Statistical Committee.

Table 6.1a: Kyrgyzstan - Total Land Area and its Allocation by Different Uses as of November 1, 1990

	Total land area	Total land under cultivation	Plowed land	of which: Tree crops	Hay	Pasture
(in thousands of hectares)						
Total land (territory)	19638.8	10522.9	1374.4	65.2	210.6	8861.0
Agricultural enterprises and farms	16046.4	10080.4	1369.4	62.4	205.1	8431.9
Collective farms	7183.8	4601.9	592.9	14.0	52.2	3936.7
Land for general use	7142.4	4565.4	563.0	8.2	51.5	3936.7
Land for employees' individual use	41.4	36.5	29.9	5.8	0.7	-
State farms	8796.2	5420.5	738.3	32.1	150.3	4494.2
Inter-farm agricultural enterprises and organizations	2.6	2.4	0.6	1.6	-	1.2
Individual use	62.7	54.8	37.6	14.7	2.6	-
City residents with farms	1.1	0.8	-	-	-	0.8
Land reserve and forest organizations	2511.8	318.3	1.3	1.3	4.5	310.9
Other land uses	1080.6	124.2	3.7	1.5	1.0	118.2

Source: Statistical Yearbook for Kyrgyzstan, 1990.

Table 6.2: Kyrgyzstan - Agricultural Production, 1985-1991

	1985	1986	1987	1988	1989	1990	1991
	(thousand tons)						
A. Crops							
Grain	1477.1	1632.7	1908.7	1757.7	1654.8	1572.9	1445.5
of which:							
Wheat	523.6	586.3	745.5	577.9	609.4	510.4	464.9
Maize	380.8	429.6	459.7	497.3	452.0	406.0	364.5
Barley	552.9	589.2	669.0	649.4	568.1	631.4	596.1
Other grain	19.8	27.6	34.5	33.1	25.3	25.1	20
Potatoes	306.5	328.9	287.9	332.3	324.4	365.1	306.6
Vegetables	445.2	512.0	490.7	553.1	585.3	487.3	338.7
Cotton	57.8	68.2	72.9	78.7	74.0	80.9	63.4
Tobacco	76.7	57.7	50.8	50.2	50.2	53.9	42.2
Fodder (maize and green sillage)	3357.6	3203.5	3101.2	2803.6	2564.7	2735.5	2432.3
Fodder (root crops)	327.0	380.5	395.8	365.3	316.3	263.1	172.9
Hay	1938.0	1972.8	2109.9	1996.3	1875.7	1854.6	1924.7
B. Livestock products							
Meat (slaughter weight)							
Beef and veal	56.4	63.7	65.7	71.9	85.4	91.2	87.5
Pork	23.0	28.2	32.3	36.4	37.6	40.5	32.7
Mutton and goat meat	59.0	66.4	67.2	71.7	75.1	77.2	70.9
Poultry	22.8	25.5	29.8	31.9	31.5	33.3	28.8
Other meat (horse, rabbit)	7.9	8.8	8.6	10.6	11.7	11.9	9.8
Milk	771.0	909.1	997.4	1063.2	1202.3	1185.0	1131.4
Eggs	532.5	573.4	612.1	665.8	704.1	713.8	649.9
Wool	32.5	35.9	37.4	38.0	38.6	39.0	36.5
	(index: 1985 = 100)						
A. Crops							
Grain	100.0	110.5	129.2	119.0	112.0	106.5	97.9
of which:							
Wheat	100.0	112.0	142.4	110.4	116.4	97.5	88.8
Maize	100.0	112.8	120.7	130.6	118.7	106.6	95.7
Barley	100.0	106.6	121.0	117.5	102.7	114.2	107.8
Other grain	100.0	139.4	174.2	167.2	127.8	126.8	101.0
Potatoes	100.0	107.3	93.9	108.4	105.8	119.1	100.0
Vegetables	100.0	115.0	110.2	124.2	131.5	109.5	76.1
Cotton	100.0	118.0	126.1	136.2	128.0	140.0	109.7
Tobacco	100.0	75.2	66.2	65.4	65.4	70.3	55.0
Fodder (maize and green sillage)	100.0	95.4	92.4	83.5	76.4	81.5	72.4
Fodder (root crops)	100.0	116.4	121.0	111.7	96.7	80.5	52.9
Hay	100.0	101.8	108.9	103.0	96.8	95.7	99.3
B. Livestock products							
Meat (slaughter weight)							
Beef and veal	100.0	112.9	116.5	127.5	151.4	161.7	155.1
Pork	100.0	122.6	140.4	158.3	163.5	176.1	142.2
Mutton and goat meat	100.0	112.5	113.9	121.5	127.3	130.8	120.2
Poultry	100.0	111.8	130.7	139.9	138.2	146.1	126.3
Other meat (horse, rabbit)	100.0	111.4	108.9	134.2	148.1	150.6	124.1
Milk	100.0	117.9	129.4	137.9	155.9	153.7	146.7
Eggs	100.0	107.7	114.9	125.0	132.2	134.0	122.0
Wool	100.0	110.5	115.1	116.9	118.8	120.0	112.4

Source: Statistical Yearbook for Kyrgyzstan, 1990 and State Statistical Committee.

Table 6.3: Kyrgyzstan - Procurement Prices for Agricultural Products Sold to the State
                          Annual Survey

	1983		1989	1990	1991	1992 a)
		(in rubles per ton)				
Crops						
Grain	109		177	337	419	10,000
Wheat	..		156	286	..	12,125
Maize	..		227	451	..	10,064
Barley	..		173	288	..	10,045
Cotton	830		854	973	2,572	10,250
Tobacco	5,210		5,997	7,418	21,225	18,000
Potatoes	191		395	383	1,284	4,000
Vegetables	281 b)		224	264	1,504	7,000
Fruits	1,031 c)		471	551	1,630	..
Grapes	467		425	625	786	..
Livestock production						
Beef d)	2,389	(4,160)	2,261	3,231	4,760	35,000
Sheep d)	1,855	(4,270)	2,116	2,766	3,590	25,000
Pigs d)	2,151	(4,340)	2,030	2,850	4,345	30,000
Poultry d)	2,240	(3,030)	2,067	1,920	4,569	30,000
Milk	396		472	378	650	12,000
Eggs	96		85	123	204	1,100
Wool	8,585		9,529	10,564	38,041	200,000
Cocoons	8,067		7,655	11,121	17,723	..

a) Preliminary as of October 1992.

b) The State Statistical Committee gives an average price of 589 rubles per ton which seem inconsistent with prices for later years. This estimate is the unit price for vegetables derived from data on the value of agricultural production at 1983 prices and volumes provided by Goskomstat.

c) This price does not appear consistent with those for later years, but we do not have basis for a revised estimate.

d) These are prices for slaughter weight; prices for dressed weight for 1983 are given in brackets.

Source: State Statistical Committee and World Bank mission estimates.

Table 6.4: Kyrgyzstan - Gross Value of Agricultural Output at 1983 Prices

	1985	1986	1987	1988	1989	1990	1991
	(in millions of rubles)						
Crops:							
Grain	161.0	178.8	208.0	191.6	180.4	173.3	159.4
Potatoes	58.5	62.8	55.0	63.5	62.0	69.8	62.4
Vegetables	125.1	143.9	137.9	155.4	164.5	136.7	110.4
Cotton	48.0	56.6	60.5	65.3	61.4	63.1	47.3
Tobacco	399.6	300.6	264.7	261.5	261.5	282.0	219.8
Fruit	51.0	136.5	70.0	94.0	64.0	100.9	65.5
Other Crops	283.7	337.8	321.6	316.5	324.3	281.1	257.0
Total Crops	1,126.9	1,217.0	1,117.7	1,147.8	1,118.1	1,106.9	921.8
Livestock Products:							
Meat							
Beef and Veal	234.6	265.0	273.3	299.1	355.3	378.6	353.3
Mutton and Lamb	251.9	283.5	286.9	306.2	320.7	330.1	297.5
Pork	99.8	122.4	138.0	155.5	160.7	101.9	94.6
Poultry	69.1	77.3	90.3	96.7	96.4	101.2	104.4
Other	136.2	66.8	117.0	96.0	60.0	40.9	40.6
Milk	305.3	360.0	395.0	421.0	476.1	470.5	449.0
Eggs	51.1	55.0	58.8	63.9	67.6	68.4	62.2
Wool	279.0	308.2	321.1	326.2	331.4	340.0	319.1
Total Livestock	1,427.0	1,538.3	1,680.4	1,764.6	1,867.1	1,916.9	1,800.7
Total Agriculture	2,553.9	2,755.3	2,798.1	2,912.4	2,985.2	3,023.8	2,722.5

Source: State Statistical Committee.

Table 6.5: Kyrgyzstan - Livestock Population, 1985-1991

Year	Cattle	of which Cows	Sheep and Goats	Pigs	Horses	Poultry
			(in thousands; at the end of the year)			
1985	1,110.0	426.9	10,200.0	349.3	276.5	12,394.1
1986	1,129.6	434.4	10,263.0	379.0	283.7	13,495.8
1987	1,161.0	460.1	10,389.8	387.6	293.4	13,927.2
1988	1,190.1	487.4	10,404.9	416.4	303.5	14,461.1
1989	1,214.3	507.4	10,483.0	444.8	310.0	15,206.7
1990	1,205.2	506.1	9,968.0	393.4	312.6	13,905.6
1991	1,190.0	518.6	9,524.9	357.7	320.5	13,363.0
			(index: 1985 = 100)			
1985	100.0	100.0	100.0	100.0	100.0	100.0
1986	101.8	101.8	100.6	108.5	102.6	108.9
1987	104.6	107.8	101.9	111.0	106.1	112.4
1988	107.2	114.2	102.0	119.2	109.8	116.7
1989	109.4	118.9	102.8	127.3	112.1	122.7
1990	108.6	118.6	97.7	112.6	113.1	112.2
1991	107.2	121.5	93.4	102.4	115.9	107.8

Source: Statistical Yearbook for Kyrgyzstan, 1990 and State Statistical Committee.

Table 6.6: Kyrgyzstan - Livestock Population, 1985-1991
By Category of Farm, at the End of the Year

Category of Farm	Year	Cattle	of which Cows	Pigs	Sheep and Goats	Poultry	Horses
			(in thousands)				
All Farms	1985	1,110.0	426.9	349.3	10,200.0	12,394.1	276.5
	1986	1,129.6	434.4	379.0	10,263.0	13,495.8	283.7
	1987	1,161.0	460.1	387.6	10,389.8	13,927.2	293.4
	1988	1,190.1	487.4	416.4	10,404.9	14,461.1	303.5
	1989	1,214.3	507.4	444.8	10,483.0	15,206.7	310.0
	1990	1,205.2	506.1	393.4	9,968.0	13,905.6	312.6
	1991	1,190.0	518.6	357.7	9,524.9	13,363.0	320.5
of which:							
Collective and State Farms	1985	734.4	204.5	236.7	8,679.0	4,898.0	205.3
	1986	739.8	206.2	282.7	8,694.6	5,234.0	207.5
	1987	735.2	204.0	289.7	8,618.9	6,227.2	208.8
	1988	731.2	205.8	311.7	8,447.4	6,223.0	215.4
	1989	735.3	208.3	335.5	8,339.8	6,923.6	220.1
	1990	717.5	201.9	318.3	7,707.8	5,914.2	211.7
	1991	645.2	187.7	275.9	6,256.0	6,237.4	185.0
Owned by Households	1985	375.6	222.4	112.6	1,521.0	7,496.1	71.2
	1986	389.8	228.2	96.3	1,568.4	8,261.8	76.2
	1987	425.8	256.1	97.9	1,770.9	7,700.0	84.6
	1988	458.9	281.6	104.7	1,957.5	8,238.1	88.1
	1989	479.0	299.1	109.3	2,143.2	8,283.1	89.9
	1990	487.0	304.2	75.1	2,260.2	7,991.4	100.9
	1991	544.8	330.9	81.8	3,268.9	7,125.6	135.5
			(index: 1985 = 100)				
All Farms	1985	100.0	100.0	100.0	100.0	100.0	100.0
	1986	101.8	101.8	108.5	100.6	108.9	102.6
	1987	104.6	107.8	111.0	101.9	112.4	106.1
	1988	107.2	114.2	119.2	102.0	116.7	109.8
	1989	109.4	118.9	127.3	102.8	122.7	112.1
	1990	108.6	118.6	112.6	97.7	112.2	113.1
	1991	107.2	121.5	102.4	93.4	107.8	115.9
of which:							
Collective and State Farms	1985	100.0	100.0	100.0	100.0	100.0	100.0
	1986	100.7	100.8	119.4	100.2	106.9	101.1
	1987	100.1	99.8	122.4	99.3	127.1	101.7
	1988	99.6	100.6	131.7	97.3	127.1	104.9
	1989	100.1	101.9	141.7	96.1	141.4	107.2
	1990	97.7	98.7	134.5	88.8	120.7	103.1
	1991	87.9	91.8	116.6	72.1	127.3	90.1
Owned by Households	1985	100.0	100.0	100.0	100.0	100.0	100.0
	1986	103.8	102.6	85.5	103.1	110.2	107.0
	1987	113.4	115.2	86.9	116.4	102.7	118.8
	1988	122.2	126.6	93.0	128.7	109.9	123.7
	1989	127.5	134.5	97.1	140.9	110.5	126.3
	1990	129.7	136.8	66.7	148.6	106.6	141.7
	1991	145.0	148.8	72.6	214.9	95.1	190.3

Source: Statistical Yearbook for Kyrgyzstan, 1990 and State Statistical Committee.

Table 6.7: Kyrgyzstan - Livestock Productivity in all Types of Farms, 1985-1991 1/

Year	Cattle			Sheep and Goats			Pigs			Horses		
	Heads (number)	Total Weight (tons)	Average Weight (kg)	Heads (number)	Total Weight (tons)	Average Weight (kg)	Heads (number)	Total Weight (tons)	Average Weight (kg)	Heads (number)	Total Weight (tons)	Average Weight (kg)
1985	227,899	70,096	308	1,828,867	65,728	36	182,923	20,378	111	:	5,689	:
1986	236,857	77,673	328	2,234,285	83,715	38	211,648	24,134	114	:	5,245	:
1987	256,578	86,230	336	2,260,192	82,941	37	232,076	26,327	113	:	5,380	:
1988	271,094	93,689	346	2,196,861	80,876	37	219,825	25,216	115	:	5,010	:
1989	261,469	92,408	353	2,251,580	82,788	37	239,988	27,124	113	:	5,965	:
1990	273,683	90,157	329	2,349,694	77,514	33	255,542	26,949	105	:	4,556	:
1991	239,777	73,119	305	1,623,793	55,357	34	167,297	16,540	99	14,397	3,628	252

1/ *Quantities bought by the State from all types of farms.*

Source: State Statistical Committee.

Table 7.1: Kyrgyzstan - Industrial Production, 1985-90

	1985	*1986*	*1987*	*1988*	*1989*	*1990*
Production Volume (comparable prices, millions of rubles)	5,545.2	5,783.9	5,875.4	6,277.9	6,584.8	6,501.2
Number of Enterprises	3,354.0	3,449.0	3,523.0	3,644.0	3,481.0	3,318.0
Number of Employees	303.1	308.9	310.8	308.2	301.3	295.8
of which Workers	247.8	253.8	264.1	262.9	257.5	252.9
Fixed Productive Assets (comparable prices, millions of rubles)	4,220.7	4,518.6	4,873.8	5,136.5	5,380.8	5,604.4
Profit (millions of rubles)	470.9	603.3	638.8	809.0	892.1	851.4

Source: Statistical Yearbook for Kyrgyzstan, 1990.

Table 7.2: Kyrgyzstan - Industrial Production, 1985-1991

	1985	1986	1987	1988	1989	1990	1991
	(in millions of 1982 rubles)						
Total Production	5545.0	5784.0	5875.0	6278.0	6585.0	6501.0	6508.0
in % to previous year	104.4	104.9	101.5	106.8	105.2	99.4	100.1
of which:							
Electric power	205.0	221.0	190.0	272.0	295.0	274.0	289.0
Fuel production	61.0	61.0	60.0	62.0	61.0	58.0	54.0
Non-ferrous metals	154.0	177.0	208.0	242.0	268.0	289.0	294.0
Machine building and metal works	1422.0	1517.0	1596.0	1688.0	1705.0	1669.0	1744.0
Timber, pulp and paper	105.0	106.0	107.0	114.0	115.0	107.0	128.0
Construction materials	246.0	268.0	276.0	305.0	304.0	310.0	303.0
Light industry products	1600.0	1626.0	1642.0	1785.0	1882.0	1873.0	1955.0
Food industry products	1289.0	1343.0	1303.0	1297.0	1395.0	1452.0	1302.0
Other industry products (residual)	463.0	465.0	493.0	513.0	560.0	469.0	439.0
	(index of output: 1985 = 100)						
Total Production	100.0	104.3	106.0	113.2	118.8	117.2	117.4
of which:							
Electric power	100.0	107.8	92.7	132.7	143.9	133.7	141.0
Fuel production	100.0	100.0	98.4	101.6	100.0	95.1	88.5
Non-ferrous metals	100.0	114.9	135.1	157.1	174.0	187.7	190.9
Machine building and metal works	100.0	106.7	112.2	118.7	119.9	117.4	122.6
Timber, pulp and paper	100.0	101.0	101.9	108.6	109.5	101.9	121.9
Construction materials	100.0	108.9	112.2	124.0	123.6	126.0	123.2
Light industry products	100.0	101.6	102.6	111.6	117.6	117.1	122.2
Food industry products	100.0	104.2	101.1	100.6	108.2	112.6	101.0
Other industry products	100.0	100.4	106.5	110.8	121.0	101.3	94.8

Source: State Statistical Committee.

Table 7.3: Kyrgyzstan - Average Monthly Wages in Industry

	1985	1986	1987	1988	1989	1990	1991
			(in rubles)				
All Industry	**188.1**	**193.8**	**198.0**	**214.7**	**237.4**	**263.7**	**428.5**
Heavy industry	**205.3**	**211.1**	**215.9**	**232.0**	**255.0**	**285.5**	**475.3**
Fuel-energy complex	233.8	238.2	249.4	265.3	288.2	315.7	622.4
Electroenergy	189.8	188.1	201.7	228.2	247.4	284.3	701.4
Fuels	262.4	271.6	282.0	289.7	317.5	342.9	564.1
Metallurgy complex	267.4	278.6	382.5	306.2	320.1	343.9	560.3
Machine building	204.4	209.7	212.8	228.1	251.3	282.2	452.0
Chemical/Forestry complex	190.9	194.8	198.1	217.4	226.5	247.8	423.9
Chemical and petrochemical	200.6	210.5	217.7	225.8	244.8	267.7	416.6
Forestry, wood processing and paper	189.3	192.0	195.8	215.5	222.4	242.2	427.2
Construction materials industry	194.6	197.8	210.7	227.3	255.6	296.9	444.8
Light industry	**155.8**	**161.2**	**160.5**	**181.6**	**205.7**	**226.7**	**402.3**
Textiles	176.8	180.8	181.1	205.6	242.1	270.5	492.4
Garment (clothing)	130.8	139.3	138.7	154.4	166.8	182.9	307.1
Leather, fur and footwear	168.6	171.0	167.6	191.7	216.8	234.7	429.7
Food industry	**157.0**	**165.7**	**177.3**	**181.8**	**199.4**	**215.3**	**351.4**
Foodstuffs	152.6	160.2	173.4	179.9	197.6	212.7	353.5
Meat and milk	166.3	177.2	185.5	185.7	204.0	213.0	347.5
Fish	144.8	153.1	154.7	170.7	176.0	194.2	314.6

Source: Statistical Yearbook for Kyrgyzstan, 1990 and State Statistical Committee.

Table 8.1: Kyrgyzstan - Indices of Wholesale Prices, 1991-92 1/

	Total	Fuels	Machinery	Forest products	Building materials	Light industry	Food industry	Milling industry
				(Index: December 1990 = 100)				
Monthly Averages:								
1991								
Jauary	131.9	118.0	161.4	110.4	241.8	121.5	107.1	100.0
February	133.9	117.6	162.9	116.7	241.8	126.0	107.1	100.0
March	136.3	117.6	162.9	169.8	241.6	129.3	107.2	100.0
April	171.6	117.5	162.9	195.3	241.6	205.4	138.4	100.0
May	246.9	116.8	162.9	198.6	241.6	248.3	139.4	100.0
June	246.8	115.9	163.2	198.6	241.6	248.3	138.8	100.0
July	283.1	116.4	163.2	198.6	241.6	321.4	171.6	100.0
August	357.8	110.8	273.2	198.6	262.1	390.4	191.7	100.0
September	362.4	113.1	315.0	198.6	261.8	362.3	191.7	100.0
October	366.4	111.5	315.0	198.6	269.4	373.2	191.7	100.0
November	429.5	110.8	384.6	198.6	269.4	408.3	213.9	100.0
December	502.9	114.4	517.6	198.6	272.1	514.4	213.9	100.0
1992								
Jauary	2429.0	1985.8	4377.5	743.9	833.5	2067.5	475.2	696.0
February	4340.7	2243.9	9739.9	743.9	2162.9	2638.2	1081.2	696.0
March	4609.8	2243.9	10665.2	1359.0	2100.2	2696.2	1164.4	696.0
April	5098.4	2800.4	10665.2	1359.0	2377.4	3329.8	1171.4	675.1
May	5246.3	4139.0	10665.2	1359.0	2396.4	3426.4	1187.8	675.1
June	7796.0	6788.0	10665.2	1357.7	2396.4	4283.0	3805.8	696.0
July	8178.0	6917.0	11977.0	1357.7	3299.9	4360.1	3817.2	696.0
August	8038.9	6854.7	11977.0	1770.4	3940.1	4072.3	3817.2	696.0
September	11929.8	6758.7	11977.0	1882.0	3940.1	4381.8	5233.4	4403.2
Quarterly Averages:								
1991								
I	134.0	117.8	162.4	132.3	241.7	125.6	107.1	100.0
II	221.8	116.7	163.0	197.5	241.6	234.0	138.9	100.0
III	334.4	113.4	250.4	198.6	255.2	358.0	185.0	100.0
IV	432.9	112.2	405.7	198.6	270.3	432.0	206.5	100.0
1992								
I	3793.1	2157.9	8260.9	948.9	1698.9	2467.3	907.0	696.0
II	6046.9	4575.8	10665.2	1358.6	2390.1	3679.7	2055.0	682.1
III	9382.2	6843.5	11977.0	1670.0	3726.7	4271.4	4289.3	1931.8
Yearly Averages:								
1991	280.8	115.0	245.4	181.7	252.2	287.4	159.4	100.0
Price Ratios:								
Mar92/Mar91	33.8	19.1	65.5	8.0	8.7	20.9	10.9	7.0
Jun92/Jun91	31.6	58.6	65.4	6.8	9.9	17.2	27.4	7.0
Sep92/Sep91	32.9	59.8	38.0	9.5	15.0	12.1	27.3	44.0
Mar92/Dec91	9.2	19.6	20.6	6.8	7.7	5.2	5.4	7.0
Jun92/Dec91	15.5	59.3	20.6	6.8	8.8	8.3	17.8	7.0
Sep92/Dec91	23.7	59.1	23.1	9.5	14.5	8.5	24.5	44.0
I-92/IV-91	8.8	19.2	20.4	4.8	6.3	5.7	4.4	7.0
II-92/I-92	1.6	2.1	1.3	1.4	1.4	1.5	2.3	1.0
III-92/II-92	1.6	1.5	1.1	1.2	1.6	1.2	2.1	2.8

1/ Based on linking month to month change starting in January 1991. In the analysis
of price changes in the Volume I of the Report, it is assumed that the Wholesale Price Index
for December 1990 was the same as the average for the year.

Source: State Statistical Committee.

Table 8.2: Kyrgyzstan – Indices of Consumer Prices, 1991-92

(Index: December 1990 = 100)

	Total 1/	Total 2/	Foods	Bread	Fruit	Sugar	Milk	Eggs	Nonfood 3/	Fabrics	Clothing	Furniture	Constr.	Services
Monthly Averages														
1991														
January	108.9	108.9	107.1	105.6	105.2	105.0	104.7	105.0	110.9	104.7	115.5	109.1	110.2	107.9
February	116.3	116.3	109.1	106.4	119.1	105.4	104.8	105.0	124.1	105.2	128.1	131.1	146.7	114.3
March	119.4	119.4	111.0	106.7	130.2	106.1	104.8	106.1	129.2	106.9	132.9	148.9	162.4	115.1
April	176.5	179.2	167.3	241.3	153.7	227.9	240.8	219.0	183.6	316.4	241.7	178.0	135.7	140.6
May	178.2	183.6	164.6	172.5	153.7	227.2	236.5	217.9	196.1	318.3	247.3	186.0	121.9	142.3
June	179.5	187.9	166.7	172.5	146.2	225.6	240.1	217.9	202.7	340.6	247.1	195.7	123.0	144.9
July	177.7	188.8	161.4	172.5	117.8	219.1	240.1	217.9	210.8	355.5	251.7	203.3	127.4	147.2
August	181.5	195.8	163.3	173.2	114.6	233.8	249.9	217.9	225.6	401.8	267.1	213.5	128.4	150.9
September	181.1	198.3	163.3	173.2	85.4	231.7	249.9	217.9	232.4	426.7	273.8	214.5	136.1	151.6
October	192.1	213.6	168.1	175.4	84.3	244.4	230.9	224.7	254.2	431.4	301.4	225.7	149.9	165.0
November	220.9	249.5	202.5	227.7	88.1	260.5	251.4	257.0	289.5	431.4	360.2	257.7	150.8	169.7
December	243.4	279.0	220.5	244.3	99.5	302.2	253.9	299.5	329.5	437.5	404.5	285.3	151.4	197.7
1992														
January	616.2	716.9	484.1	941.5	114.6	841.1	1659.3	1809.0	660.9	1603.3	836.5	484.7	913.9	602.5
February	785.4	927.7	529.1	805.0	130.6	884.0	1743.9	1680.6	735.6	1608.1	1086.6	516.2	913.9	782.1
March	895.8	1074.3	557.7	829.9	136.5	984.8	1850.3	1709.2	865.8	1741.6	1471.3	760.4	1348.9	988.5
April	.	1266.5	624.6	860.6	138.4	1051.8	2344.3	1811.8	1011.3	1743.3	1952.4	796.9	1381.3	1261.3
May	.	1321.0	649.6	959.6	140.2	1079.1	2445.1	1862.5	1080.0	1753.8	2034.4	883.8	1529.1	1342.1
June	.	1389.7	662.6	1000.8	127.0	1134.1	2552.7	1922.1	1137.3	1774.8	2087.3	966.0	1781.4	1598.4
July	.	1462.0	730.8	1018.8	118.8	1848.6	2552.8	1974.0	1216.9	1783.7	2145.7	995.0	1827.7	2082.7
August	.	1532.1	769.6	1074.8	101.3	2113.5	2598.6	2141.8	1258.3	1792.6	2227.3	1014.9	1957.5	2259.7
September	.	1944.3	1166.7	2020.6	104.0	5112.5	4791.9	2274.6	1361.5	1805.1	2436.6	1081.9	2305.9	2637.1
Quarterly Averages														
1991														
I	114.9	114.9	109.1	106.2	118.1	105.5	104.8	105.0	121.4	105.6	124.8	130.4	139.7	112.4
II	178.1	183.6	166.2	195.4	151.2	226.9	239.1	218.3	194.1	325.1	245.4	186.5	126.9	142.6
III	180.1	194.3	162.7	173.0	106.0	228.2	246.6	217.9	222.9	394.6	264.2	210.4	130.7	149.9
IV	218.8	247.3	197.0	215.8	90.6	269.1	252.1	260.4	291.1	433.4	355.4	256.2	150.7	177.5
1992														
I	765.8	906.3	523.6	858.8	127.2	903.3	1751.2	1732.9	754.1	1651.0	1151.5	587.1	1058.9	791.0
II	.	1325.7	645.6	940.3	135.2	1088.3	2447.4	1865.5	1076.2	1757.3	2024.7	882.2	1563.9	1400.6
III	.	1646.1	889.0	1371.4	108.0	3024.9	3314.4	2130.1	1278.9	1793.8	2269.9	1030.6	2030.4	2326.5
Yearly Averages														
1991	173.0	185.0	158.7	172.6	116.5	207.4	210.6	200.4	207.4	314.7	247.4	195.9	137.0	145.6
Price Ratios														
Mar92/Mar91	7.5	9.0	5.0	7.8	1.0	9.3	17.7	16.3	6.7	16.3	11.1	5.1	8.3	8.6
Jun92/Jun91	.	7.4	4.0	5.8	0.9	5.0	10.6	8.8	5.6	5.2	8.4	4.9	14.5	11.0
Sep92/Sep91	.	9.8	7.1	11.7	1.2	22.1	19.2	10.4	5.9	4.2	8.9	5.0	16.9	17.4
Mar92/Dec91	3.7	3.9	2.5	3.4	1.4	3.3	7.3	5.7	2.6	4.0	3.6	2.7	8.9	5.0
Jun92/Dec91	.	5.0	3.0	4.1	1.3	3.8	10.1	6.4	3.5	4.1	5.2	3.4	11.8	8.1
Sep92/Dec91	.	7.0	5.3	8.3	1.0	16.9	18.9	7.6	4.1	4.1	6.0	3.8	15.2	13.3
I-92/IV-91	3.5	3.7	2.7	4.0	1.4	3.4	6.9	6.7	2.6	3.8	3.2	2.3	7.0	4.5
II-92/I-92	1.5	1.5	1.2	1.1	1.1	1.2	1.4	1.1	1.4	1.1	1.8	1.5	1.5	1.8
III92/II92	1.2	1.2	1.4	1.5	0.8	2.8	1.4	1.1	1.2	1.0	1.1	1.2	1.3	1.7

1/ Chained index interpolated to conform to published ratio of March 1992 to March 1991 prices.
2/ Index chained from ratios of each month to the preceding month.
3/ Includes items not shown separately.

Source: State Statistical Committee and World Bank estimates.

Table 8.3: Kyrgyzstan - Price Control Regulations as of January 4, 1992
Maximum Allowable Ratios of Consumer Prices
Beginning January 4, 1992 to Prices as of January 3, 1992. 1/

Article	Maximum Ratio	Article	Maximum Ratio
Foods:		**Other:**	
Bread	6.2	Alcohol	7.0
Milk and		Pharmaceuticals	5.0
milk products	5.6	Transportation	5.0
Vodka	4.0		
		Water and sewage	6.0
Flour	6.2	Residential heating 2/	1.0
Salt	5.0	Residential rents 2/	1.0
Sugar	3.6		
Oil	4.0	Electricity	
Baby food	4.0	Rural	.06r/KWH
		Urban	.10r/KWH
Fuels:			
Gasoline	5.0		
Diesel fuel	4.8		
Kerosene	12.0		
Propane	4.8		
Natural gas	7.4		

1/ Ceilings were also announced for several wholesale commodities.
2/ No change permitted.

Source: State Statistical Committee.

Table 8.4: Kyrgyzstan - Selected Consumer Prices, December 1991, April and October 1992

| | December 1991 Average | | April 6, 1992 | | October 8, 1992 | | Ratio of April to December: | | Ratio of October to December: | |
	State Stores	City Markets	State Stores	City Markets	State Stores	City Markets	State Stores	City Markets	State Stores	City Markets
				(in rubles per unit of quantity)						
Foods:										
Beef (kg)	8.4	15.0	54.9	52.0	-	90.0	6.5	3.5	-	6.0
Bread (kg)	0.8	-	6.4	6.2	18.2	-	8.0	-	-	-
Milk (liter)	0.4	-	2.2	2.5	12.2	25.0	4.9	-	27.7	-
Cottage cheese (k	1.6	3.0	26.3	20.0	37.5	30.0	16.8	6.7	24.0	10.0
Eggs (per 10)	2.3	3.0	11.1	12.4	25.8	35.0	4.8	4.1	11.2	11.7
Potatoes (kg)	1.3	3.0	3.9	6.4	12.8	17.3	3.0	2.1	10.1	5.8
Apples (kg)	6.0	15.0	26.0	47.5	11.4	19.8	4.3	3.2	1.9	1.3
Tea (kg)	36.0	-	75.2	-	243.2	-	2.1	-	6.8	-
Vodka (liter)	40.0	-	80.0	-	224.0	-	2.0	-	5.6	-
Nonfoods:										
Men suits (piece)	420.0		2052.0		2134.8		4.9		5.1	
Women shoes (pai	290.0		460.0		2309.6		1.6		8.0	
Cigarettes (pack)	3.0		10.0		-		3.3		-	
Gasoline (liter)	1.3		6.0		23.9		4.6		18.4	

Source: State Statistical Committee.

Table 8.5: Kyrgyzstan - Average Monthly Wages in National Economy by Sector

	1985	1986	1987	1988	1989	1990	1991	1992 Jan-Aug	1992 August
					(in rubles)				
Total National Economy	162.6	166.4	171.4	183.6	197.5	219.2	349.1	995.0	1,723.0
Industry	188.1	193.8	198.0	214.7	237.4	263.7	428.5	1,809.0	2,555.0
Agriculture	150.5	150.9	152.3	161.6	180.0	197.7	330.2	687.0	1,062.0
Forestry	117.1	115.6	118.5	118.3	138.7	144.6	208.8	627.0	963.0
Transport	184.8	192.1	197.5	210.8	222.5	239.1	342.4	1,311.0	2,123.0
Communication	141.5	146.7	153.3	173.6	186.8	213.5	372.6	1,381.0	2,057.0
Construction	199.3	205.1	211.7	237.9	247.9	273.9	421.4	1,643.0	2,219.0
Trade	133.5	135.5	136.9	144.9	159.5	193.6	304.9	942.0	1,326.0
Computing Services	132.3	139.8	147.0	163.9	194.0	228.5	355.9	1,111.0	1,633.0
Municipal Services	136.2	138.9	143.5	154.2	160.9	179.8	280.6	991.0	1,473.0
Public Health, Social Security	121.0	121.9	130.1	138.3	143.1	166.8	266.7	906.0	1,334.0
Education	146.1	150.9	163.3	165.6	166.2	167.8	268.1	870.0	1,068.0
Culture and Arts	119.2	119.9	123.4	125.2	128.1	136.9	245.4	993.0	1,076.0
Science and Science Services	190.5	197.5	206.0	235.5	269.1	301.4	411.5	1,503.0	2,076.0
Credit and Insurance	156.6	165.4	174.4	179.9	188.2	319.3	665.3	1,827.0	3,075.0
Administration	152.4	161.8	167.3	180.9	207.3	297.3	393.5	1,385.0	2,212.0

Source: Statistical Yearbook for Kyrgyzstan, 1990 and State Statistical Committee.

Table 9.1: Kyrgyzstan - Capital Stock, Capital Formation and Depreciation, 1990

	Assets (begin. of the year)	Increase of Assets during the year	of which:				Decrease of Assets during the year	of which:			Level of Assets (end of the year)
			New Assets	Capital Repair	Free of Charge	Other Sources		Depreciation	Remaining Value of Liquidated Asstes	Transfer	
(in millions of rubles)											
All Assets	16,701	2,971	1,947	514	481	29	2,351	1,325	431	595	17,321
of which owned by:											
State	13,264	2,212	1,354	435	423		1,869	1,142	173	554	13,607
Co-operatives	488	87	48	10	29		44	25	2	17	531
Production co-ops	24	34	1	1	6	26	5	5			53
Collective farms	1,559	283	225	35	23		243	84	135	24	1,599
Private citizens	1,366	355	319	33		3	190	69	121		1,531
of which:											
Workers and Employees	897	227	208	19			30	30			1,094
Collective farmers	469	128	111	14		3	160	39	121		437
Productive Assets	11,086	2,011	1,276	327	379	29	1,773	981	422	370	11,324
of which owned by:											
State	9,040	1,481	860	295	326		1,392	876	167	349	9,129
Co-operatives	289	69	34	7	28		41	25	2	14	317
Production co-ops	24	34	1	1	6	26	5	5			53
Collective farms	1,297	238	195	24	19		214	75	132	7	1,321
Private citizens	436	189	186			3	121		121		504
of which:											
Workers and Employees	275	118	118								393
Collective farmers	161	71	68			3	121		121		111
Non-Productive Assets	5,615	960	671	187	102		578	344	9	225	5,997
of which owned by:											
State	4,224	731	494	140	97		477	266	6	205	4,478
Co-operatives	199	18	14	3	1		3			3	214
Production co-ops											
Collective farms	262	45	30	11	4		29	9	3	17	278
Private citizens	930	166	133	33			69	69			1,027
of which:											
Workers and Employees	622	109	90	19			30	30			701
Collective farmers	308	57	43	14			39	39			326
Productive Assets by Branches of National Economy:											
Industry	3,882	635	360	143	125	7	581	429	11	141	3,936
of which owned by:											
State	3,759	588	334	140	114		571	420	11	140	3,776
Co-operatives	58	28	21	2	5		2	2			84
Production co-ops	24	14	1		6	7	3	3			35
Collective farms	41	5	4	1			5	4		1	41
Construction	282	158	72	27	47	12	181	120	5	56	259
of which owned by:											
State	254	141	70	25	46		177	177	5	55	218
Co-operatives	15	4	2	1	1		3	2		1	16
Production co-ops		13		1		12	1	1			12
Collective farms	13										13
Agriculture (excluding livestock)	3,650	373	211	69	93		321	203	22	96	3,702
of which owned by:											
State	2,681	241	121	46	74		229	132	7	90	2,693
Co-operatives	5	2	2								7
Production co-ops											
Collective farms	938	115	73	23	19						961
Private citizens	26	15	15								41
of which:											
Workers and Employees	14	10	10								24
Collective farmers	12	5	5								17
Value of Livestock	1,052	431	428			3	381	3	378		1,102
of which owned by:											
State	343	140	140				143	3	140		340
Production co-ops											
Collective farms	299	117	117				117		117		299
Private citizens	410	174	171			3	121		121		463
of which:											
Workers and Employees	261	108	108								369
Collective farmers	149	63	63				121		121		94

(continued)

Table 9.1: Kyrgyzstan - Capital Stock, Capital Formation and Depreciation, 1990

	Assets (begin. of the year)	Increase of Assets during the year	of which:				Decrease of Assets during the year	of which:			Level of Assets (end of the year)
			New Assets	Capital Repair	Free of Charge	Other Sources		Depre-ciation	Remaining Value of Liquidated Asstes	Transfer	
(in millions of rubles)											
Forestry	8	2	2				1				9
of which owned by:											
State	8	2	2				1				9
Transport and Roads	1,473	209	94	70	45		170	150	2	18	1,512
of which owned by:											
State	1,473	209	94	70	45		170	150	2	18	1,512
Railroads	51	7	2	5			7	7			51
Sea Transport											
River Transport	6	1	1				1	1			6
Oil Pipelines											
Gas Pipelines	47	9	9				2	2			54
Car Transport	162	47	5	21	21		65	54	2	9	144
Other Transport	83	27	18	9			25	24		1	85
Road Management	25	5	2	1	2		6	3		3	24
Assets in Roads	1,099	113	57	34	22		64	59		5	1,148
Communication	176	43	26	5	12		36	16		20	183
of which owned by:											
State	176	43	26	5	12		36	16		20	183
Collective farms											
State Purchases	63	44	15	3	23	3	17	9	2	6	90
of which owned by:											
State	31	33	13	2	18		12	6	2	4	52
Co-operatives	32	8	2	1	5		4	2		2	36
Production co-ops		3				3	1	1			2
Material-Technical Supply and Sale	115	23	14	3	6		19	13		6	119
of which owned by:											
State	115	23	14	3	6		19	13		6	119
Trade and Public Food Service	345	61	30	4	27		59	31	2	26	347
of which owned by:											
State	160	33	22	1	10		27	12		15	166
Co-operatives	179	27	7	3	17		32	19	2	11	174
Production co-ops											
Collective farms	6	1	1								7
Information Services	10	8	3	1		4	3	2		1	15
of which owned by:											
State	10	4	3	1			3	2		1	11
Production co-ops		4				4					4
Other Branches of Material Production	30	24	21	2	1		4	4			50
of which owned by:											
State	30	24	21	2	1		4	4			50
Non-Productive Assets by Branches of National Economy											
Housing	3,457	595	456	92	47		285	182	7	96	3,767
Communal services	739	110	71	18	21		147	49		98	702
Public Health, Social Security	353	53	26	19	8		39	31	1	7	367
National Education	637	85	37	44	4		55	48		7	667
Science and Scientific Service	115	22	18	4			9	8		1	128
Culture and Art	148	41	22	5	14		18	14	1	3	171
Other Non-Productive Branches	166	54	41	5	8		25	12		13	195

(continued)

*Table 9.1: **Kyrgyzstan - Capital Stock, Capital Formation and Depreciation, 1990***

	Assets (begin. of the year)	Increase of Assets during the year	of which:				Decrease of Assets during the year	of which:			Level of Assets (end of the year)
			New Assets	Capital Repair	Free of Charge	Other Sources		Depre-ciation	Remaining Value of Liquidated Asstes	Transfer	
(in millions of rubles)											
All Assets (without livestock)	15,649	2,540	1,519	514	481	26	1,970	1,322	53	595	16,219
of which owned by:											
State	12,921	2,072	1,214	435	423		1,726	1,139	33	554	13,267
Co-operatives	488	87	48	10	29		44	25	2	17	531
Production co-ops	24	34	1	1	6	26	5	5			53
Collective farms	1,260	166	108	35	23		126	84	18	24	1,300
Private citizens	956	181	148	33			69	69			1,068
All Productive Assets											
(without livestock)	10,034	1,580	848	327	379	26	1,392	978	44	370	10,222
of which owned by:											
State	8,697	1,341	720	295	326		1,249	873	27	349	8,789
Co-operatives	289	69	34	7	28		41	25	2	14	317
Production co-ops	24	34	1	1	6	26	5	5			53
Collective farms	998	121	78	24	19		97	75	15	7	1,022
Private citizens	26	15	15								41
Agriculture (including livestock)	4,702	804	639	69	93	3	702	206	400	96	4,804
of which owned by:											
State	3,024	381	261	46	74		372	135	147	90	3,033
Co-operatives	5	2	2								7
Production co-ops											
Collective farms	1,237	232	190	23	19		209	71	132	6	1,260
Private citizens	436	189	186			3	121		121		504

Source: State Statistical Committee.

Table 9.2: Kyrgyzstan - Capital Investments, 1981-91

	1981-1985	1985	1986-1990	1990	1991
	(in millions of 1991 rubles)				
Total Capital Investments	**9,373**	**2,073**	**12,041**	**2,734**	**2,270**
of which in:					
Productive Sphere	**6,712**	**1,471**	**7,836**	**1,707**	**1,412**
Industry	2,497	587	3,397	737	723
Agriculture	2,954	626	2,914	551	447
Construction	295	66	428	102	84
Transport	454	89	498	119	66
Communication	130	27	153	31	21
Other	382	76	446	167	71
Non-Productive Sphere	**2,661**	**602**	**4,205**	**1,027**	**858**
Housing	1,611	376	2,453	614	502
Other	1,050	226	1,752	413	356
	(in percent of total)				
Total Capital Investments	**100.0**	**100.0**	**100.0**	**100.0**	**100.0**
of which in:					
Productive Sphere	**71.6**	**71.0**	**65.1**	**62.4**	**62.2**
Industry	26.6	28.3	28.2	27.0	31.9
Agriculture	31.5	30.2	24.2	20.2	19.7
Construction	3.1	3.2	3.6	3.7	3.7
Transport	4.8	4.3	4.1	4.4	2.9
Communication	1.4	1.3	1.3	1.1	0.9
Other	4.1	3.7	3.7	6.1	3.1
Non-Productive Sphere	**28.4**	**29.0**	**34.9**	**37.6**	**37.8**
Housing	17.2	18.1	20.4	22.5	22.1
Other	11.2	10.9	14.6	15.1	15.7

Source: State Statistical Committee.

Table 9.3: Kyrgyzstan - Capital Investments in 1988-1991 and Forecast for 1992

	1988	1989	1990	1991	1992 a)
	(in millions of rubles)				
A. Breakdown by Sector					
Total Capital Investments	1539	1603	1704	2229	12238
of which:					
Electric Power	78	105	109	221	1548
Non-Ferrous Metallurgy	76	90	82	80	361
Machine Building	87	28	30	93	409
Agriculture and Processing	513	444	458	496	2350
Construction Materials	55	86	78	88	467
Light Industry	31	28	48	40	383
Local Industry	6	2	8	26	42
Road Construction	26	25	21	14	56
Housing Construction	176	212	234	579	4140
Communal Construction	46	53	62	115	524
Public Education	76	87	92	156	667
Public Health	33	42	46	75	425
Culture	15	15	17	25	93
Miscellaneous	321	386	419	212	773
B. Breakdown by Source of Financing					
Total Capital Investments	1539	1603	1704	2229	12238
of which:					
Government Investments from the Budget	953	755	763	1036	857
of which: from Republican Budget	390	345	469	568	859
Government Investments from Enterprise Funds	290	553	613	735	8199
Investments from Public Organizations Funds	7	5	7	9	32
Investments from Construction Cooperative Funds	13	15	19	32	338
Investments from Collective Farms Funds	127	133	108	134	453
Investments from Consumer Cooperative Funds	28	39	41	37	217
Investments from Individual Funds for					
Construction of Private Housing (estimate)	122	103	153	247	2140

a) Forecast as of January 1992.

Note: Expenditure growth in 1991-92 is related to inflationary processes.

Source: Ministry of Economy, Kyrgyzstan.

Table 10.1: Kyrgyzstan - Household Monetary Incomes and Outlays, 1987-90

	1987	1988	1989	1990
	(in millions of rubles)			
INCOMES				
A. TOTAL LABOR INCOME	3517	3827	4305	4755
1. Regular Wages	2719	2891	3177	3474
1.a Wages Paid by Cooperatives	..	32	101	139
2. Other Wages and Compensations	92	105	119	140
3. Income Paid by Collective Farms	365	380	401	455
4. Income from Sale of Farm Products	341	419	507	547
B. TOTAL TRANSFER RECEIPTS	895	1066	1043	1284
5. Pensions and Allowances	632	671	714	818
6. Scholarships	37	38	38	44
7. Income from the Financial System (insurance, interest, etc.)	138	231	163	293
8. Other Income	88	126	128	129
9. Adjustment	0	0	0	0
C. TOTAL INCOME	4412	4893	5348	6039
OUTLAYS				
A. TOTAL PURCHASES	3675	4109	4536	5031
1. Retail Trade Purchases	3302	3689	4091	4560
2. Purchased Services	373	420	445	471
of which:				
Rent and Utilities	89	90	92	93
Communications	27	30	33	36
Health and Other Services	11	13	12	14
Cooperatives	0	12	12	20
B. TRANSFERS AND SAVINGS	609	698	819	912
of which:				
3. Taxes, Fees, Dues and Other	424	466	550	599
4. Savings	184	228	269	313
5. Other	2	4	0	0
6. Adjustment	0	0	0	0
C. TOTAL OUTLAYS	4285	4807	5355	5943
7. Income less Expenditure	127	86	0	96
8. Account Balance	4412	4893	5355	6039

Source: State Statistical Committee.

Table 10.2: Kyrgyzstan - Household Monetary Incomes and Outlays, 1987-90

	1987	1988	1989	1990
	(in percent of Total Income)			
INCOMES				
A. TOTAL LABOR INCOME	79.7	78.2	80.5	78.7
1. Regular Wages	61.6	59.1	59.4	57.5
1.a Wages Paid by Cooperatives	..	0.7	1.9	2.3
2. Other Wages and Compensations	2.1	2.1	2.2	2.3
3. Income Paid by Collective Farms	8.3	7.8	7.5	7.5
4. Income from Sale of Farm Products	7.7	8.6	9.5	9.1
B. TOTAL TRANSFER RECEIPTS	20.3	21.8	19.5	21.3
5. Pensions and Allowances	14.3	13.7	13.4	13.5
6. Scholarships	0.8	0.8	0.7	0.7
7. Income from the Financial System (insurance, interest, etc.)	3.1	4.7	3.0	4.9
8. Other Income	2.0	2.6	2.4	2.1
9. Adjustment	0.0	0.0	0.0	0.0
C. TOTAL INCOME	100.0	100.0	100.0	100.0
	(in percent of Total Outlays)			
OUTLAYS				
A. TOTAL PURCHASES	85.8	85.5	84.7	84.7
1. Retail Trade Purchases	77.1	76.7	76.4	76.7
2. Purchased Services	8.7	8.7	8.3	7.9
of which:				
Rent and Utilities	2.1	1.9	1.7	1.6
Communications	0.6	0.6	0.6	0.6
Health and Other Services	0.3	0.3	0.2	0.2
Cooperatives	0.0	0.2	0.2	0.3
B. TRANSFERS AND SAVINGS	14.2	14.5	15.3	15.4
of which:				
3. Taxes, Fees, Dues and Other	9.9	9.7	10.3	10.1
4. Savings	4.3	4.7	5.0	5.3
5. Other	0.0	0.1	0.0	0.0
6. Adjustment	0.0	0.0	0.0	0.0
C. TOTAL OUTLAYS	100.0	100.0	100.0	100.0
7. Income less Expenditure	3.0	1.8	0.0	1.6
8. Account Balance	103.0	101.8	100.0	101.6

Source: Table 10.1.

Distributors of World Bank Publications

ARGENTINA
Carlos Hirsch, SRL
Galeria Guemes
Florida 165, 4th Floor-Ofc. 453/465
1333 Buenos Aires

AUSTRALIA, PAPUA NEW GUINEA, FIJI, SOLOMON ISLANDS, VANUATU, AND WESTERN SAMOA
D.A. Information Services
648 Whitehorse Road
Mitcham 3132
Victoria

AUSTRIA
Gerold and Co.
Graben 31
A-1011 Wien

BANGLADESH
Micro Industries Development
    Assistance Society (MIDAS)
House 5, Road 16
Dhanmondi R/Area
Dhaka 1209

   Branch offices:
   Pine View, 1st Floor
   100 Agrabad Commercial Area
   Chittagong 4100

   76, K.D.A. Avenue
   Kulna 9100

BELGIUM
Jean De Lannoy
Av. du Roi 202
1060 Brussels

CANADA
Le Diffuseur
C.P. 85, 1501B rue Ampère
Boucherville, Québec
J4B 5E6

CHILE
Invertec IGT S.A.
Americo Vespucio Norte 1165
Santiago

CHINA
China Financial & Economic
    Publishing House
8, Da Fo Si Dong Jie
Beijing

COLOMBIA
Infoenlace Ltda.
Apartado Aereo 34270
Bogota D.E.

COTE D'IVOIRE
Centre d'Edition et de Diffusion
    Africaines (CEDA)
04 B.P. 541
Abidjan 04 Plateau

CYPRUS
Center of Applied Research
Cyprus College
6, Diogenes Street, Engomi
P.O. Box 2006
Nicosia

DENMARK
SamfundsLitteratur
Rosenoerns Allé 11
DK-1970 Frederiksberg C

DOMINICAN REPUBLIC
Editora Taller, C. por A.
Restauración e Isabel la Católica 309
Apartado de Correos 2190 Z-1
Santo Domingo

EGYPT, ARAB REPUBLIC OF
Al Ahram
Al Galaa Street
Cairo

The Middle East Observer
41, Sherif Street
Cairo

FINLAND
Akateeminen Kirjakauppa
P.O. Box 128
SF-00101 Helsinki 10

FRANCE
World Bank Publications
66, avenue d'Iéna
75116 Paris

GERMANY
UNO-Verlag
Poppelsdorfer Allee 55
D-5300 Bonn 1

HONG KONG, MACAO
Asia 2000 Ltd.
46-48 Wyndham Street
Winning Centre
2nd Floor
Central Hong Kong

INDIA
Allied Publishers Private Ltd.
751 Mount Road
Madras - 600 002

   Branch offices:
   15 J.N. Heredia Marg
   Ballard Estate
   Bombay - 400 038

   13/14 Asaf Ali Road
   New Delhi - 110 002

   17 Chittaranjan Avenue
   Calcutta - 700 072

   Jayadeva Hostel Building
   5th Main Road, Gandhinagar
   Bangalore - 560 009

   3-5-1129 Kachiguda
      Cross Road
   Hyderabad - 500 027

   Prarthana Flats, 2nd Floor
   Near Thakore Baug, Navrangpura
   Ahmedabad - 380 009

   Patiala House
   16-A Ashok Marg
   Lucknow - 226 001

   Central Bazaar Road
   60 Bajaj Nagar
   Nagpur 440 010

INDONESIA
Pt. Indira Limited
Jalan Borobudur 20
P.O. Box 181
Jakarta 10320

IRELAND
Government Supplies Agency
4-5 Harcourt Road
Dublin 2

ISRAEL
Yozmot Literature Ltd.
P.O. Box 56055
Tel Aviv 61560

ITALY
Licosa Commissionaria Sansoni SPA
Via Duca Di Calabria, 1/1
Casella Postale 552
50125 Firenze

JAPAN
Eastern Book Service
Hongo 3-Chome, Bunkyo-ku 113
Tokyo

KENYA
Africa Book Service (E.A.) Ltd.
Quaran House, Mfangano Street
P.O. Box 45245
Nairobi

KOREA, REPUBLIC OF
Pan Korea Book Corporation
P.O. Box 101, Kwangwhamun
Seoul

MALAYSIA
University of Malaya Cooperative
    Bookshop, Limited
P.O. Box 1127, Jalan Pantai Baru
59700 Kuala Lumpur

MEXICO
INFOTEC
Apartado Postal 22-860
14060 Tlalpan, Mexico D.F.

NETHERLANDS
De Lindeboom/InOr-Publikaties
P.O. Box 202
7480 AE Haaksbergen

NEW ZEALAND
EBSCO NZ Ltd.
Private Mail Bag 99914
New Market
Auckland

NIGERIA
University Press Limited
Three Crowns Building Jericho
Private Mail Bag 5095
Ibadan

NORWAY
Narvesen Information Center
Book Department
P.O. Box 6125 Etterstad
N-0602 Oslo 6

PAKISTAN
Mirza Book Agency
65, Shahrah-e-Quaid-e-Azam
P.O. Box No. 729
Lahore 54000

PERU
Editorial Desarrollo SA
Apartado 3824
Lima 1

PHILIPPINES
International Book Center
Suite 1703, Cityland 10
Condominium Tower 1
Ayala Avenue, H.V. dela
    Costa Extension
Makati, Metro Manila

POLAND
International Publishing Service
Ul. Piekna 31/37
00-677 Warzawa

For subscription orders:
IPS Journals
Ul. Okrezna 3
02-916 Warszawa

PORTUGAL
Livraria Portugal
Rua Do Carmo 70-74
1200 Lisbon

SAUDI ARABIA, QATAR
Jarir Book Store
P.O. Box 3196
Riyadh 11471

SINGAPORE, TAIWAN, MYANMAR, BRUNEI
Information Publications
    Private, Ltd.
Golden Wheel Building
41, Kallang Pudding, #04-03
Singapore 1334

SOUTH AFRICA, BOTSWANA
For single titles:
Oxford University Press
    Southern Africa
P.O. Box 1141
Cape Town 8000

For subscription orders:
International Subscription Service
P.O. Box 41095
Craighall
Johannesburg 2024

SPAIN
Mundi-Prensa Libros, S.A.
Castello 37
28001 Madrid

Librería Internacional AEDOS
Consell de Cent, 391
08009 Barcelona

SRI LANKA AND THE MALDIVES
Lake House Bookshop
P.O. Box 244
100, Sir Chittampalam A.
    Gardiner Mawatha
Colombo 2

SWEDEN
For single titles:
Fritzes Fackboksforetaget
Regeringsgatan 12, Box 16356
S-103 27 Stockholm

For subscription orders:
Wennergren-Williams AB
P. O. Box 1305
S-171 25 Solna

SWITZERLAND
For single titles:
Librairie Payot
Case postale 3212
CH 1002 Lausanne

For subscription orders:
Librairie Payot
Service des Abonnements
Case postale 3312
CH 1002 Lausanne

THAILAND
Central Department Store
306 Silom Road
Bangkok

TRINIDAD & TOBAGO, ANTIGUA BARBUDA, BARBADOS, DOMINICA, GRENADA, GUYANA, JAMAICA, MONTSERRAT, ST. KITTS & NEVIS, ST. LUCIA, ST. VINCENT & GRENADINES
Systematics Studies Unit
#9 Watts Street
Curepe
Trinidad, West Indies

TURKEY
Infotel
Narlabahçe Sok. No. 15
Cagaloglu
Istanbul

UNITED KINGDOM
Microinfo Ltd.
P.O. Box 3
Alton, Hampshire GU34 2PG
England

VENEZUELA
Libreria del Este
Aptdo. 60.337
Caracas 1060-A